The Super Cute Drawing Course

Step-By-Step Lovely Illustrations

Tanja Geier

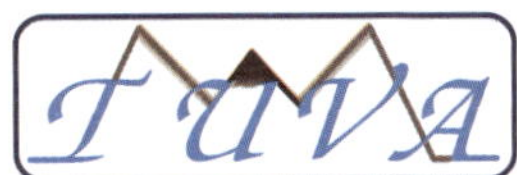

Content

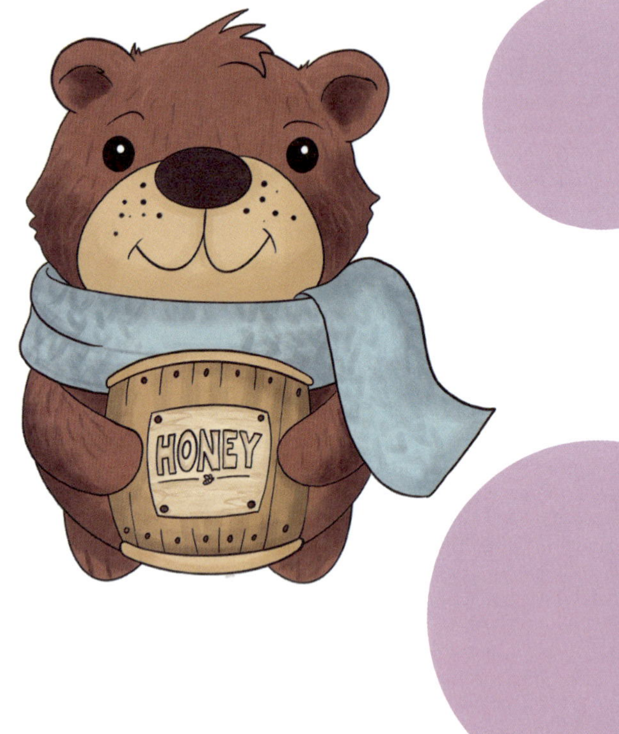

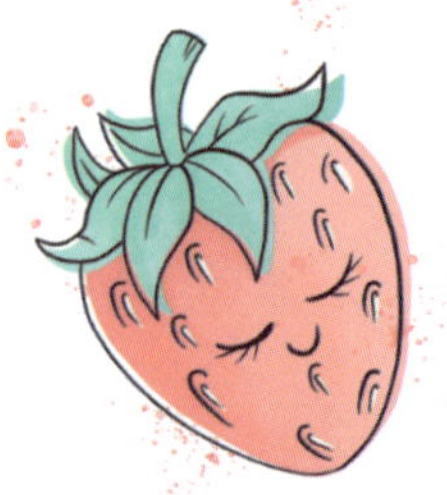

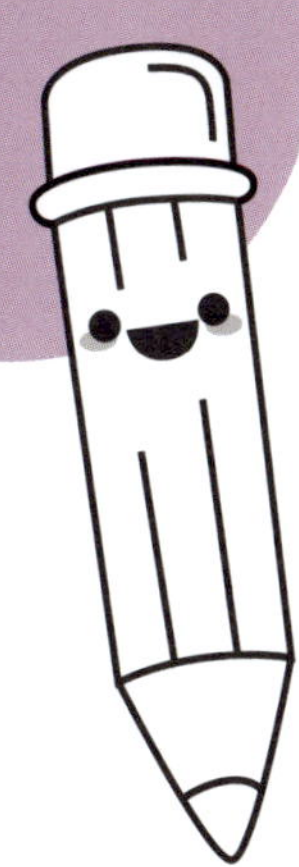

Level of Difficulty

All drawings in this book are given a pencil rating to show how challenging they will be.

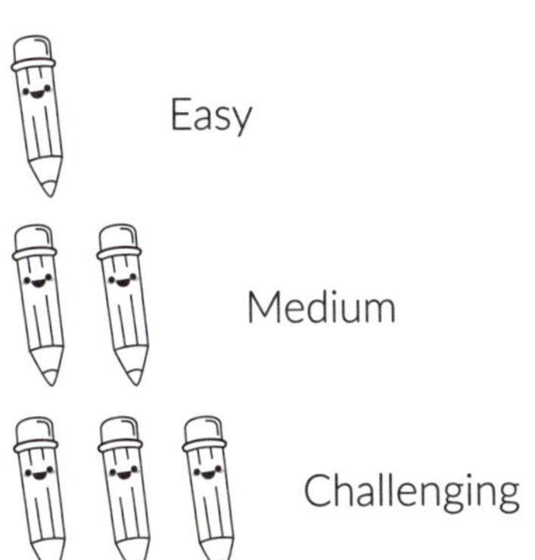

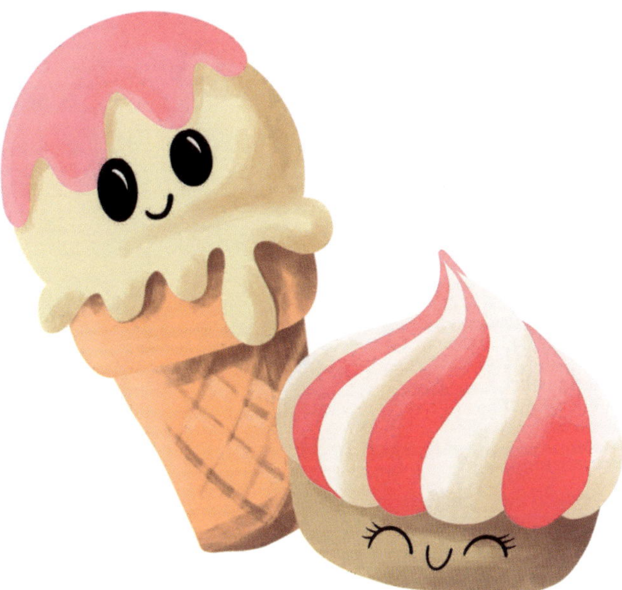

Drawing Lovely Illustrations Is Not Difficult

Do you want to draw? Do you see little, enchanting illustrations all over the place and ask yourself if you too could also create such lovely doodles?

Have no fear - drawing can be learnt. With a few tricks, a little practice and much inspiration, you will soon find it easy to draw the most beautiful illustrations.

There are so many different drawing materials. It makes no difference whether you use pencils, fineliners, biros or coloured pencils. Pick your favourite and create your own little works of art.

Let the following pages inspire you.

Happy drawing!!!

Tanja

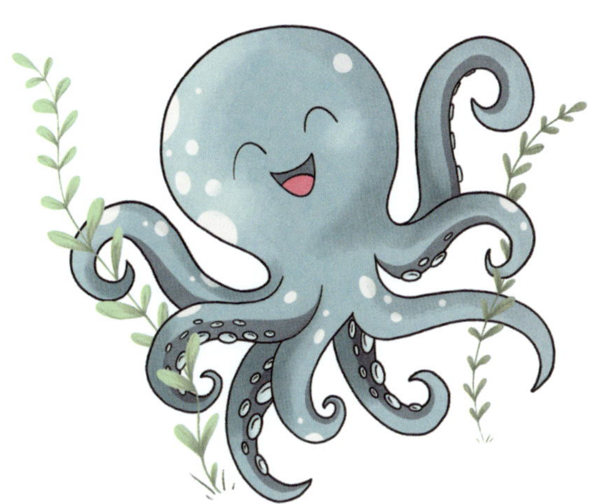

Materials

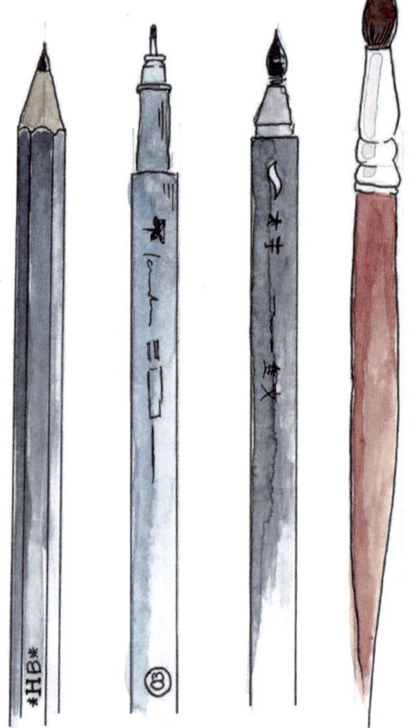

You don't need much to draw beautiful illustrations - a pencil and paper are enough. But the possibilities are endless.

Drawing means using strokes and lines to create art. And you can do exactly that with a wide variety of materials: pencils, fineliners, drawing ink, coloured pencils, biros, chalk, charcoal and so many more.

Your basic equipment should include:

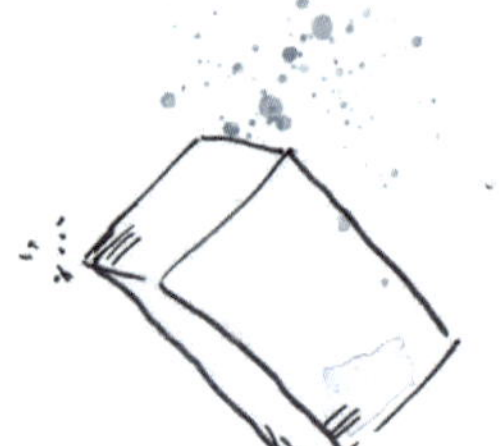

- Pencil
- Eraser
- Pencil sharpener
- Paper
- And maybe even a fineliner

Pencils

When you are just starting to learn drawing, sketching your motif first is a big help. With the right pencil, it won't be any problem. You can buy pencils with different degrees of hardness that are categorised with the letters H and B. H stands for hard and B stands for black or soft. The number before the letter shows the level of hardness.

Pencils range from 9H (very hard) to 9B (very soft). HB (medium) is in the very middle and describes a medium hard pencil, which can be used for many things.

I like to use a hard 2H pencil to sketch outlines. However, you can also use a normal HB pencil. Your own preference plays a big role in this decision. The only important thing to remember is that you should not press too hard so that if you have to, you can still erase and correct the outline.

To shade illustrations, I start with a HB pencil and then move on to a B pencil. My favourite is the 5B pencil - you can use it to easily draw very dark areas without needing to apply much pressure.

For all your drawings it is important that you do not erase too much! You can easily damage the paper and too soft pencils are hard to remove without leaving marks.

Tip:

It is easy to smudge pencil drawings, in particular if you are working with a B pencil. For all your drawings ensure that you are always working from left to right, otherwise you may smudge your beautiful illustrations with your hand. If you are left-handed, then work the other way round.

Fineliners

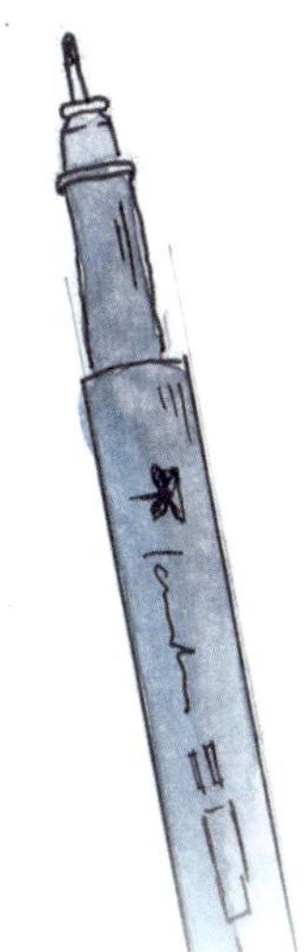

Unlike pencils, you can't create shades of grey with a fineliner, just black. It is also not possible to use layers, as you can with the pencil technique. However, the white paper and the black stroke of a fineliner always creates the starkest contrast.

There are numerous brands and producers of fineliners, all with different tips and different sizes from thick to thin. It is simply a case of trying and testing which pen suits you best.

Personally, I like to work with waterproof fineliners. It means that I can also paint my sketches and illustrations with watercolour paints without any of the ink running.

The biggest disadvantage of fineliners is that every stroke must be right. Once it is on the paper, it cannot be erased. Therefore, when using them, it is best to sketch out with a hard pencil first.

Brush Pens

Since hand lettering has gained in popularity, many people are aware of brush pens. They are pens with brush-like tips. By using pressure on the tip, you can create lines with different thicknesses from thick to thin. When working with these pens particularly smooth paper gives you the best result for your illustrations.

Paper

There are innumerable types of paper, from different shades of ultra white and cream to coloured and black paper. The surface varies from very smooth to very rough, for example watercolour paper. The grammage (the weight of the paper) is calculated in grams per square meter and is used to measure how robust the paper is.

Paper that is too light can be easily damaged with an eraser. I like to use smooth paper that is heavier than 200g/m^2 best. It works well with pencils and fineliners, and I can even add a smattering of watercolours to the mix.

Colours

I love colour. I absolutely love adding a few colourful highlights to a beautiful illustration or colouring it completely.

There are thousands of possibilities to enhance your art with colours. My favourite media are watercolour paints. I use them to bring life to simple and straight-forward sketches with a few brush strokes and to create tension with light and dark.

You are also always free to incorporate your own favourite media, such as coloured pencils, watercolour pencils, chalk or alcohol markers.

There are absolutely no limits, so let off steam and have fun!

Drawing with Circles

A shape is always the beginning of any drawing. Every illustration must be planned. There are several important points to consider: shape, proportion, perspective and shadow.

All objects, animals and plants can be constructed with the help of basic geometric shapes, such as circles, triangles, squares and rectangles. The majority of organic shapes consist of circles.

In the beginning, it is easier if you use a pencil to first sketch out your illustration with the help of a few circles. They help you to quickly capture the correct shape and create harmonious drawings. This technique works for objects as well as for plants and animals.

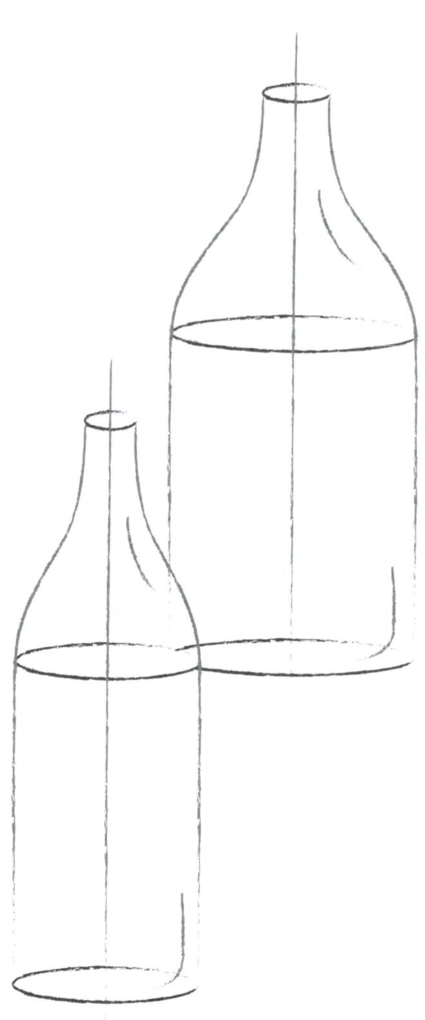

Let's start with a simple example: a bottle.

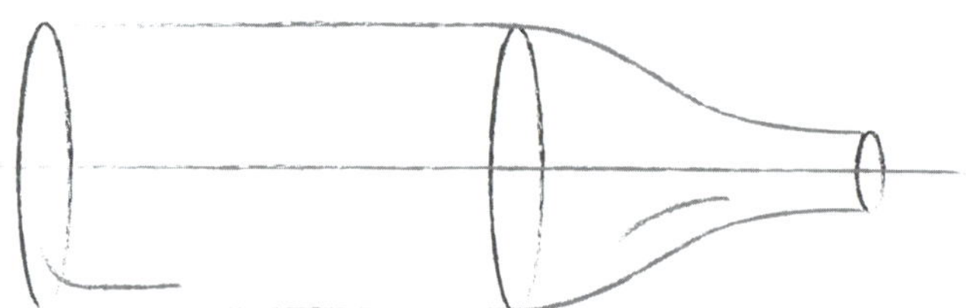

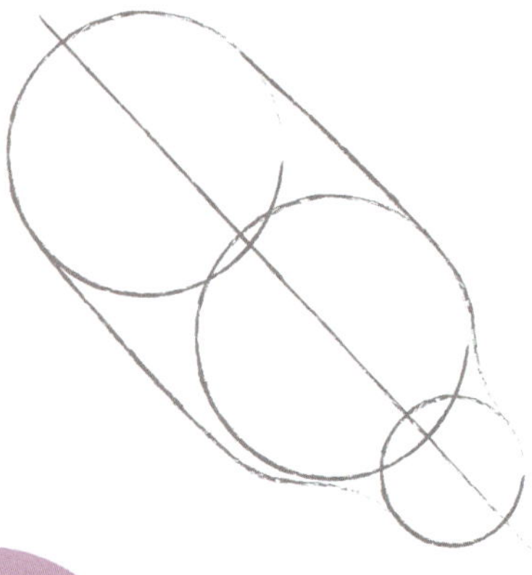

No matter whether the bottle is narrow or wide, whether it is drawn on its side, standing up or even from a difficult angle, the bottle can always be easily drawn with the aid of three parallel circles.

In the beginning, objects are the easiest to draw. We can place them on the table, move and turn them, and have time to clearly trace their shape.

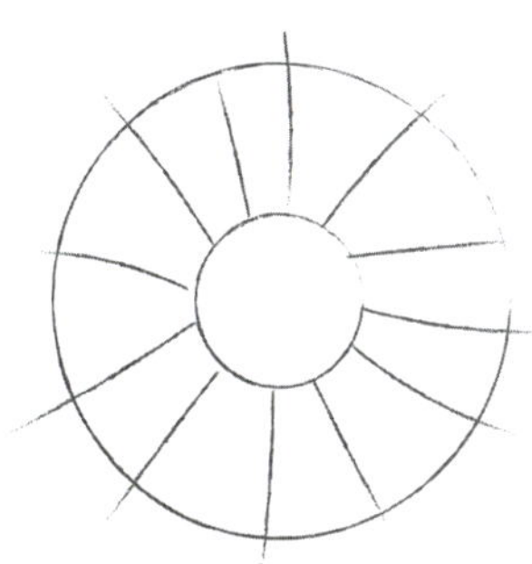

It is more difficult with plants and animals because they often won't stay still or because we can't simply place them on the table to draw them.

However, the technique with circles also works for them too. Let's use a daisy as an example. We all remember this flower from childhood and we can see them almost everywhere.

And just as the circle trick works for daisies, it works for animals and even for people. All animal shapes can be broken down into circles and therefore they can be drawn easily.

Just give it a try.

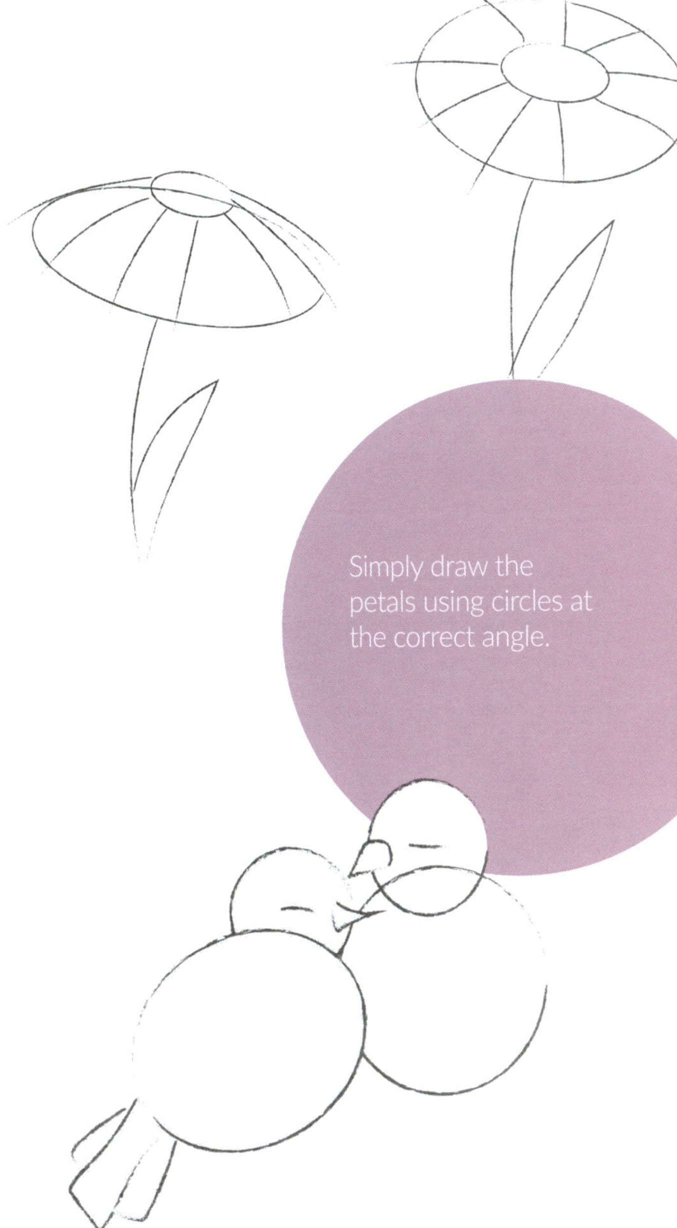

Simply draw the petals using circles at the correct angle.

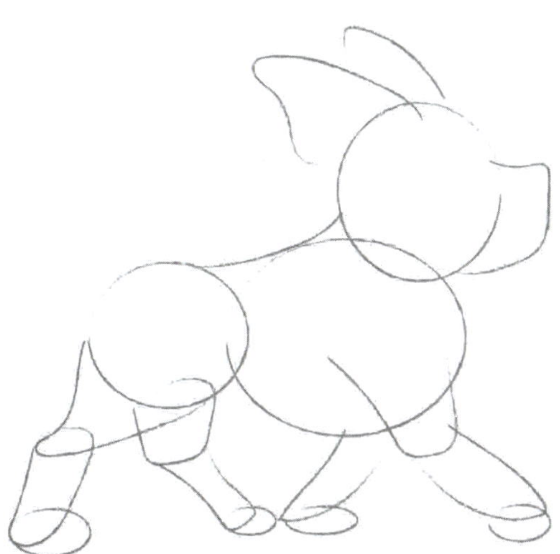

Animals can be drawn from circles for the head, body and limbs.

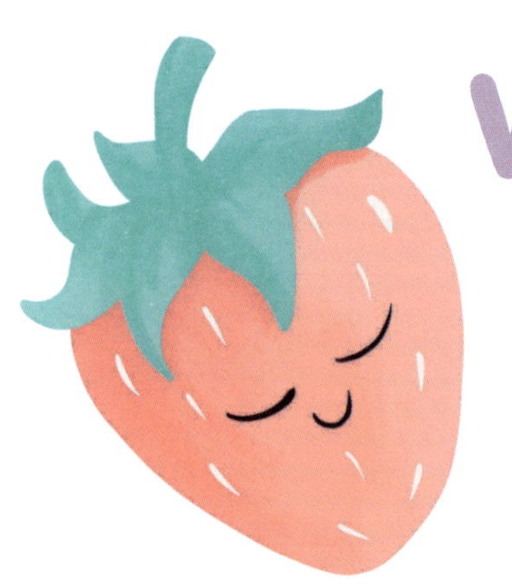

What Is Kawaii

Kawaii has its origins in Japan and means something like "cute", "tiny" or even "pretty".

In Japan, these cute illustrations and shapes can be found everywhere in daily life. Above all food, especially sweets and fruit, get a really cute make-over as "Kawaii" illustrations. However, everyday objects, such as cars or kitchen utensils and accessories, are often illustrated with big round eyes, friendly faces and cuddly shapes.

How Do I Draw Kawaii

If you want to draw cute Kawaii illustrations, then you are certainly wondering what is typical for Kawaii style.

Here are a few simple tricks that you can use:
- The shapes are predominantly round,
- You can achieve the typical facial expressions using eyes, mouth and cheeks,
- All illustrations always appear very emotional (happy, sad, annoyed...) and
- The colours are mainly friendly pastel-like shades.

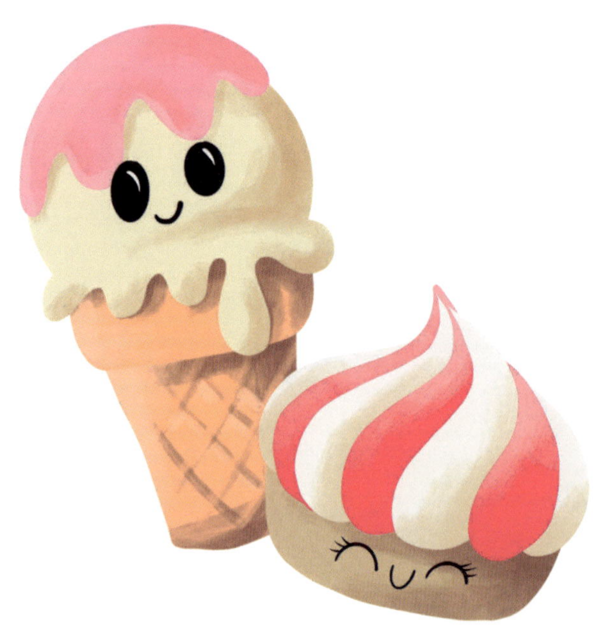

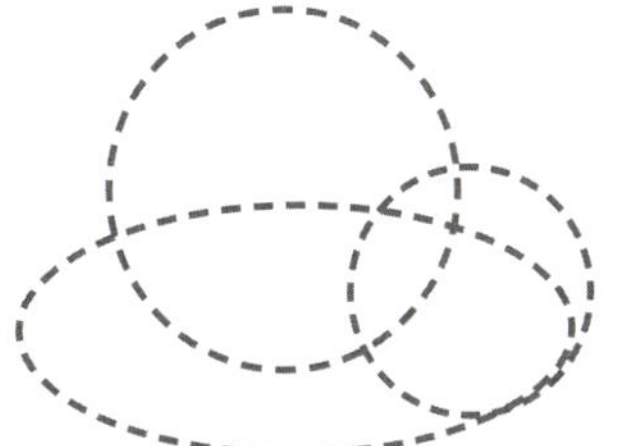

Round shapes can be easily drawn by sketching circles.

They can then be turned into really cute shapes.

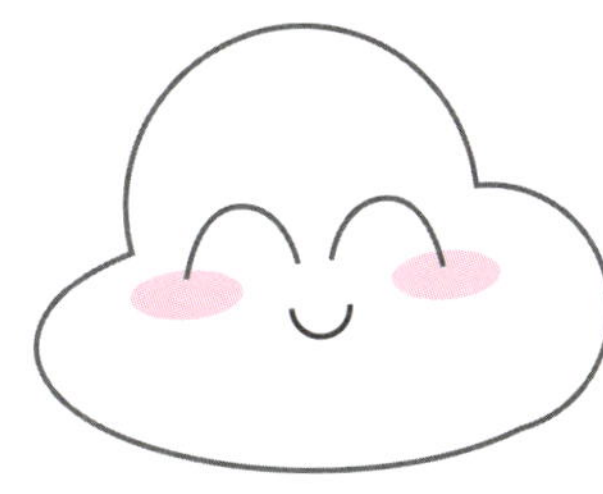

Draw half circles for the eyes and mouth, and add round cheeks.

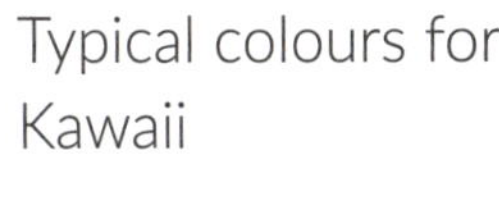

Typical colours for Kawaii

Emotions

You can simply give your Kawaii characters emotions with just a few strokes. You only need to pay attention to the eyes, mouth and maybe the eyebrows in order to make an emotion clearer. Here are a few examples:

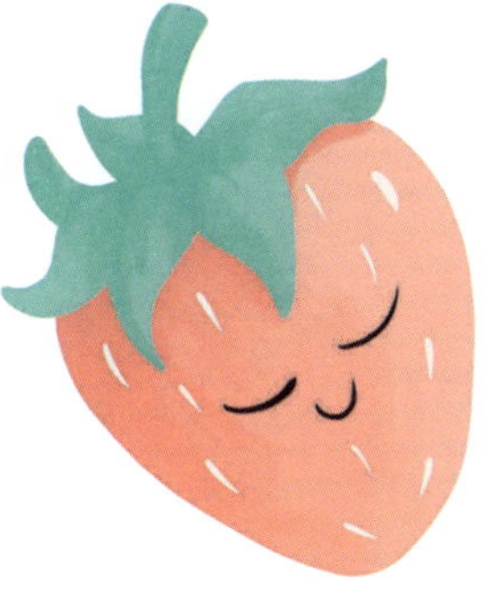

Closed eyes and a smile = content

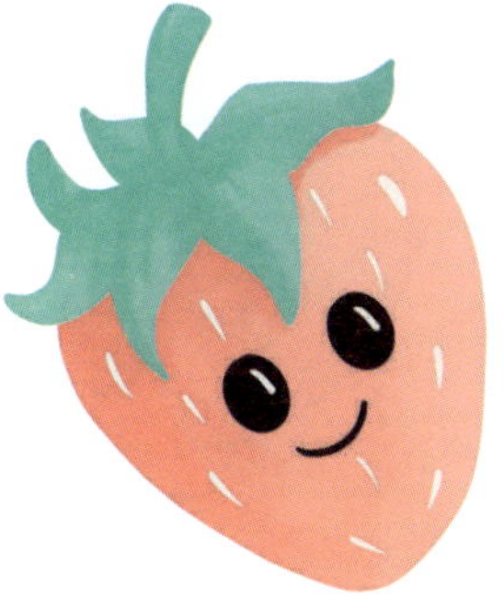

Open eyes and a smile = Good mood

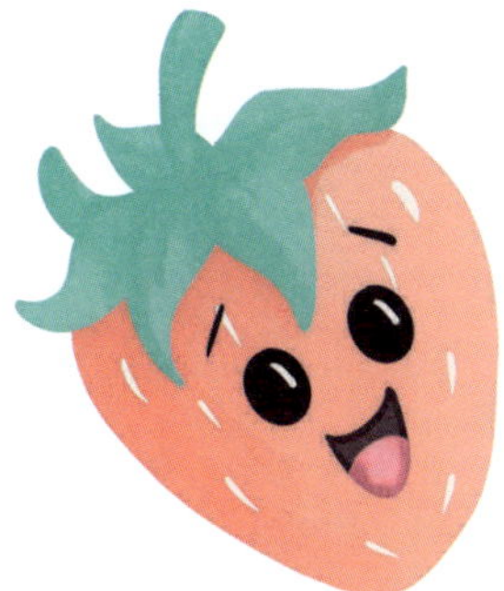

Closed eyes and a laughing mouth = Happy

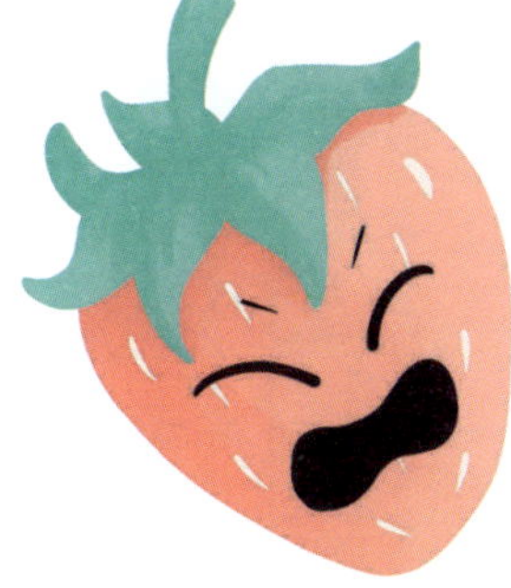

Scrunched eyes and twisted mouth = Angry

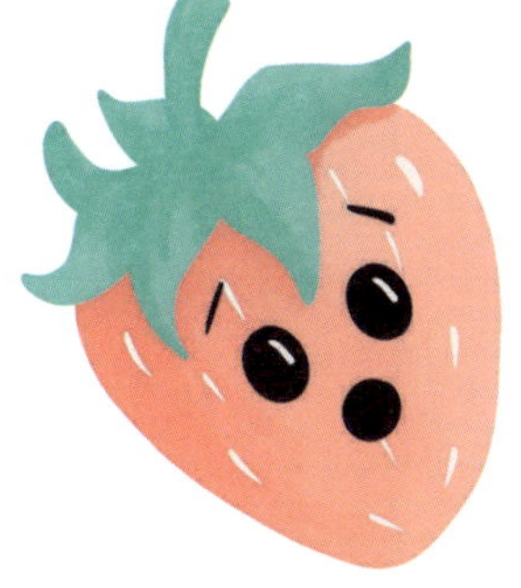

Open eyes and circle mouth = Surprised / Shocked

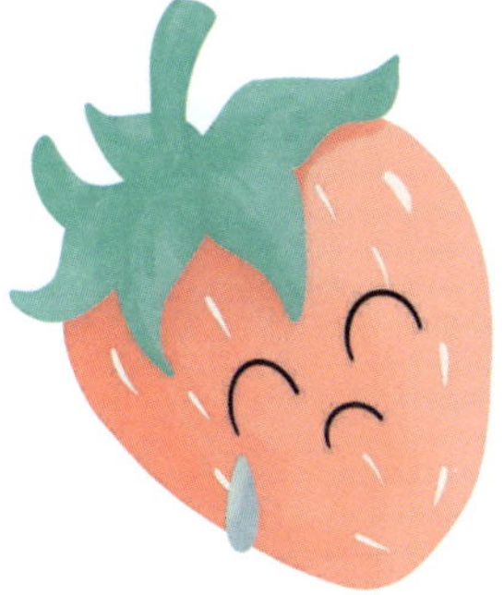

Closed eyes and sad mouth = Sad

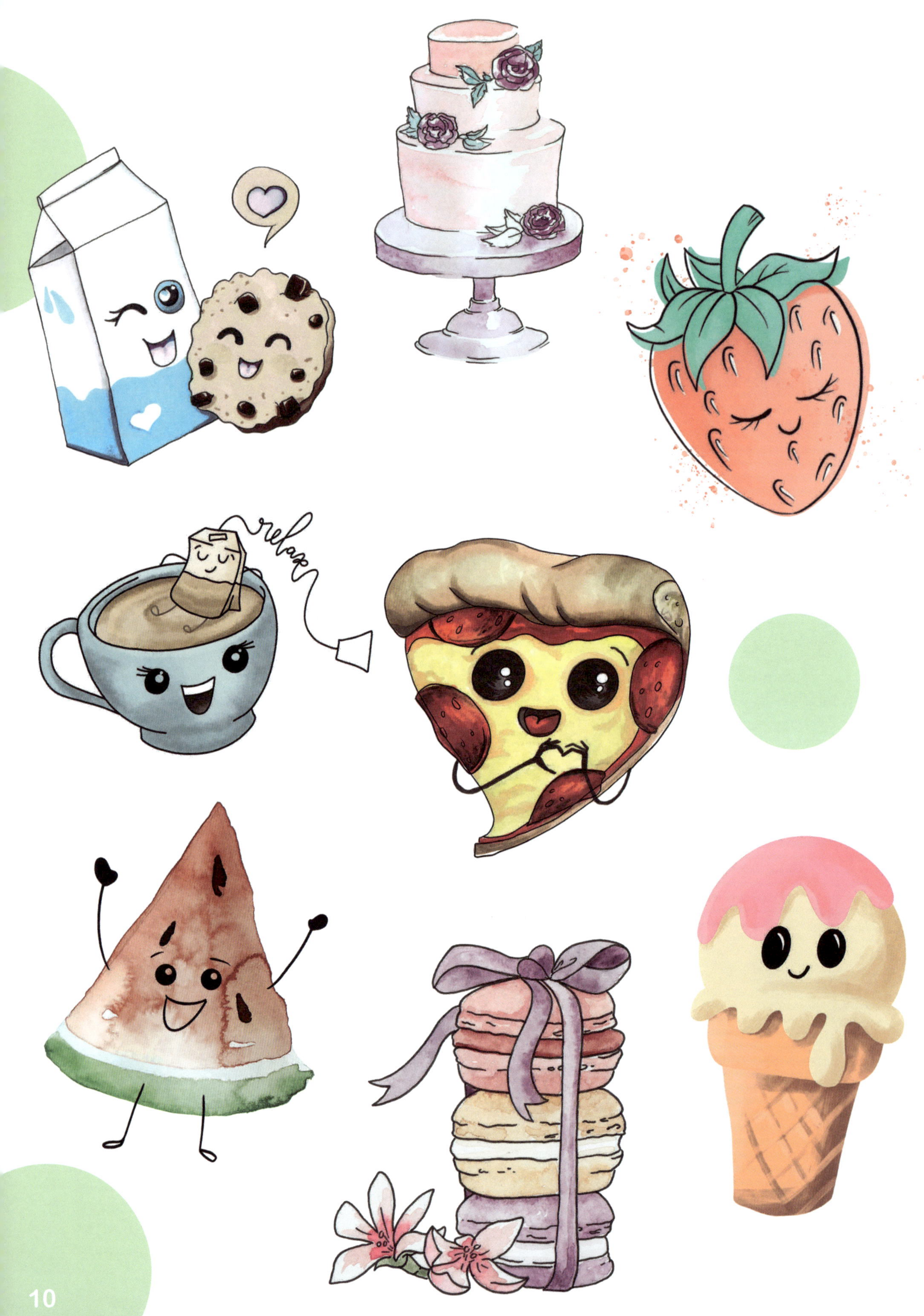
relax

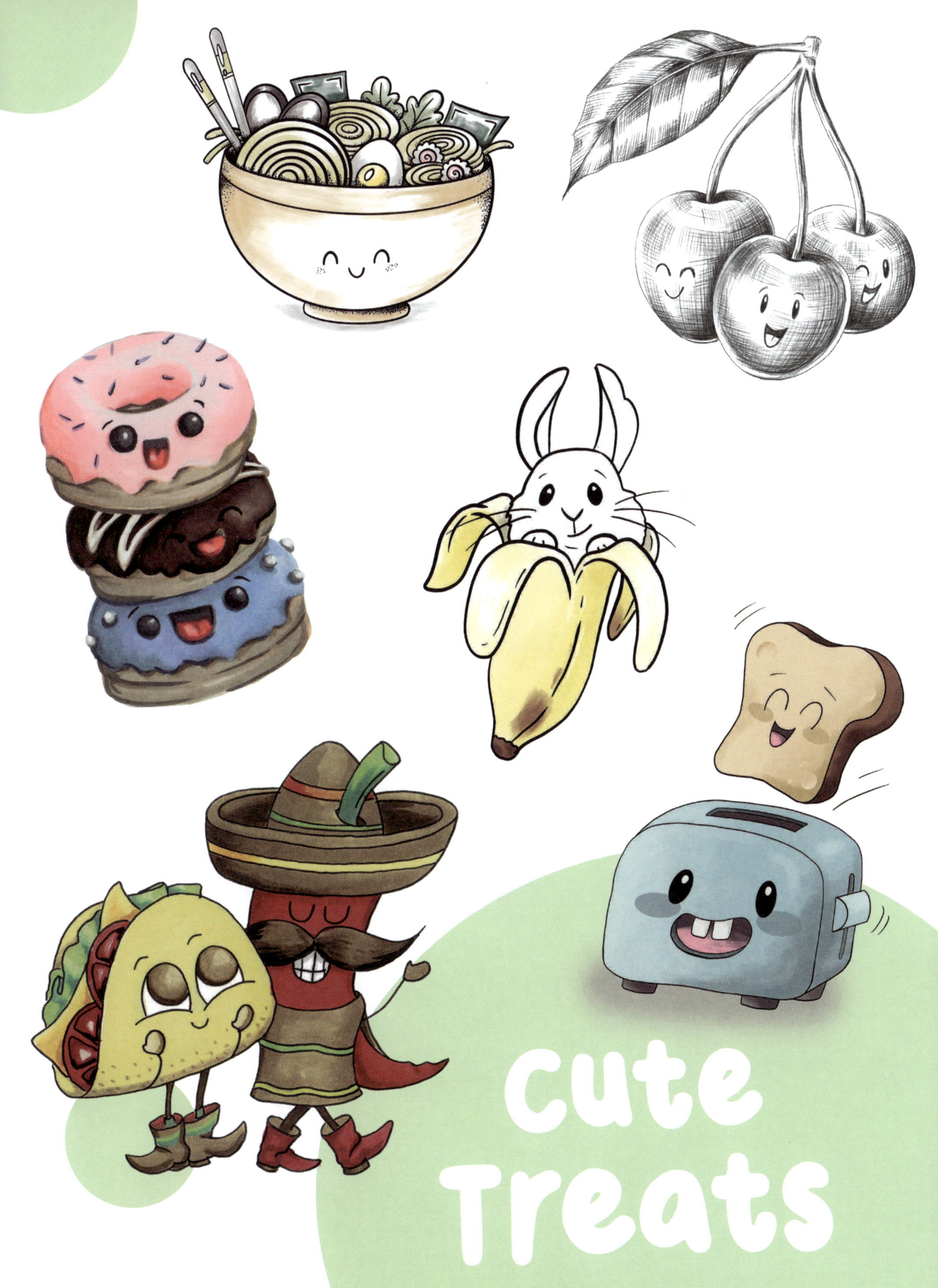
Cute
Treats

Drills

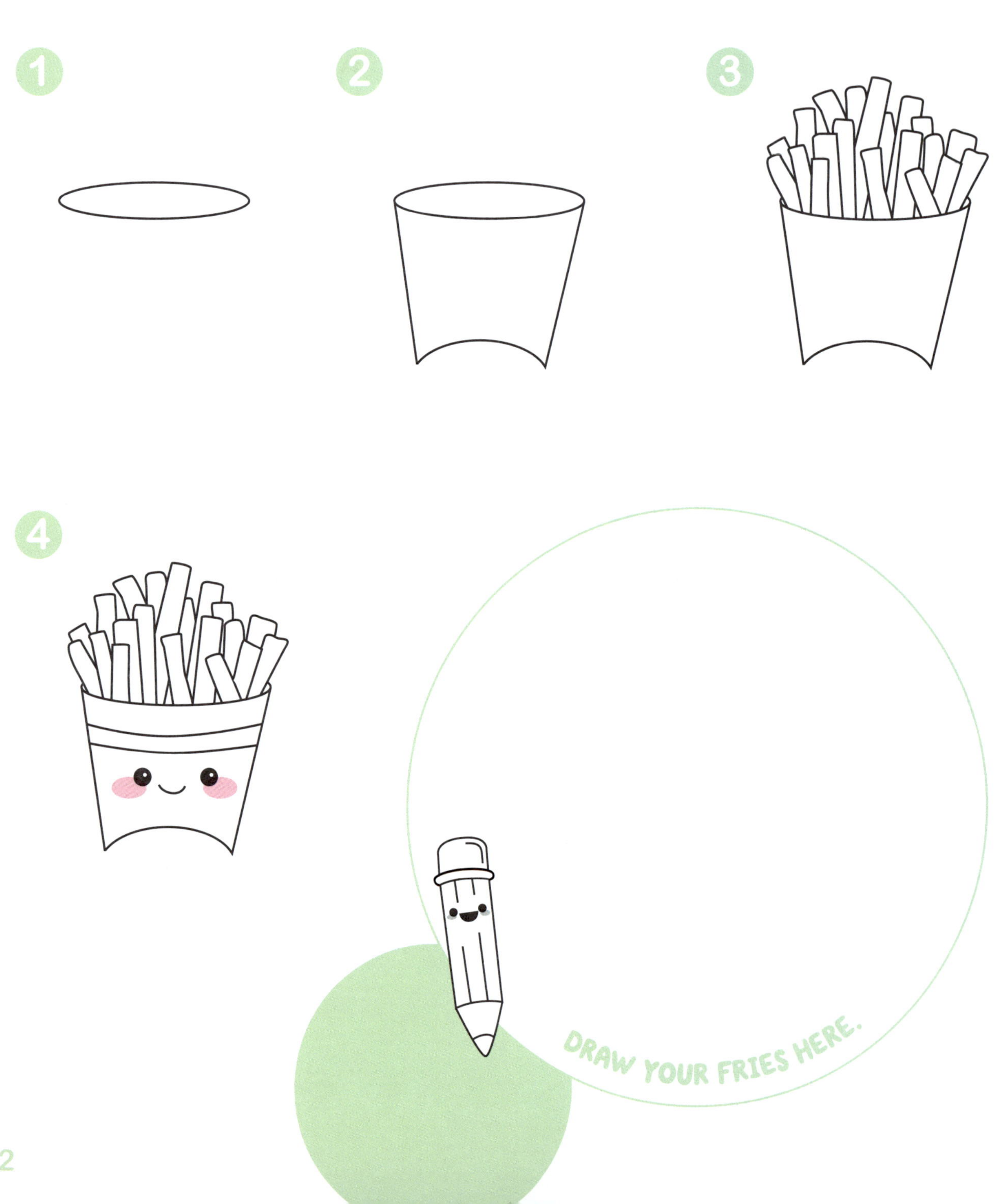

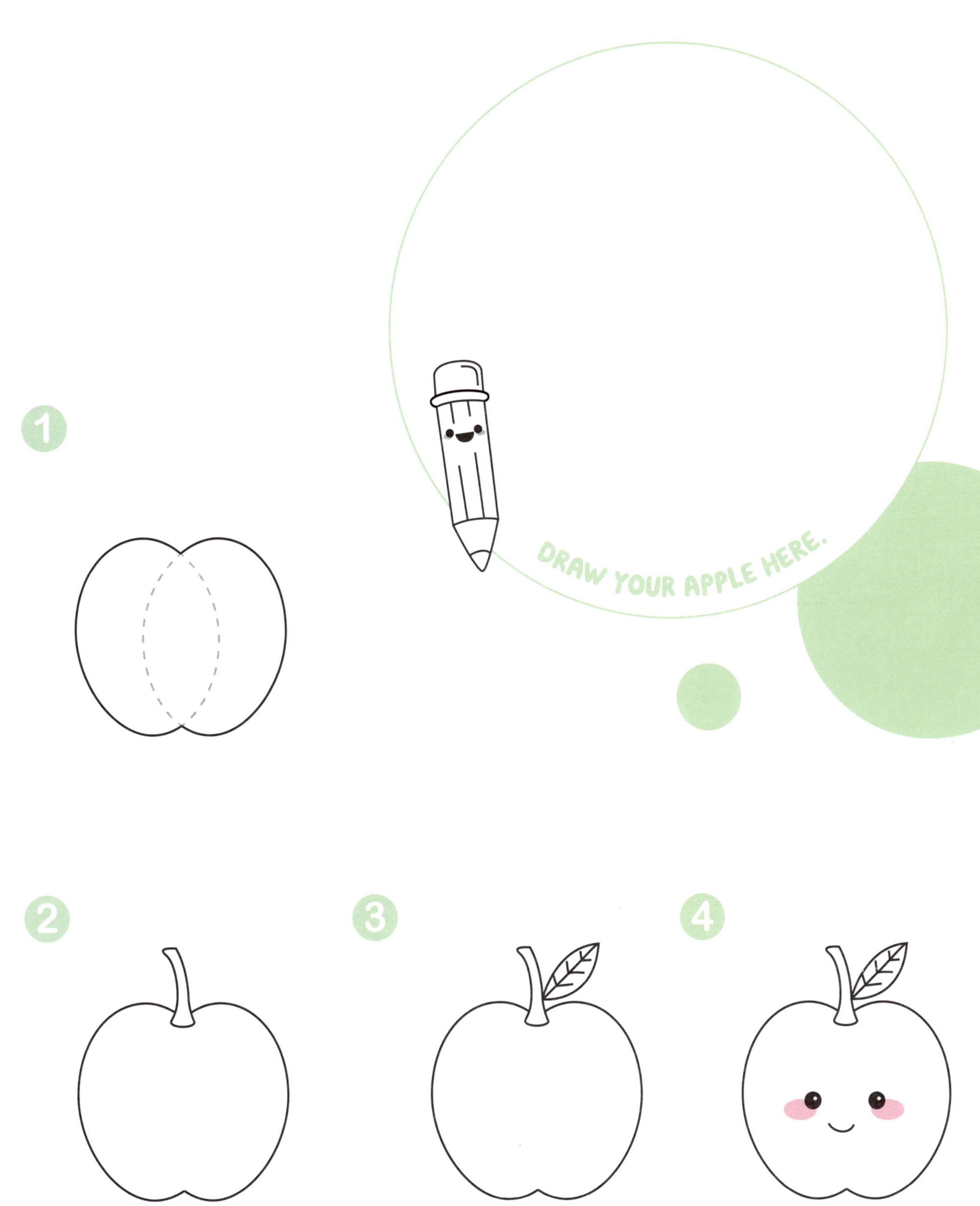
DRAW YOUR APPLE HERE.
1
2
3
4

Drills

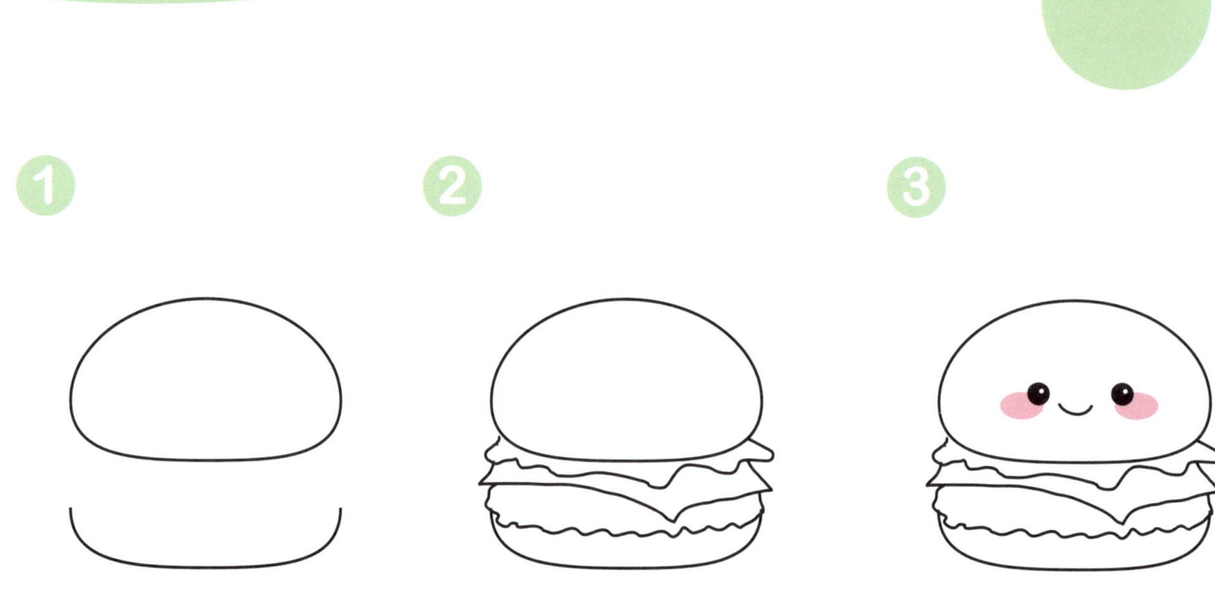

4

DRAW YOUR HAMBURGER HERE

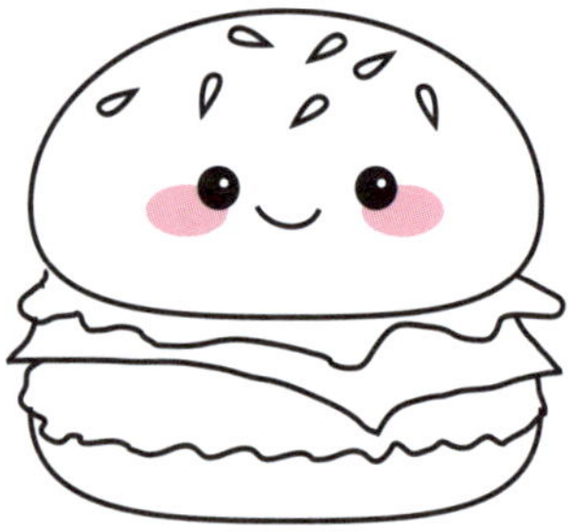

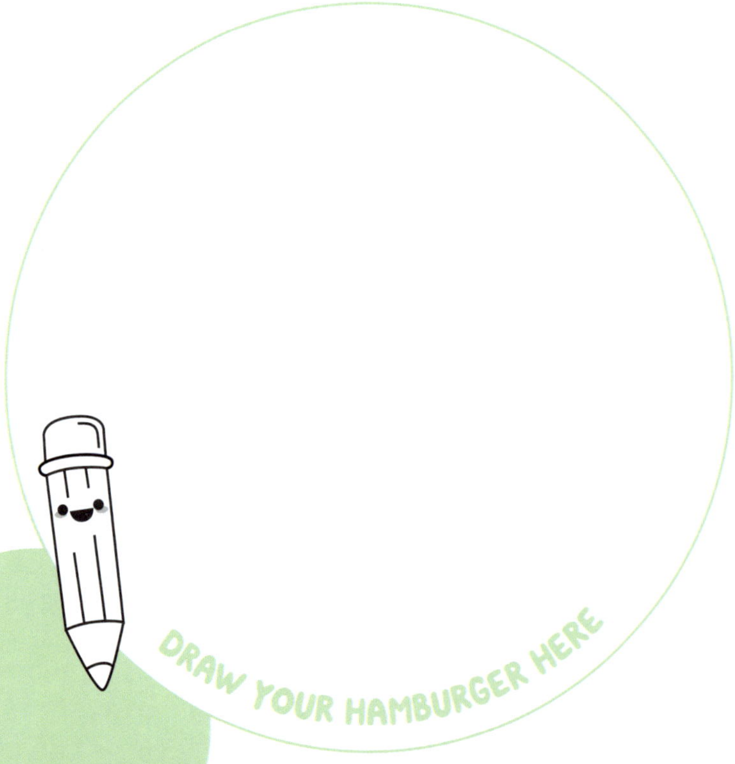

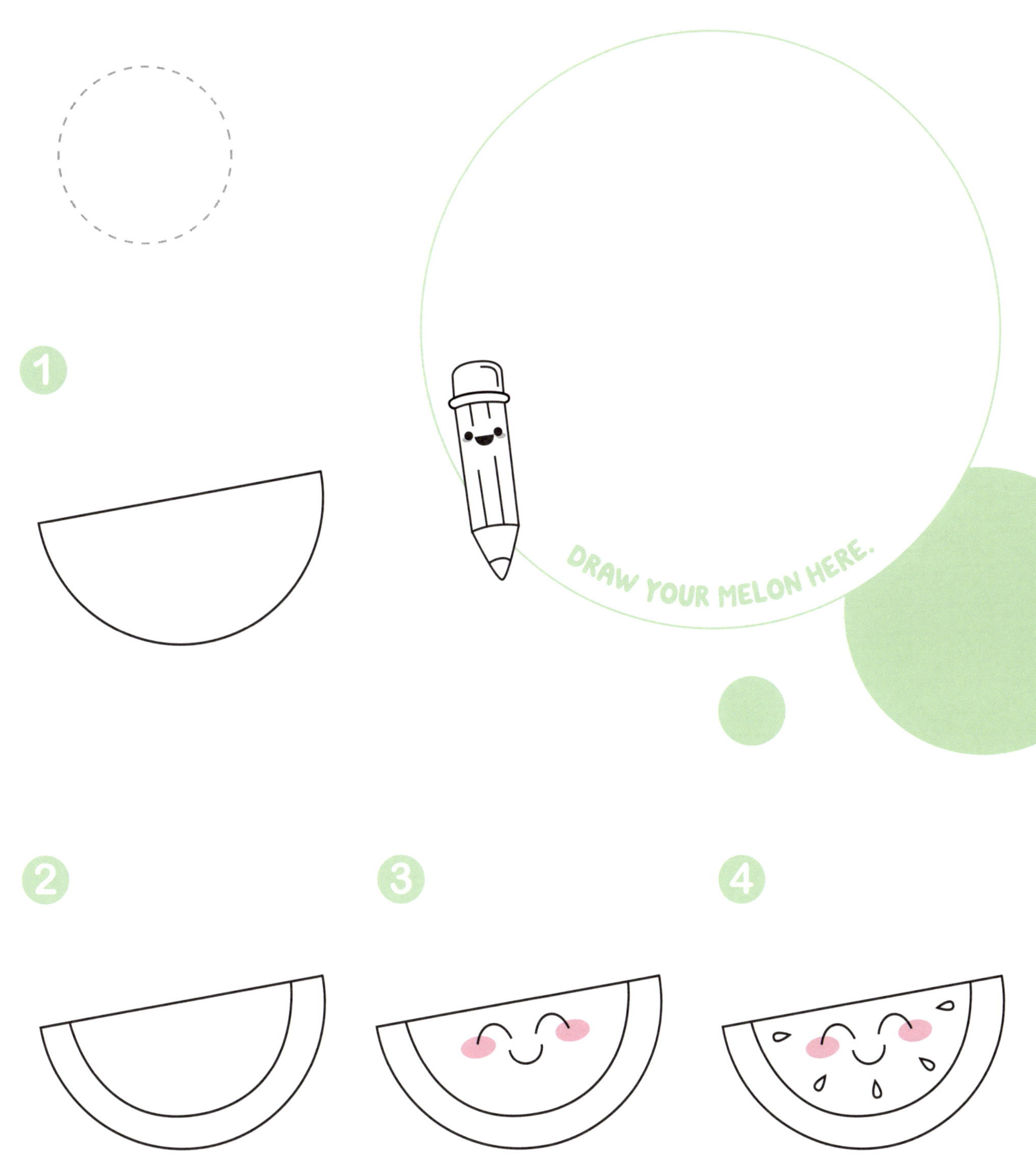
1
DRAW YOUR MELON HERE.
2
3
4

Drills

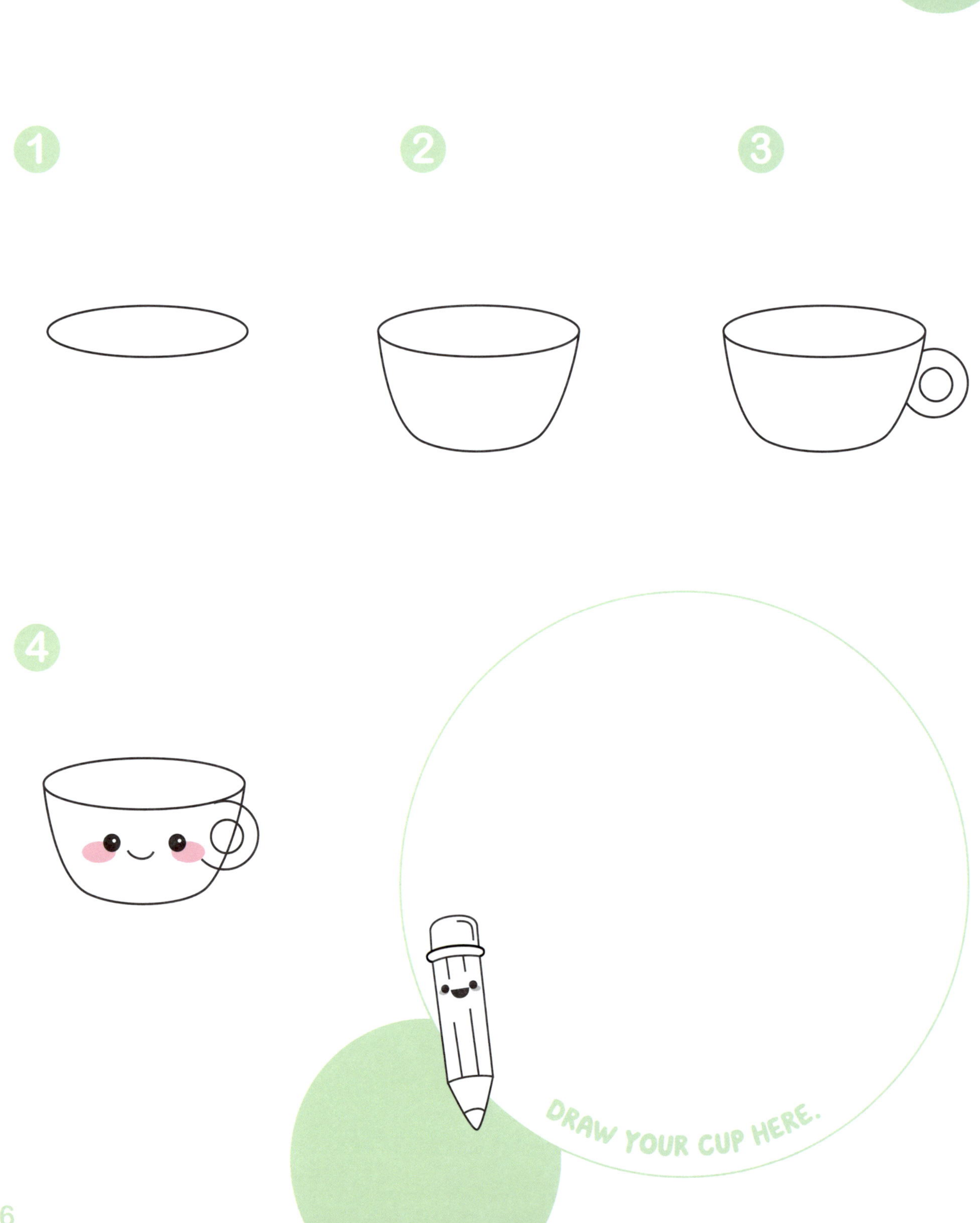

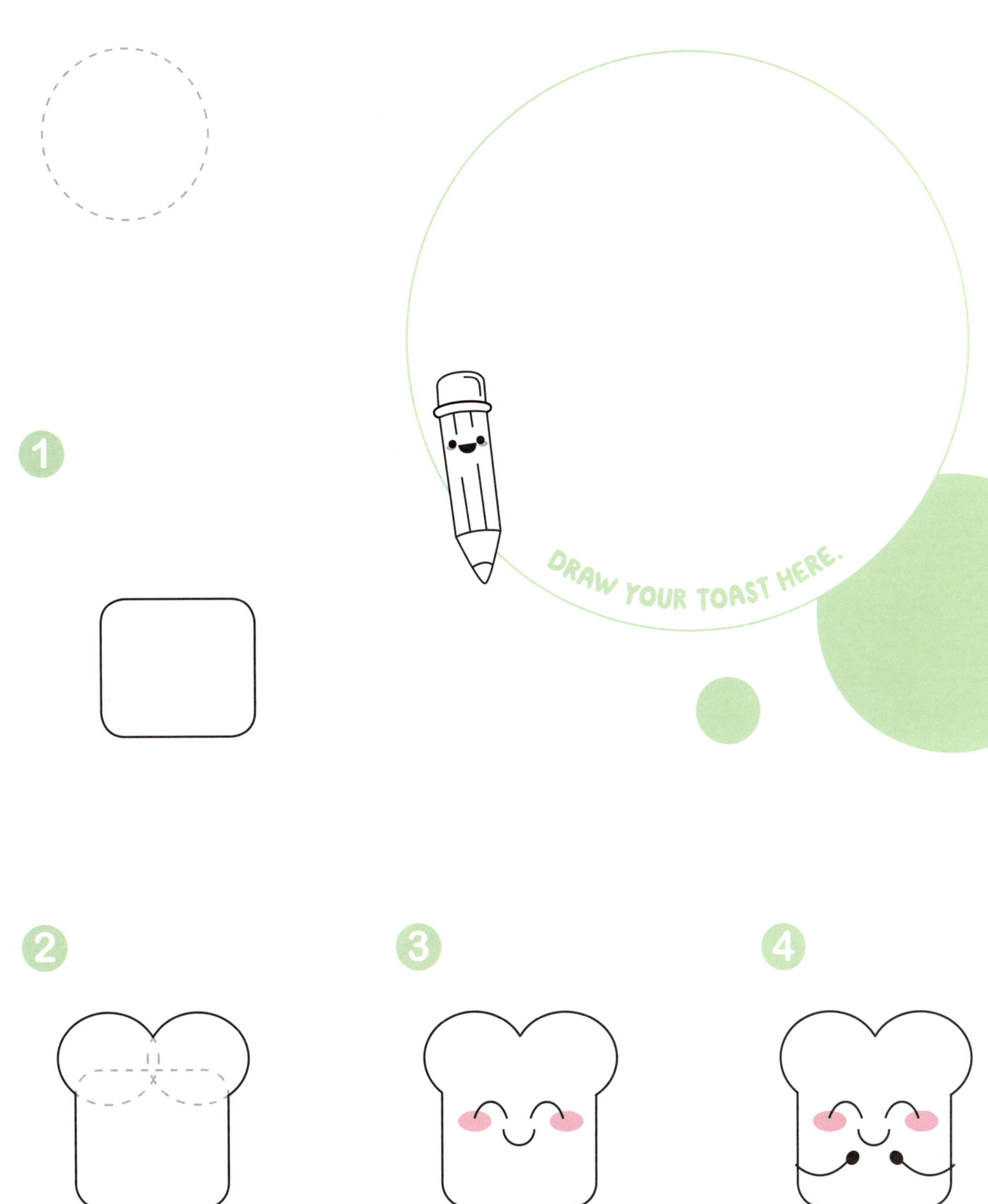
DRAW YOUR TOAST HERE.
1
2
3
4

watermelon

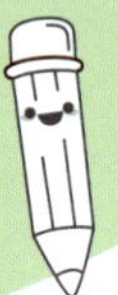

1

Draw the shape of a piece of cake.

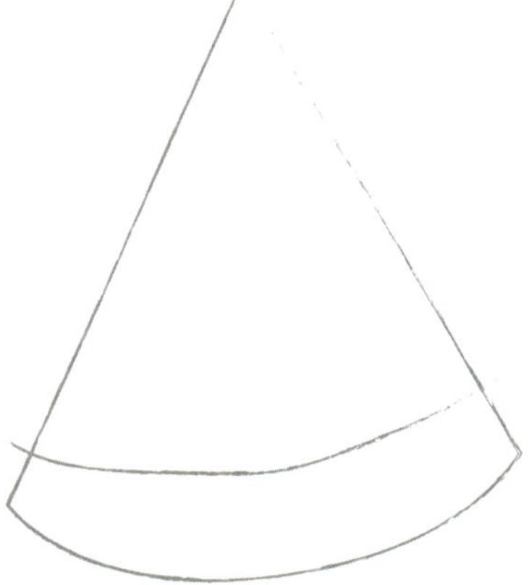

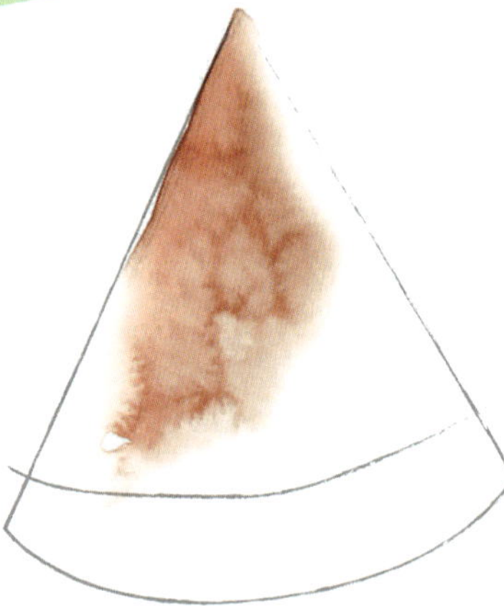

2 Start to wet the area that is to be red and add some red watercolour to it.

Paint the whole area red.

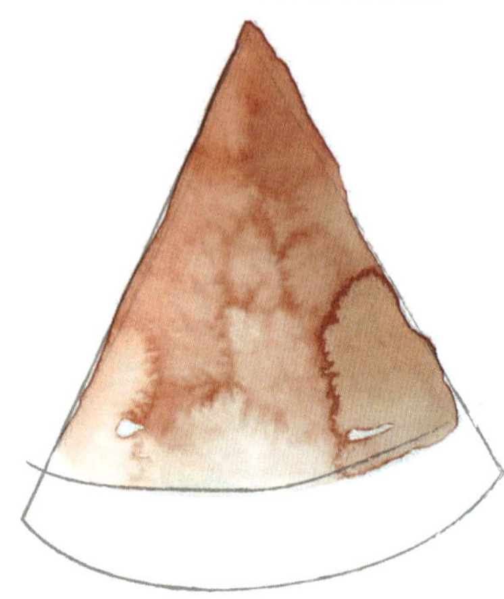

4 Allow the red to dry and wet the area that is to be green later. Add some green watercolour to the edge.

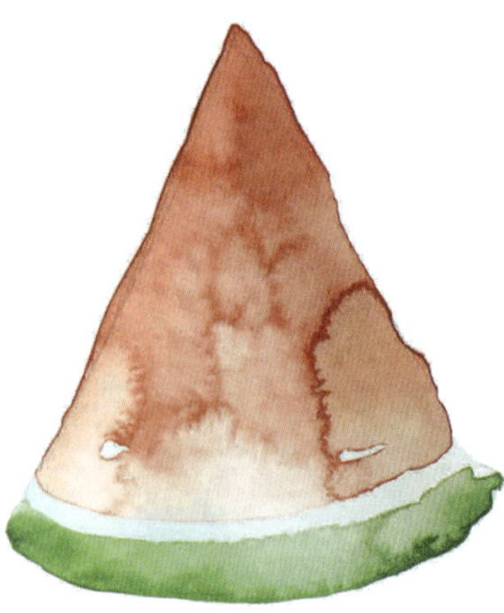

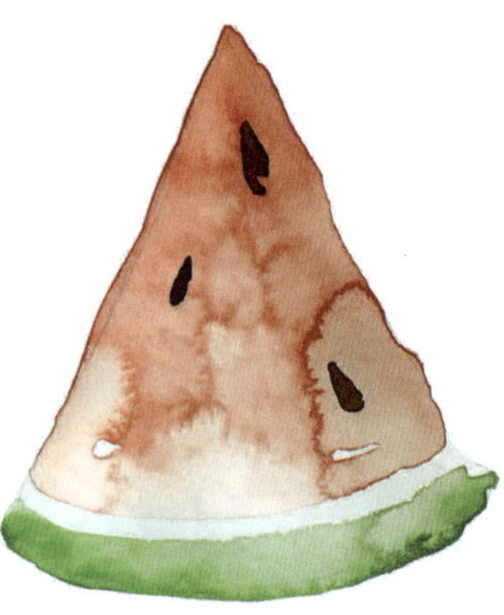

5

Once the red has completely dried, you can paint the seeds.

Take a black felt tip to draw a face and legs on your melon.

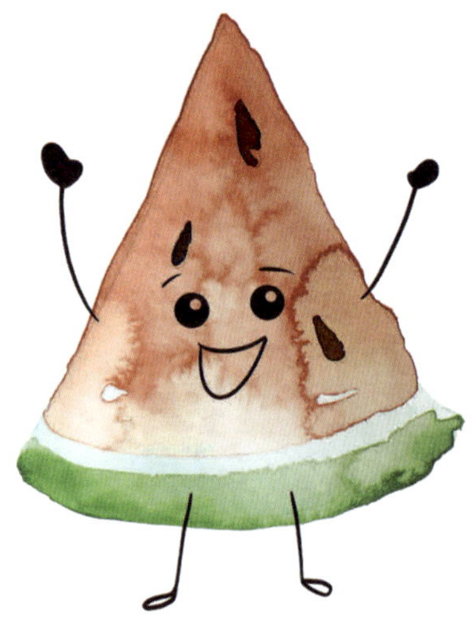

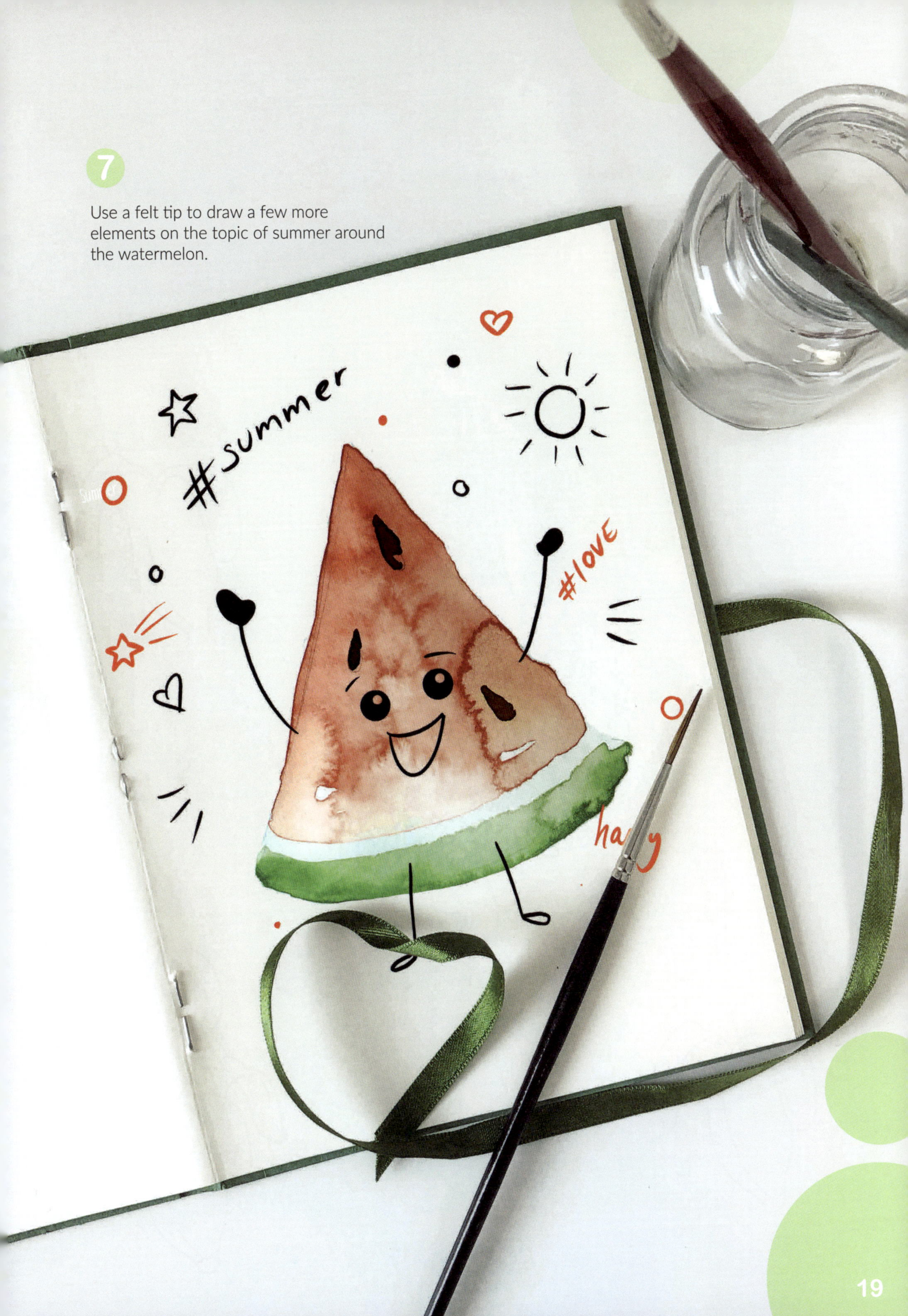

7

Use a felt tip to draw a few more elements on the topic of summer around the watermelon.

Bunana

Draw two circles and use them to plan your banana.

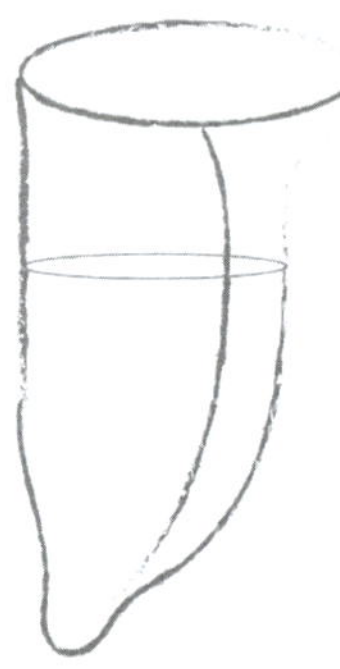

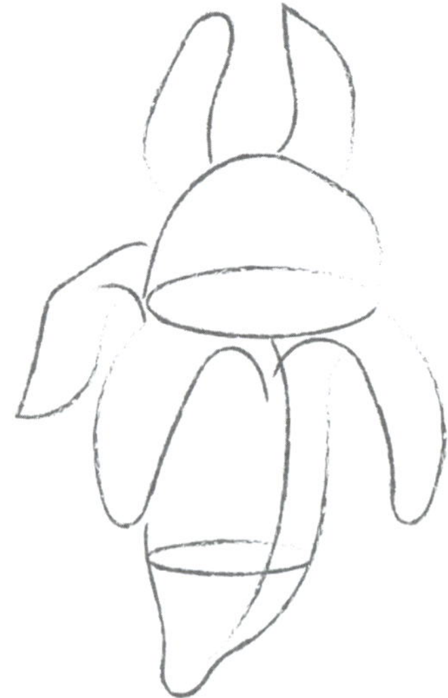

2 Sketch the bunny and the parts of the banana skin that hang down.

Use a fineliner to start drawing the outlines of the banana.

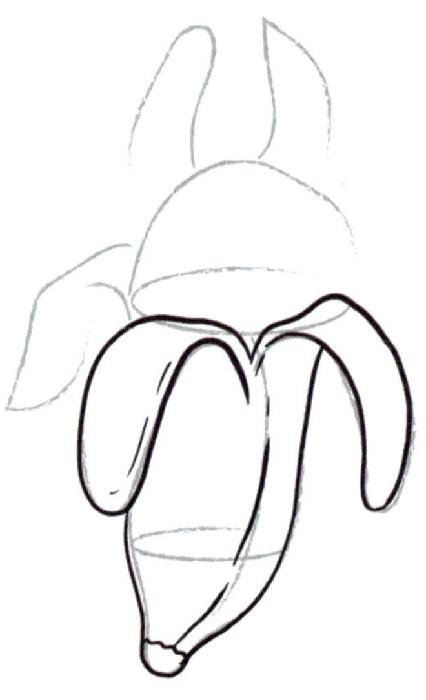

4 Also draw in the parts of the banana skin that are in the background.

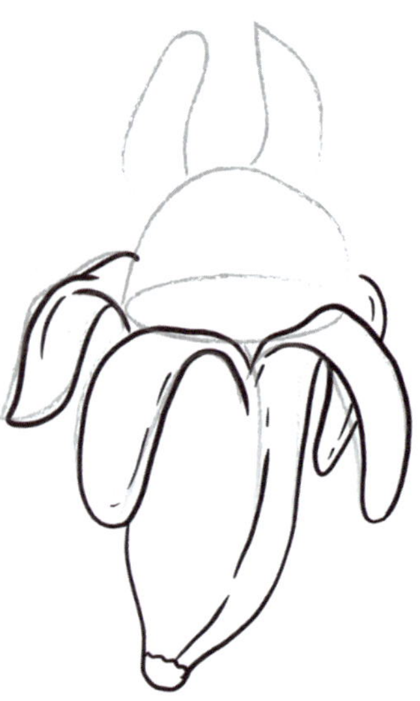

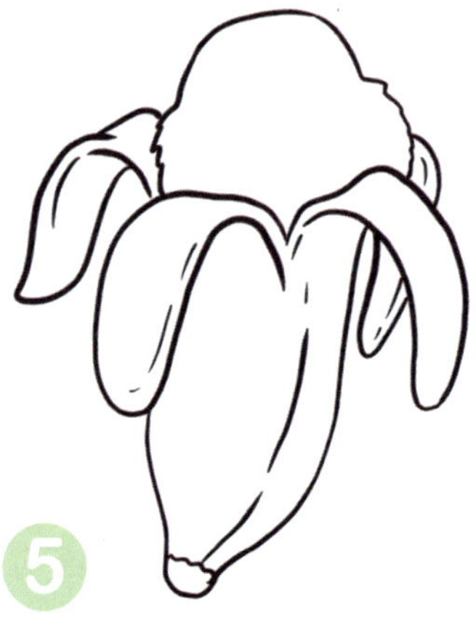

5

Draw your bunny's head.

Complete your bunny with ears, face and paws.

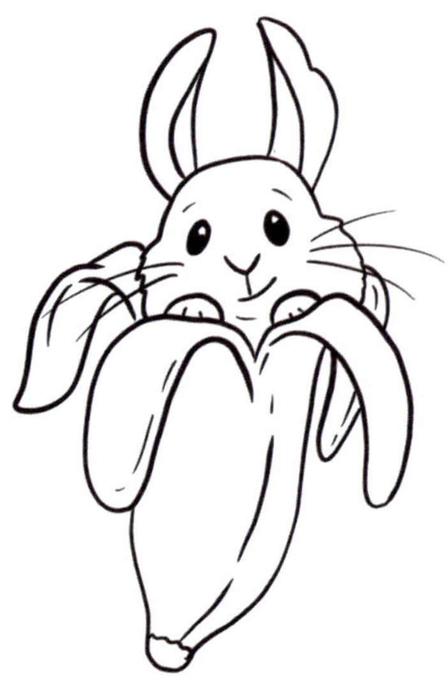

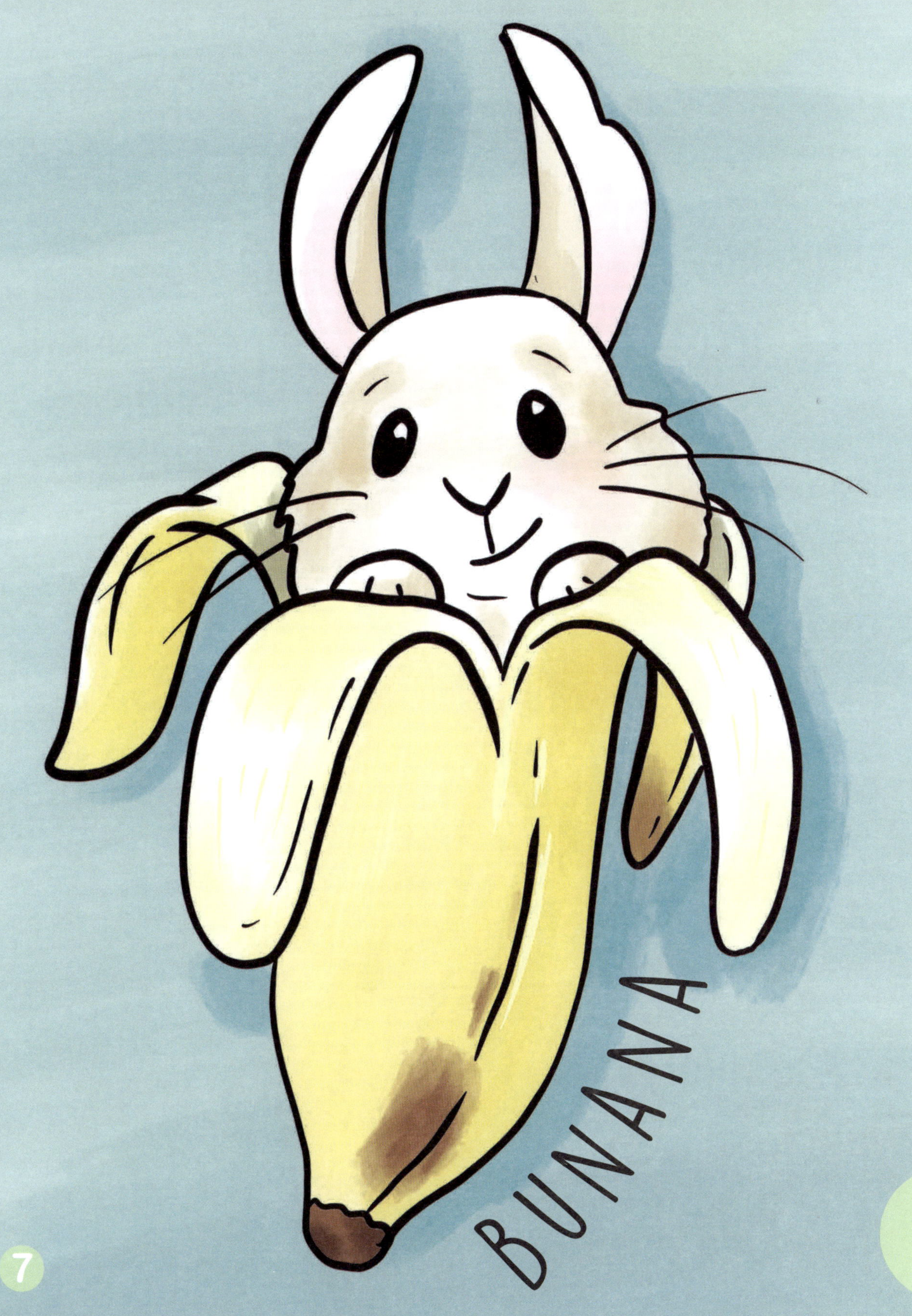

7

Use cheerful colours to paint your bunny and banana to complete your Bunana.

Cake

For each tier of the cake, draw two parallel ellipses.

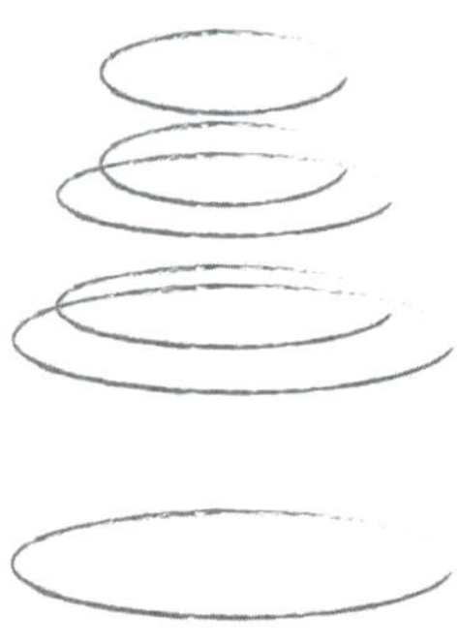

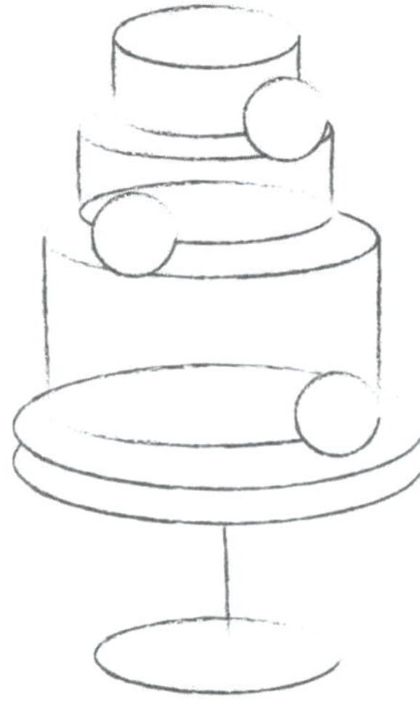

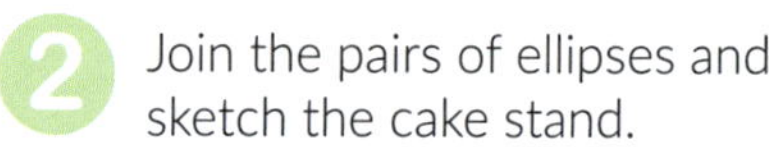

2 Join the pairs of ellipses and sketch the cake stand.

Use a fineliner to draw the first tier.

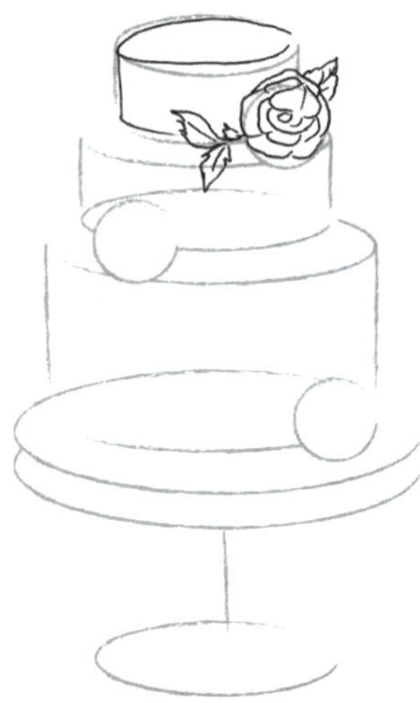

4 Draw the second tier and position the flower on the other side.

5 Now for the third tier.

6 Finally add a fancy foot to the cake stand. Then carefully erase the pencil sketch.

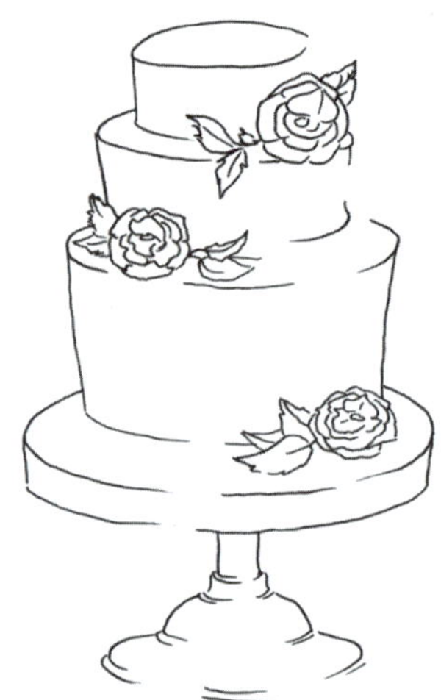

CAKE IS THE ANSWER NO MATTER THE QUESTION

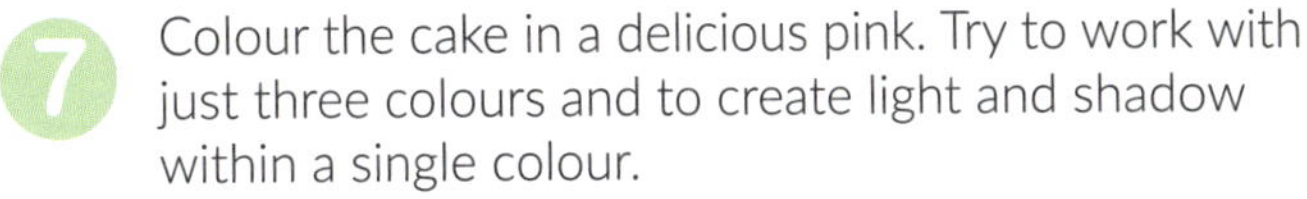

7 Colour the cake in a delicious pink. Try to work with just three colours and to create light and shadow within a single colour.

Strawberry

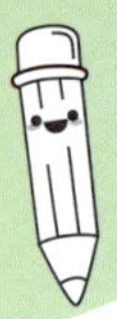

1

Start with a large circle with a rounded tip.

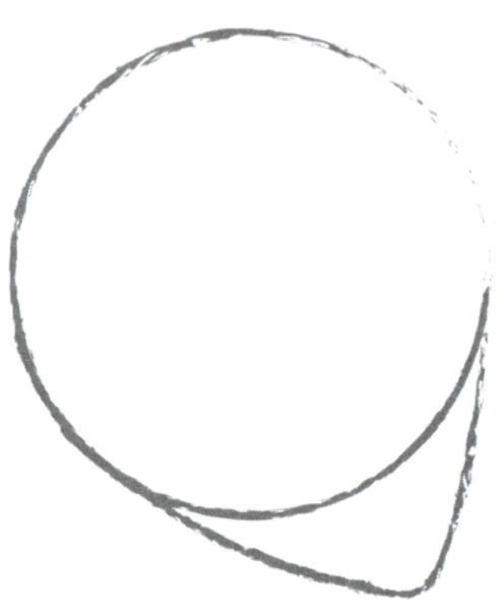

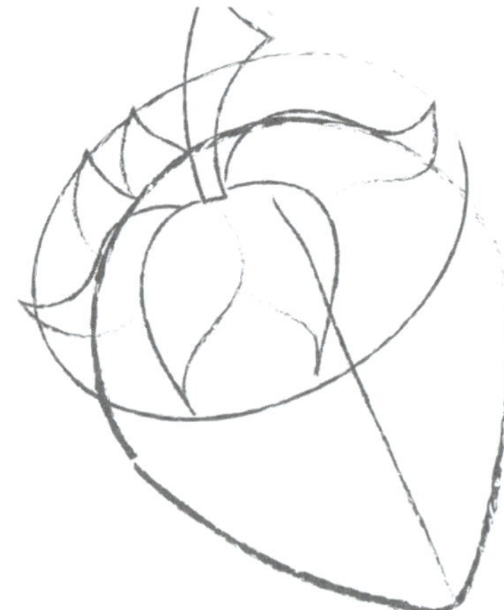

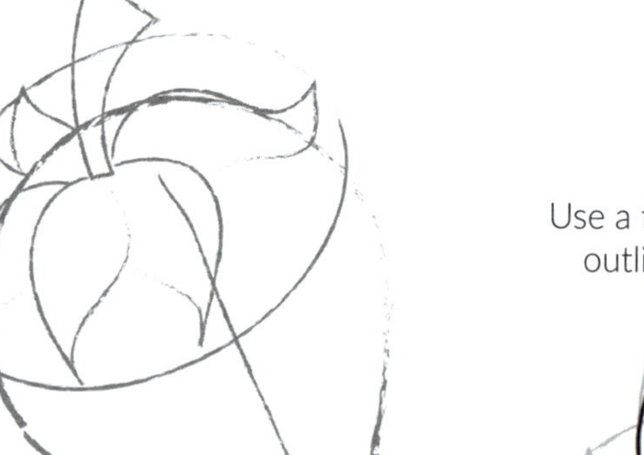

2 Sketch an oval to plan and shape the strawberry's stalk and leaves.

3

Use a fineliner to draw the outlines of the leaves.

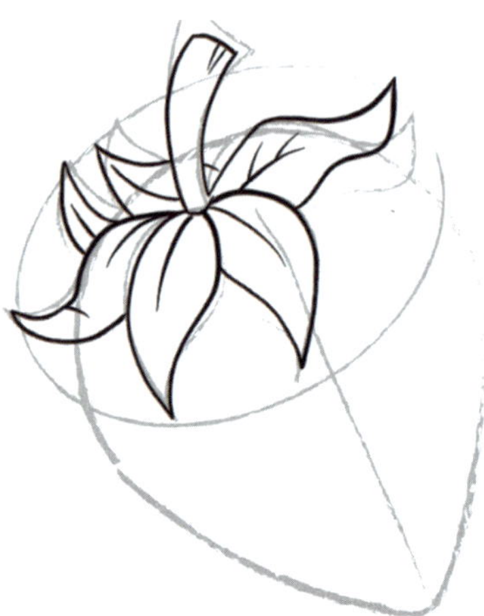

4 Draw the outline of your strawberry and its face. Carefully erase the pencil sketch.

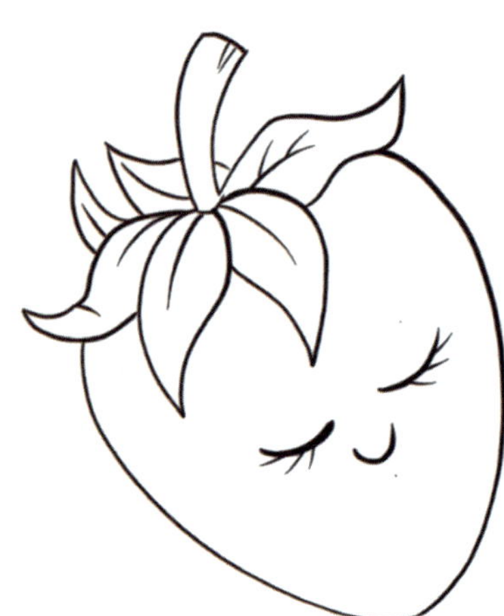

5

Position the strawberry seeds around the face.

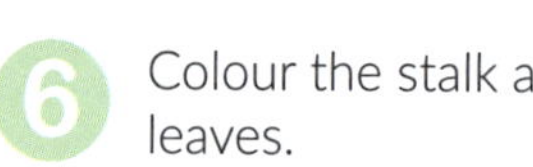

6 Colour the stalk and the leaves.

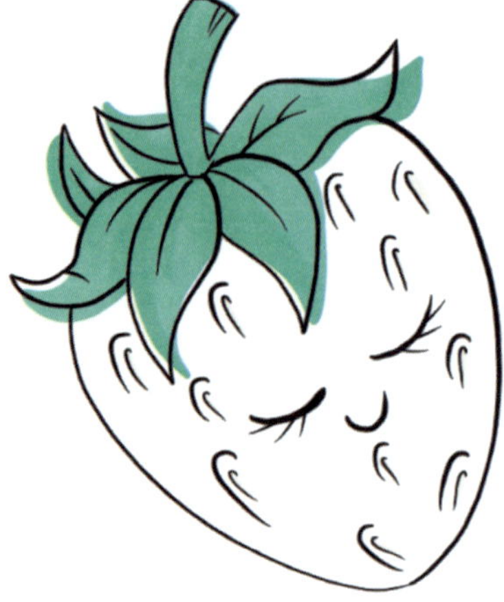

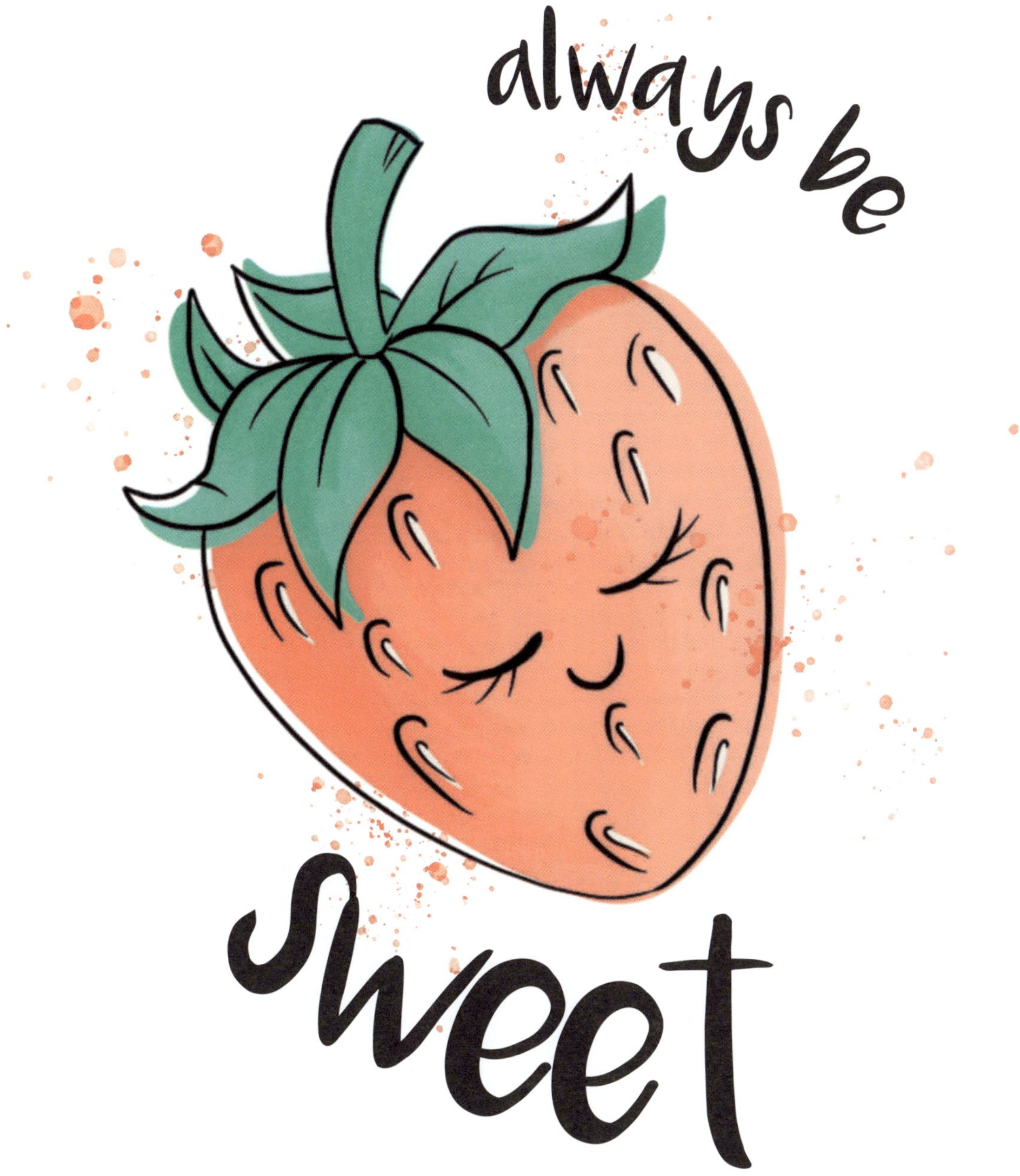

always be

sweet

Fully paint the strawberry - you can go over the white seeds with a white gel pen later.

Macarons

Sketch three parallel ellipses for the first macaron.

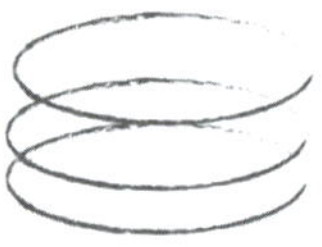

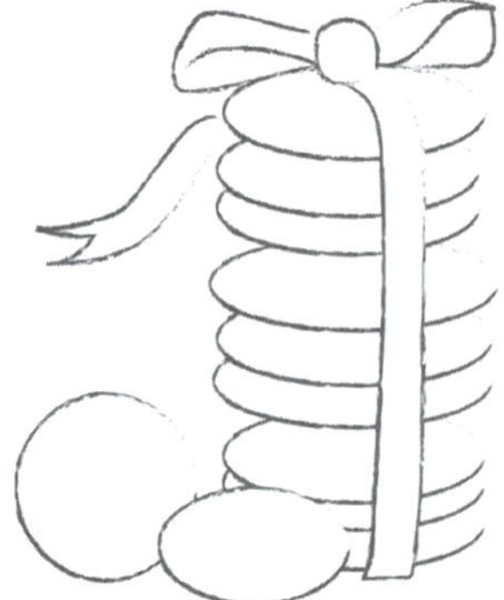

2 Complete your sketch with two more macarons, a ribbon and two circles for the flowers.

Use a fineliner to draw the outline of the ribbon and the top macaron.

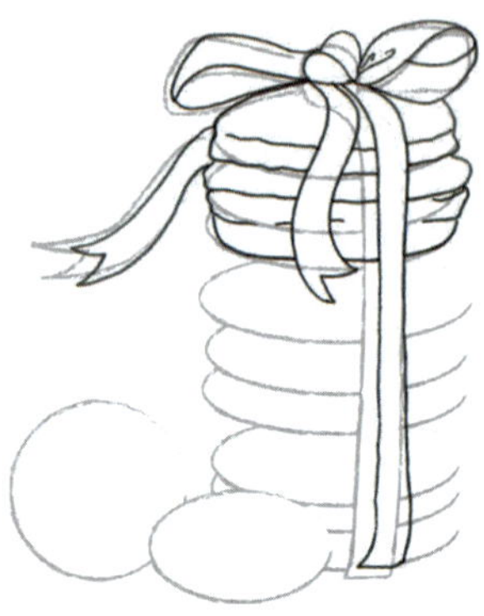

4 Draw the second macaron.

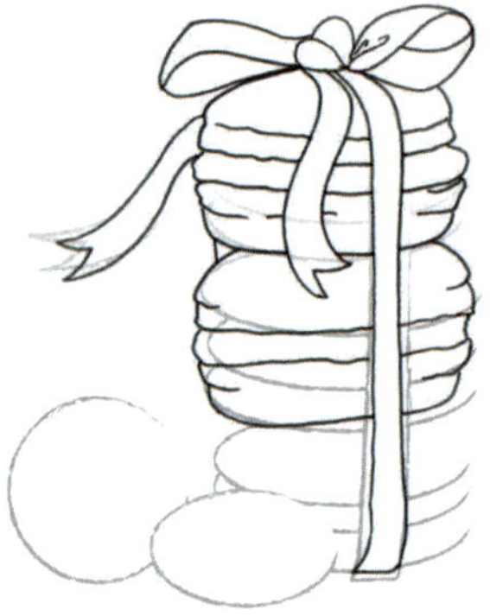

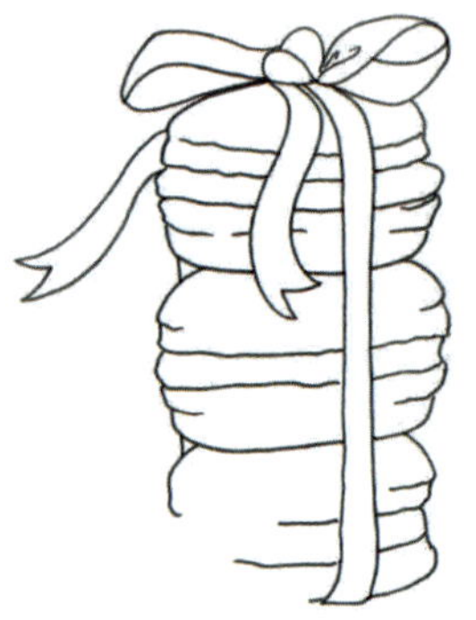

5 And now the third and final macaron.

6 Finish the illustration by adding two flowers.

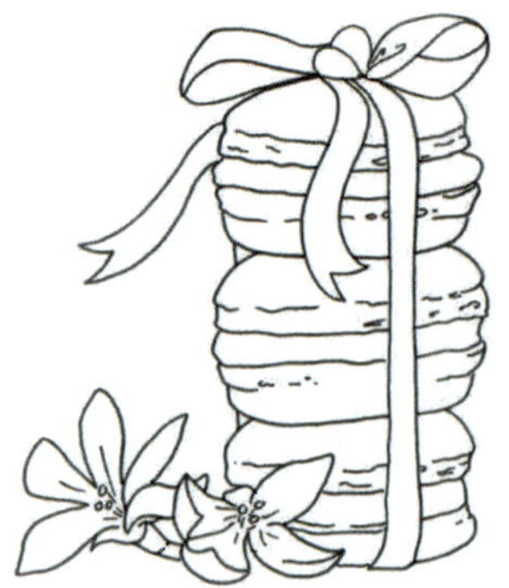

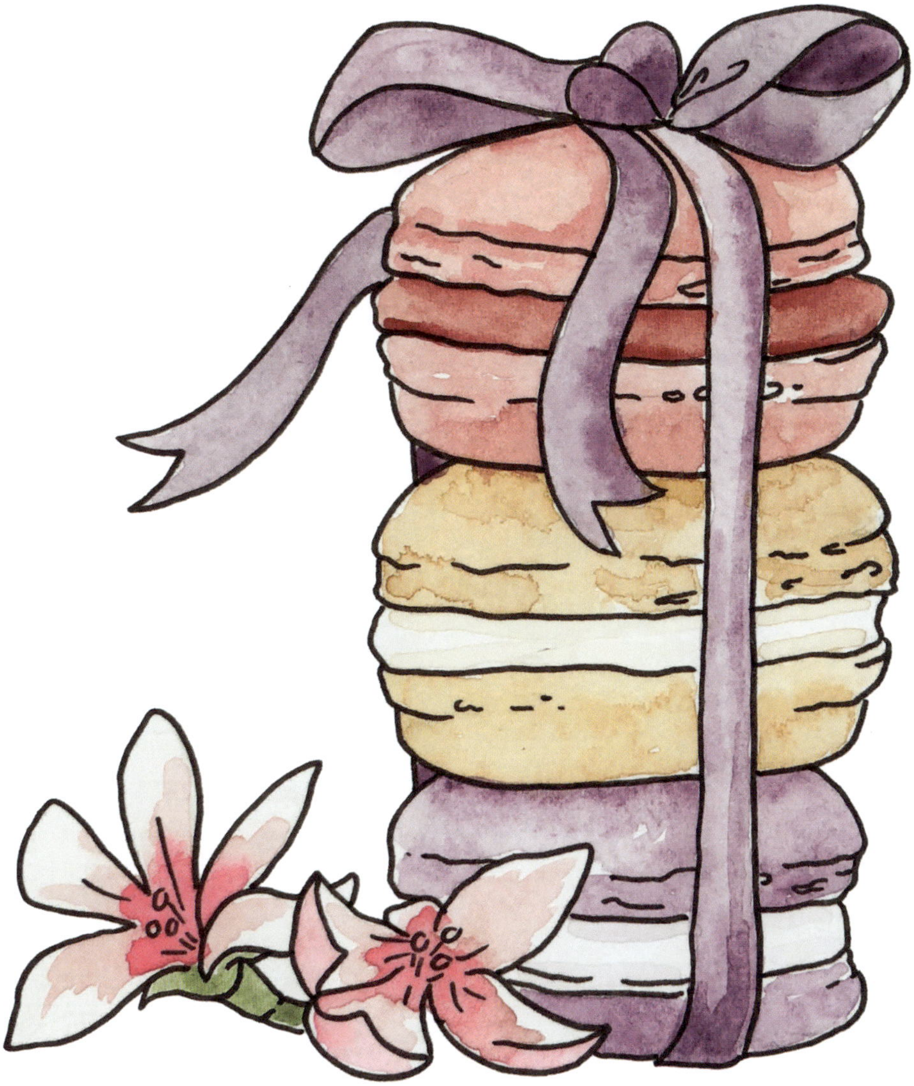

Pretty pastel shades are typical for macarons. Paint with your favourite colours.

Ramen Soup

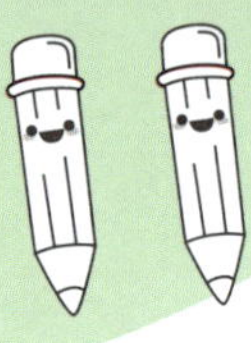

1

Sketch two ellipses: one large and a small one underneath it. Connect them so that they create the shape of a bowl.

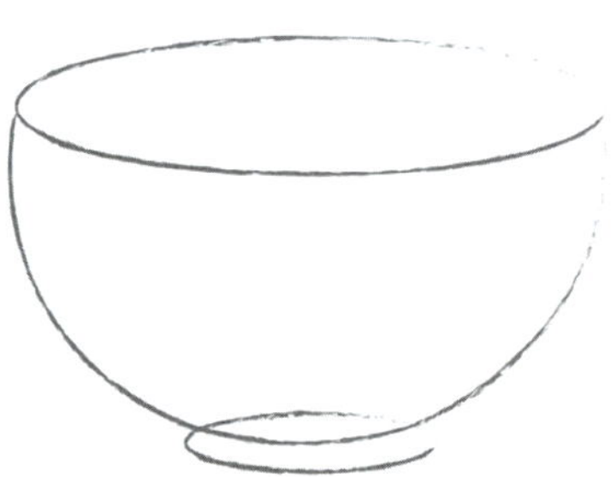

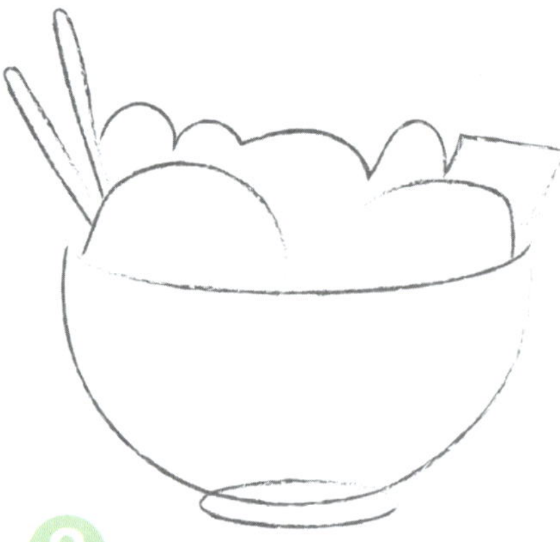

2

Lightly sketch the content of the bowl to make the layout easier for you.

3

Use a fineliner to go over the outlines.

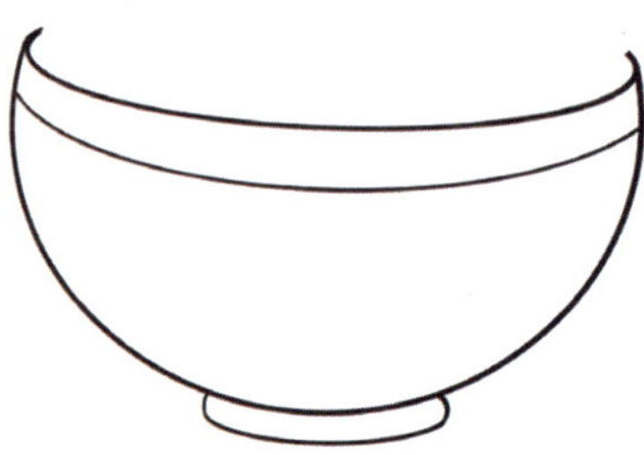

4

Start to draw the soup ingredients. Start on the left-hand side and draw chop sticks, noodles and the egg.

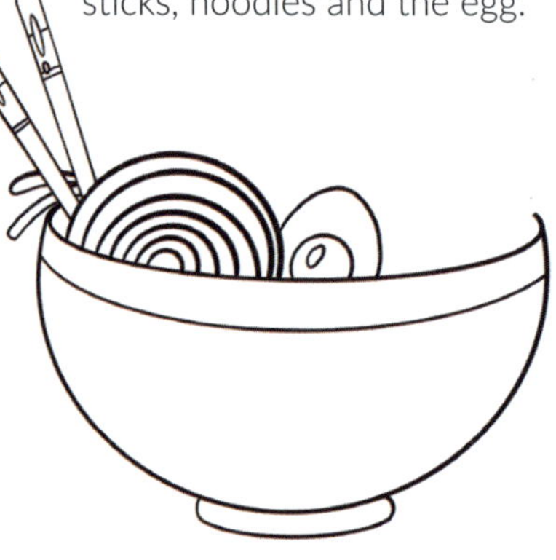

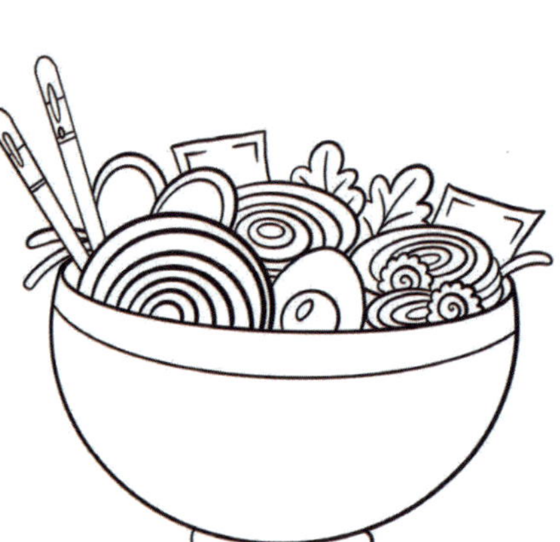

5

Fill the whole bowl with yummy food.

6

Use small dots to add shading to your illustration.

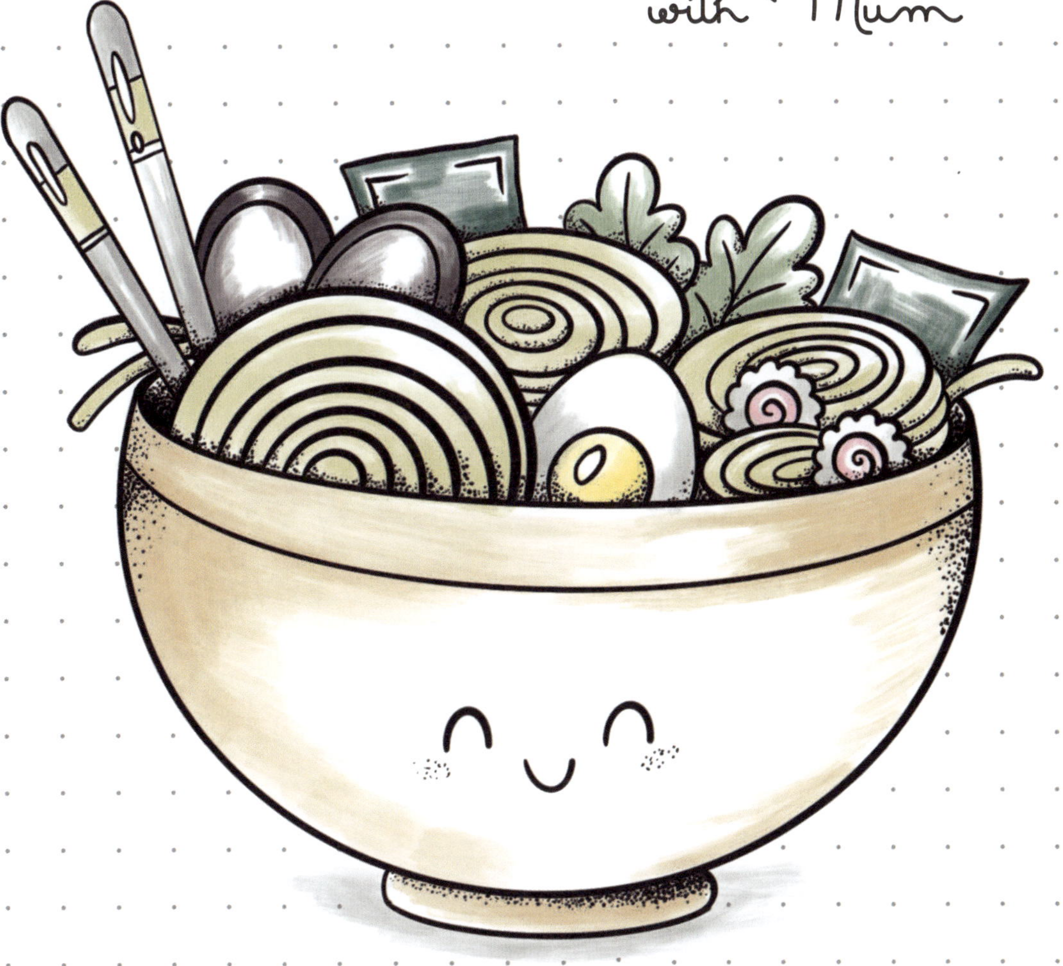

7 Add a little colour to complete your super cute ramen soup bowl.

Milk & Cookies

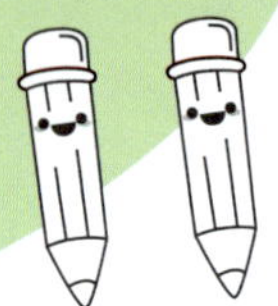

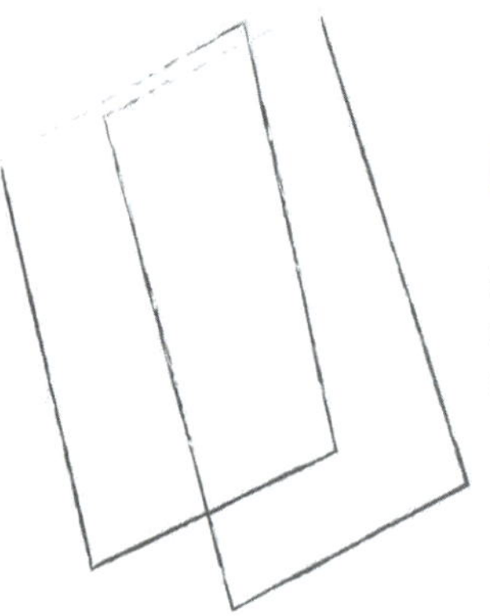

1 Sketch two slightly offset rectangles for the milk carton.

3 Add a final edge to the milk carton and leave the circle blank for the time being.

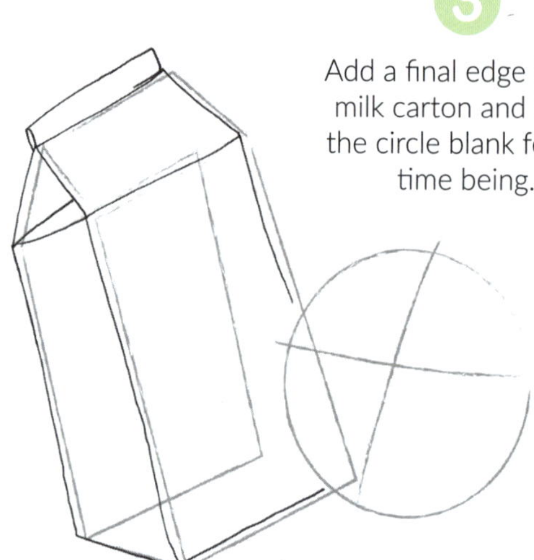

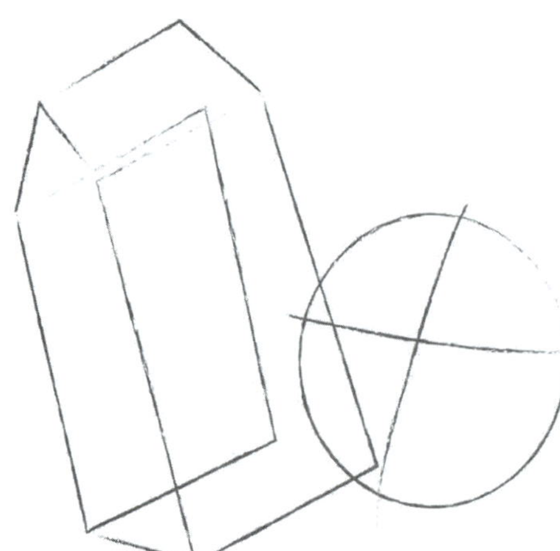

2 Connect the rectangles and sketch a circle for the biscuit.

5 Add a face and a few chocolate chips to the cookie.

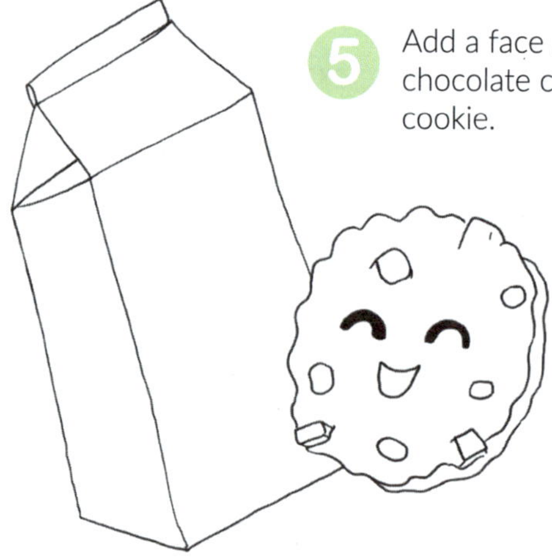

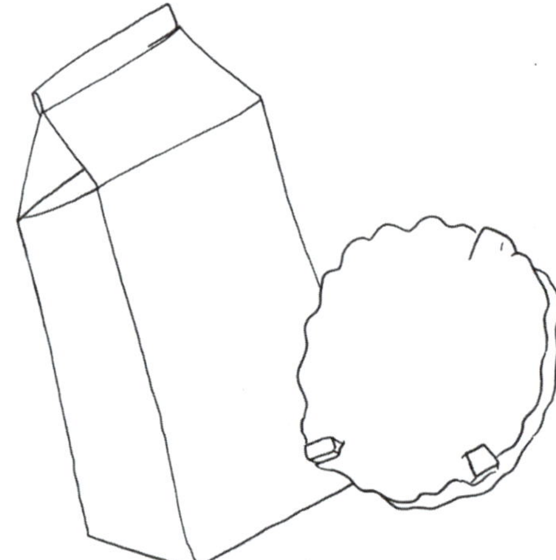

4 Use a fineliner to draw a cookie with a wavy edge and carefully erase the sketch.

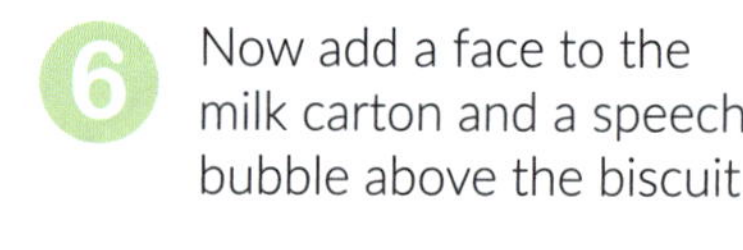

6 Now add a face to the milk carton and a speech bubble above the biscuit.

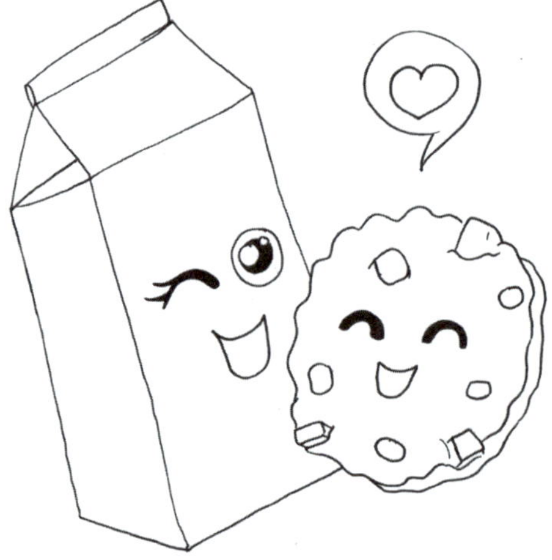

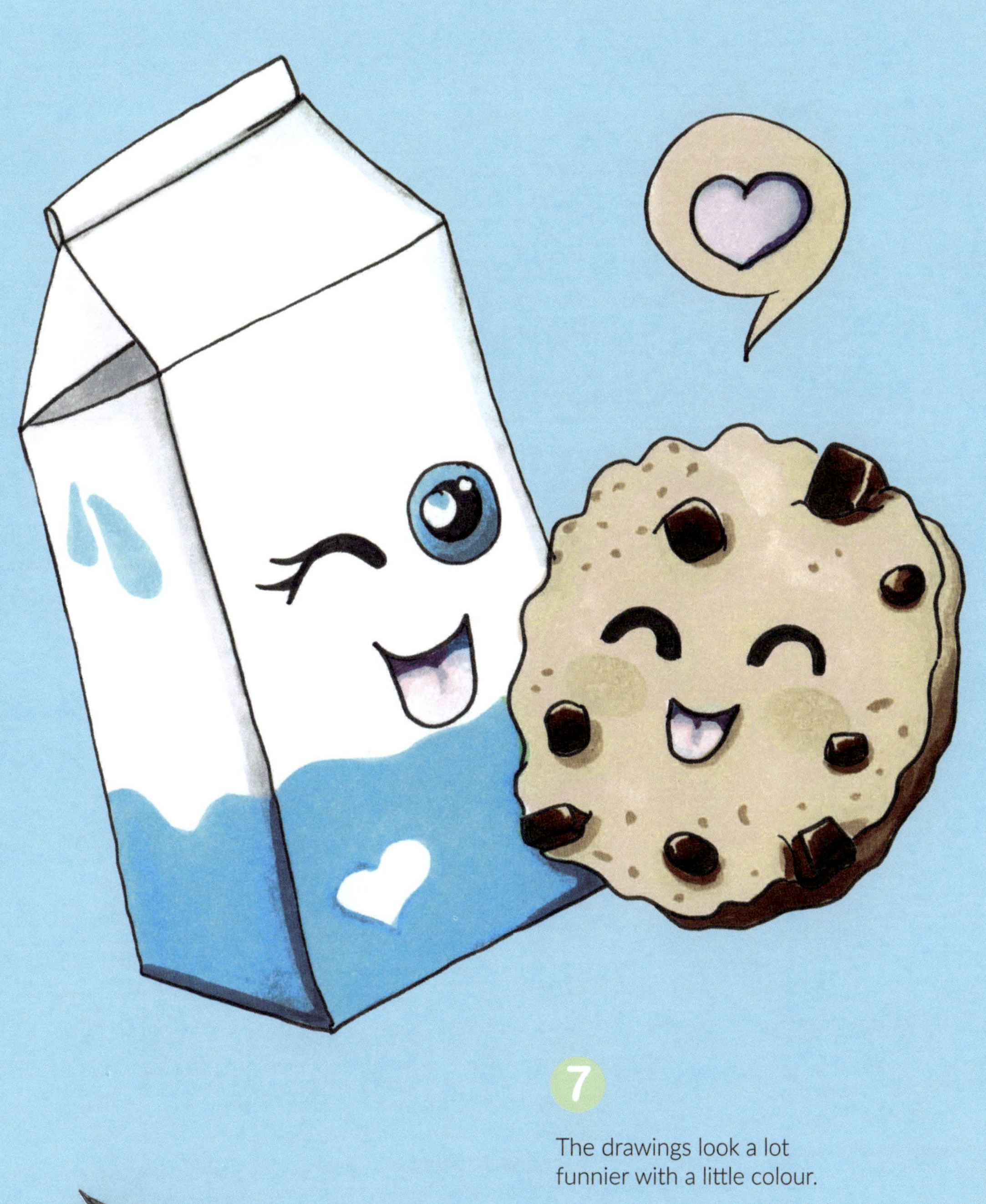

7

The drawings look a lot funnier with a little colour.

Avocados

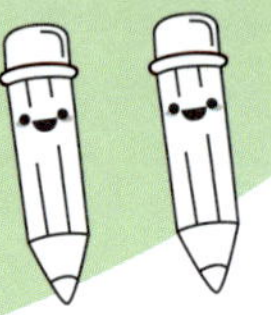

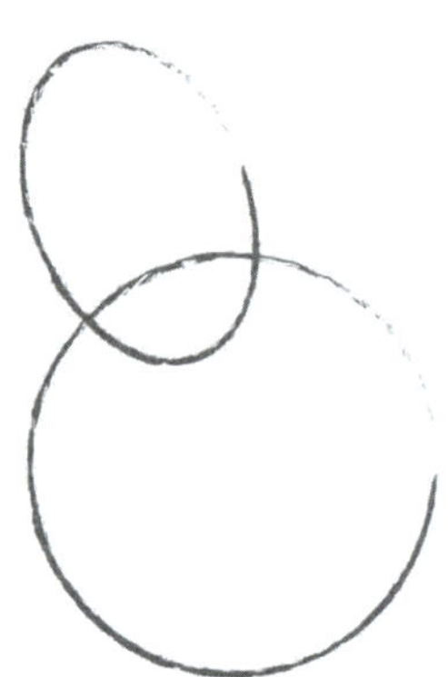

1 Sketch two ellipses for your avocado.

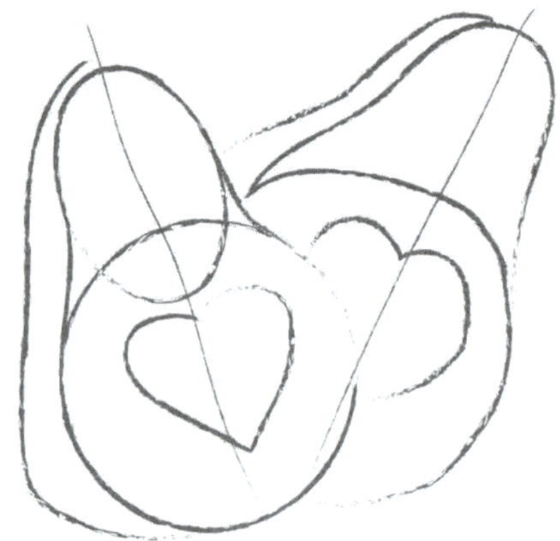

2 Draw guidelines for the placement of the faces and the stones. Sketch the second avocado.

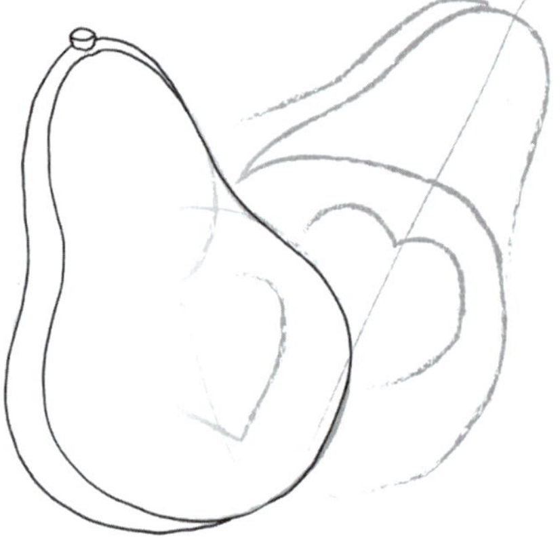

3 Use a fineliner to draw the outlines of the first avocado.

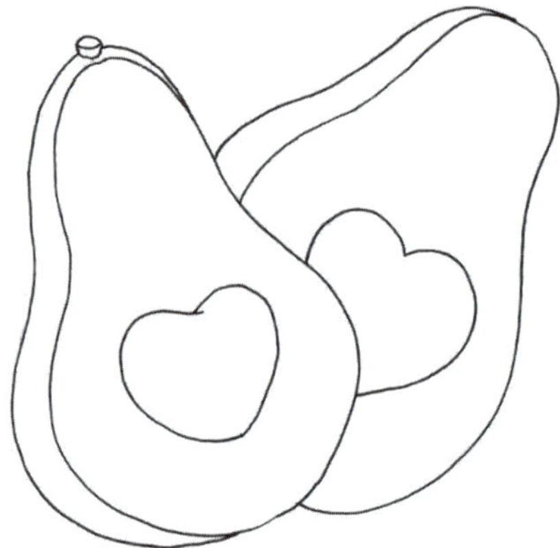

4 Draw the outline of the second avocado.

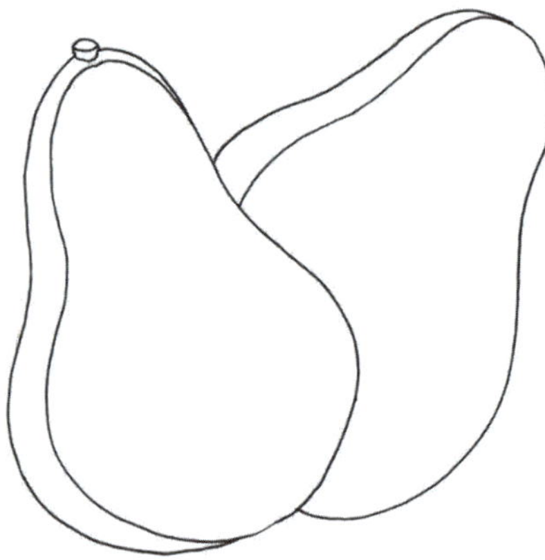

5 Draw a heart-shaped stone in both halves - the shapes should be very similar.

6 Give your avocados friendly faces.

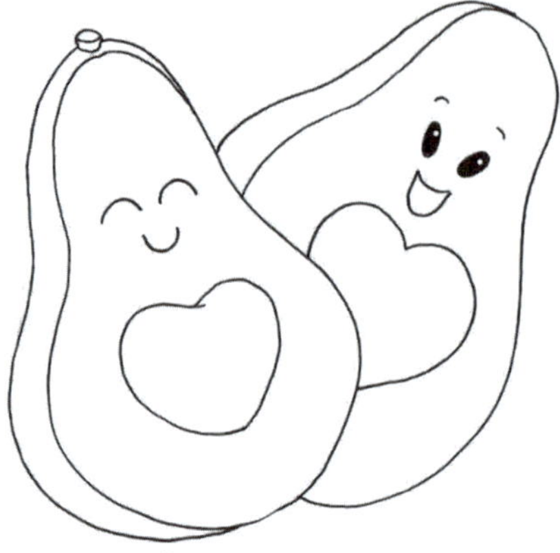

Paint your avocado in light shades of green with the stone in brown - now it is clear how they complete each other.

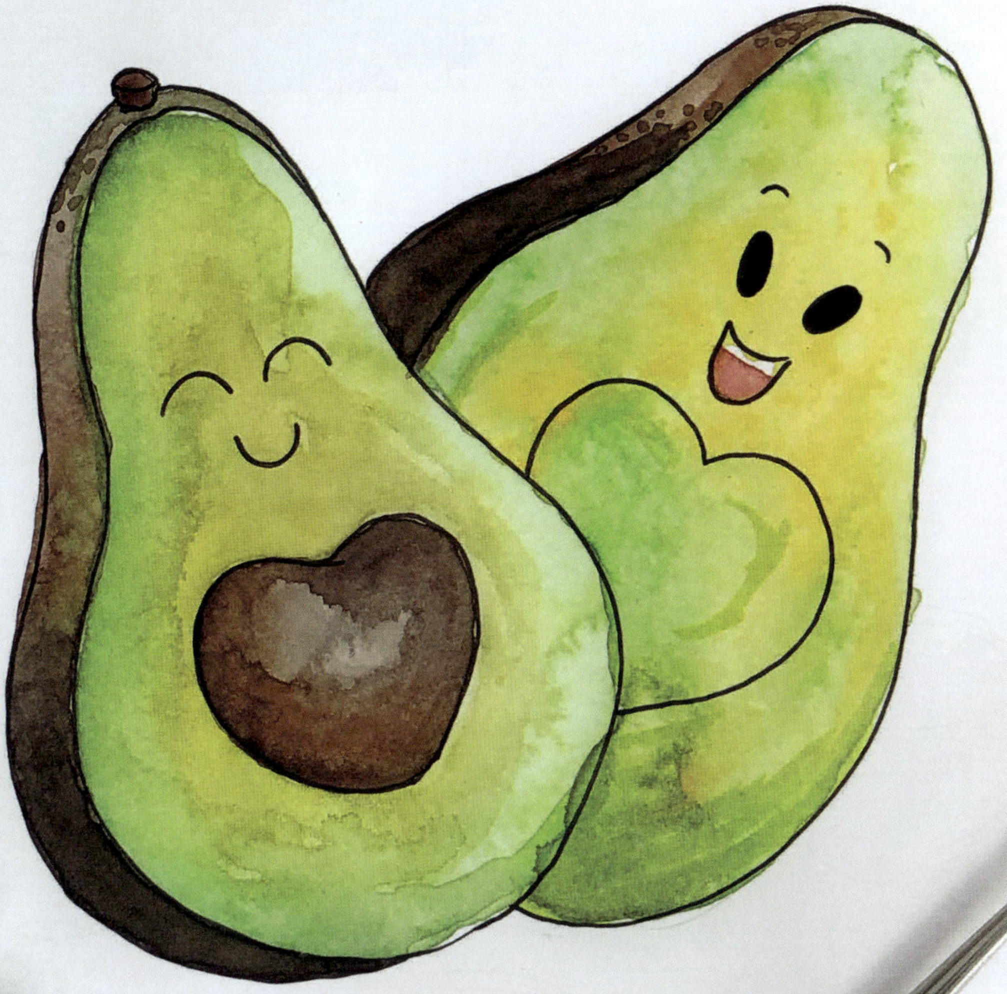

YOU COMPLETE ME

Cup of Tea

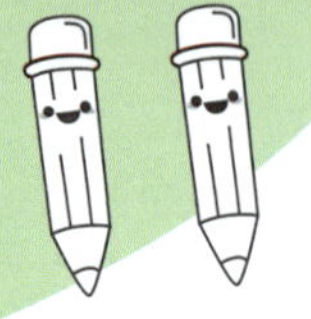

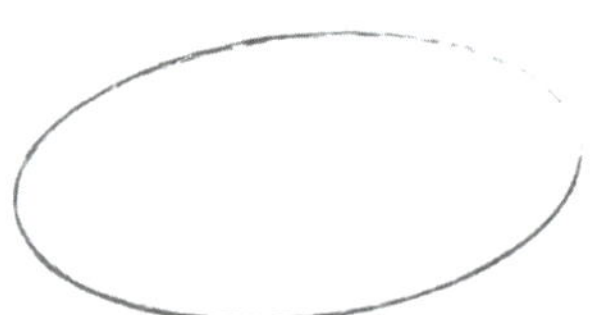

1 Start with two ellipses for your cup.

Connect the circles so that the shape of a cup is created.

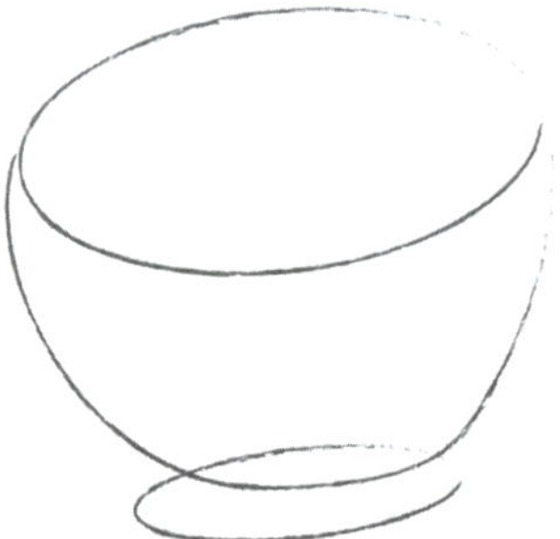

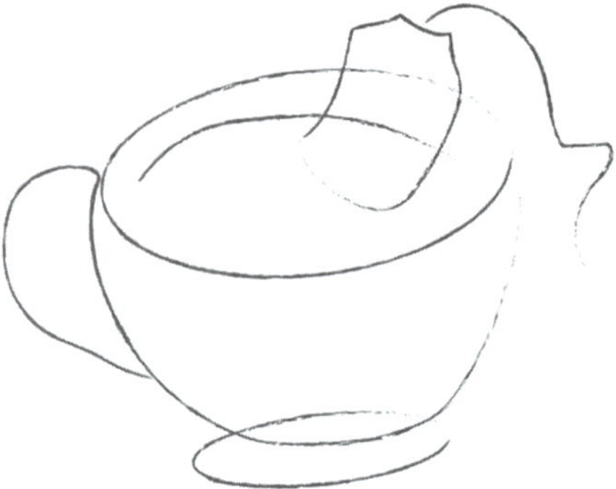

3 Add a handle and sketch the tea bag.

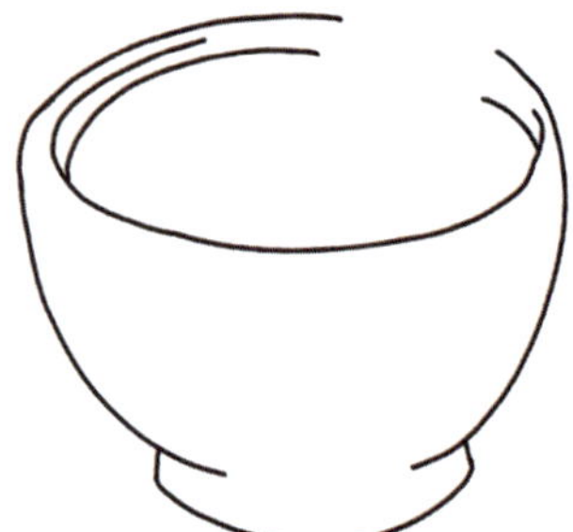

4 Use a fineliner to start going round the cup.

Add the handle and the tea bag.

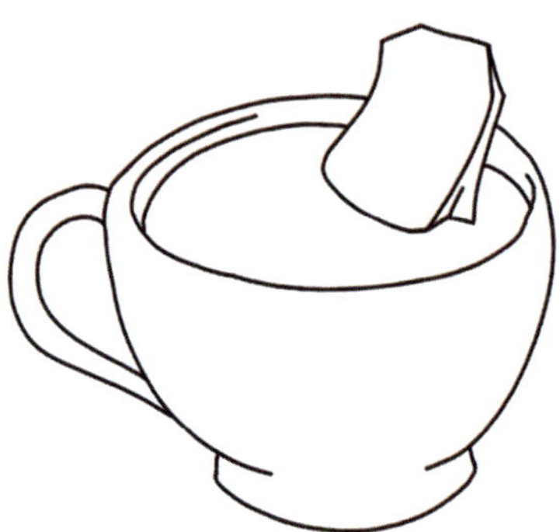

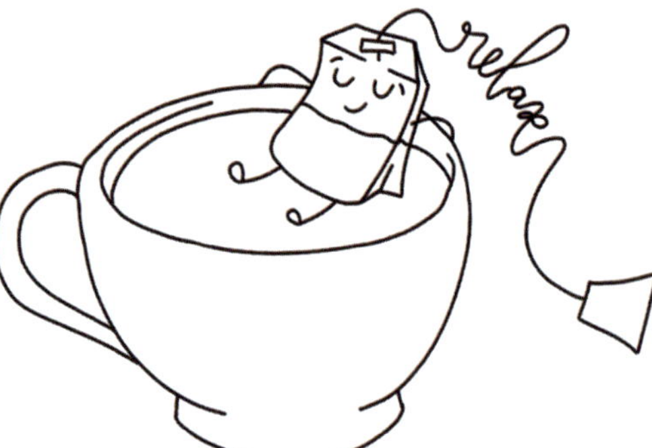

6 Draw further details, such as the faces and the string on the tea bag.

7 Add cheerful colours to your cup of tea and if you like, add a jolly slogan!

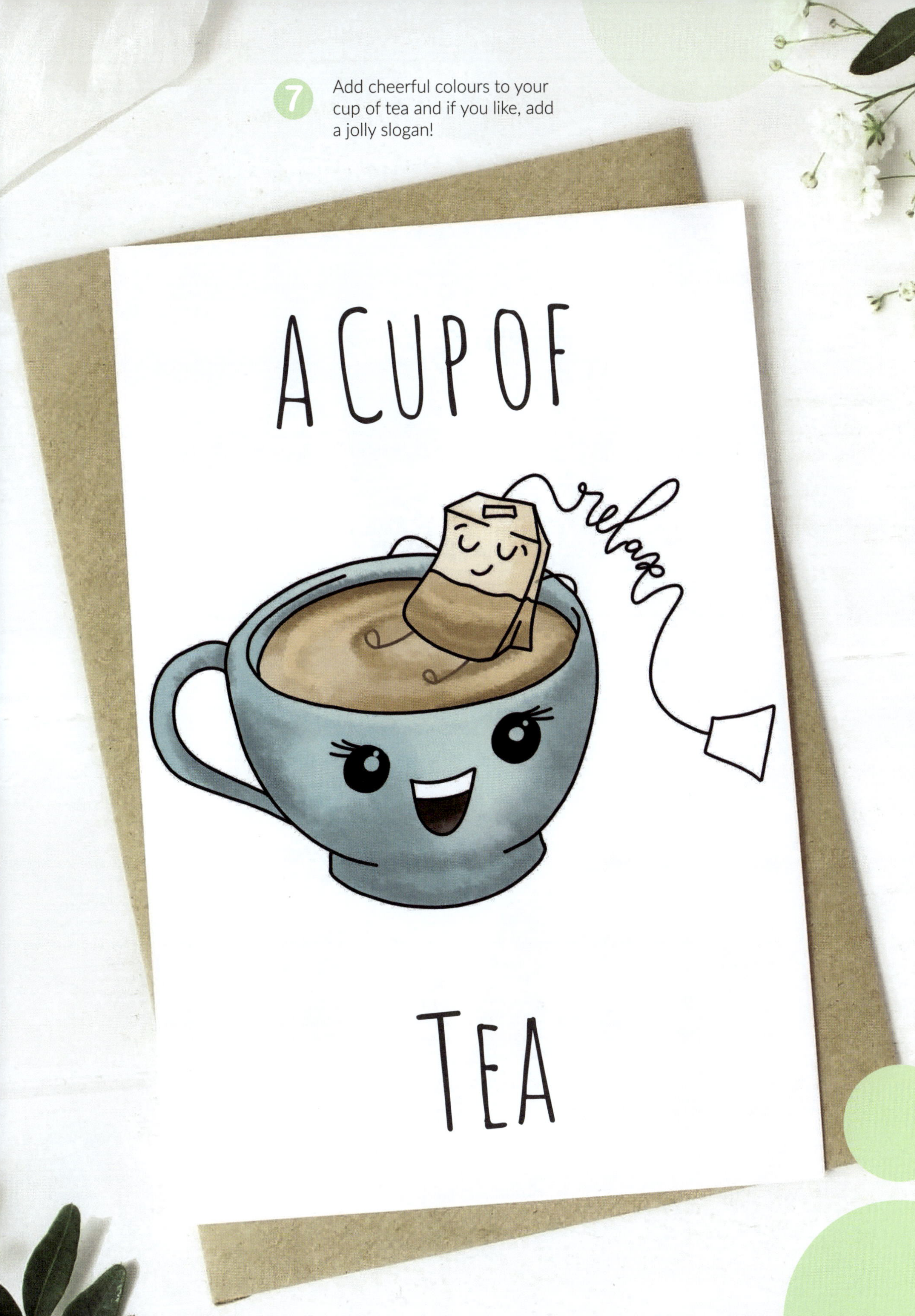

Ice Ice Baby

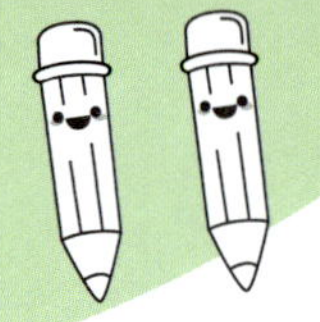

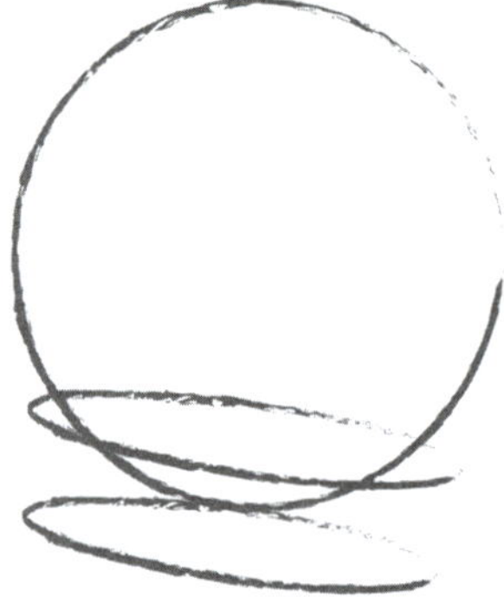

1 Start your sketch with a large circle for the scoop of ice cream and three ellipses for the cone.

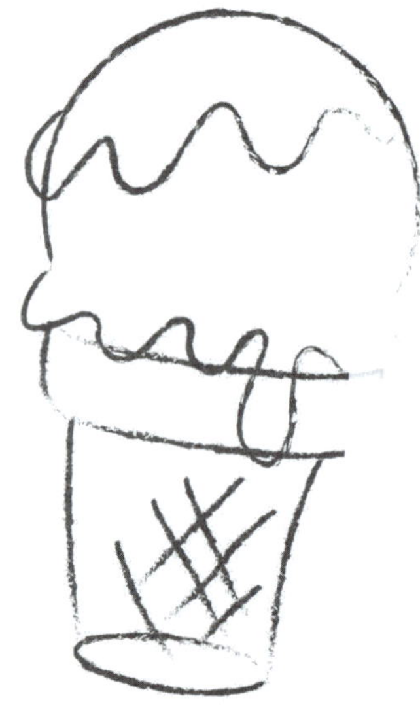

2 Connect the ellipses and sketch the outline of the ice cream.

3 Paint the scoop in two bright colours.

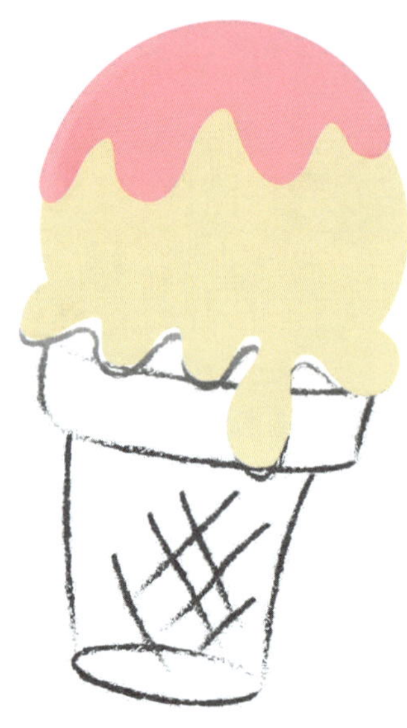

4 Use darker colours to add some shadows to the scoop.

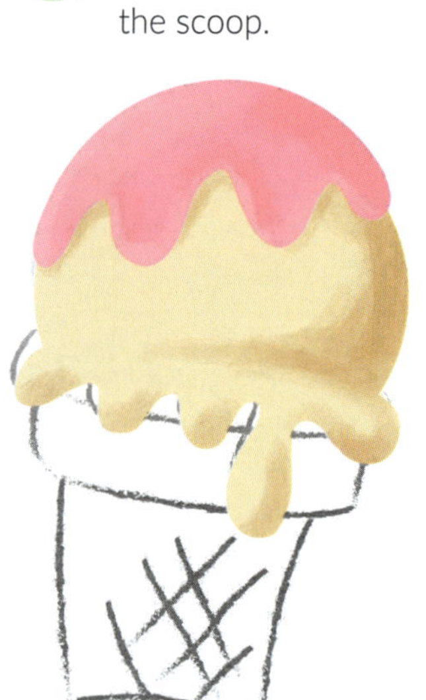

5 Paint the cone in brown.

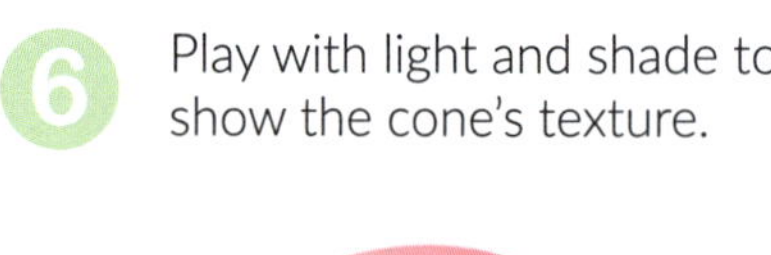

6 Play with light and shade to show the cone's texture.

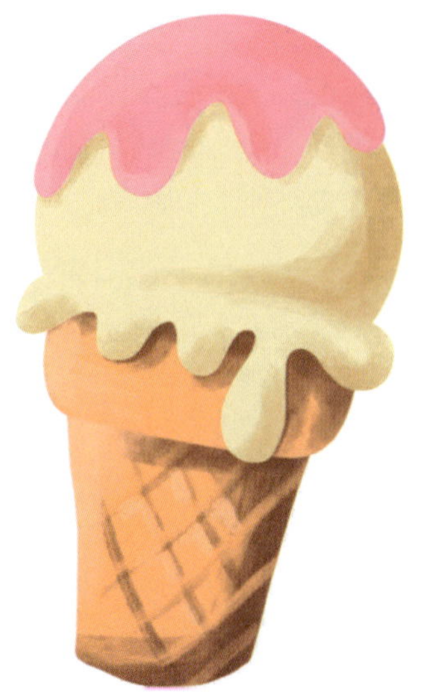

Ice Ice Baby

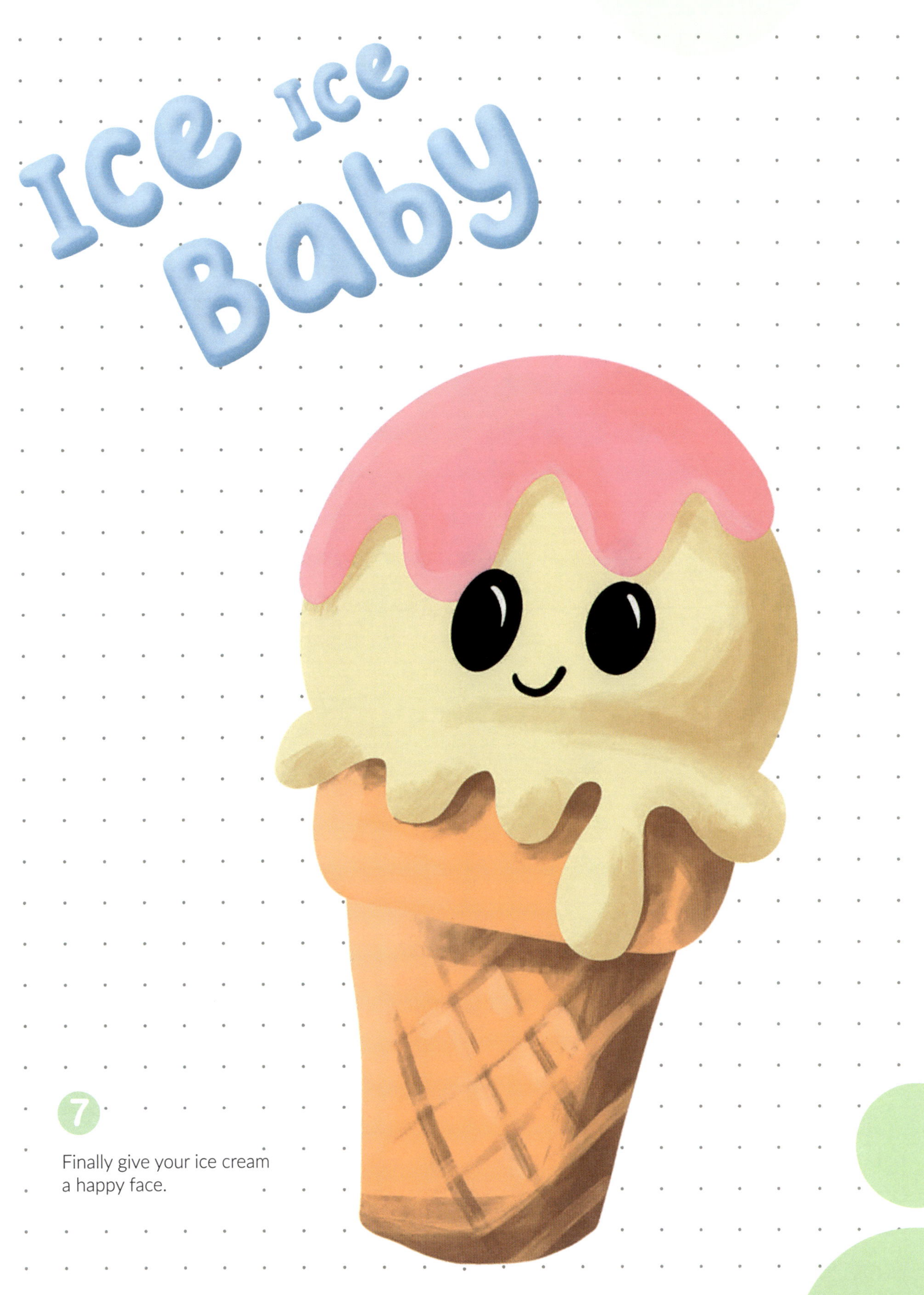

7

Finally give your ice cream a happy face.

Toast Buddies 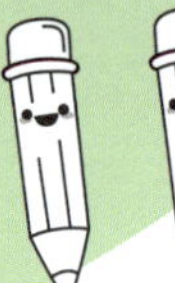 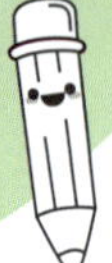 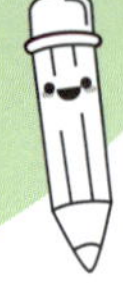

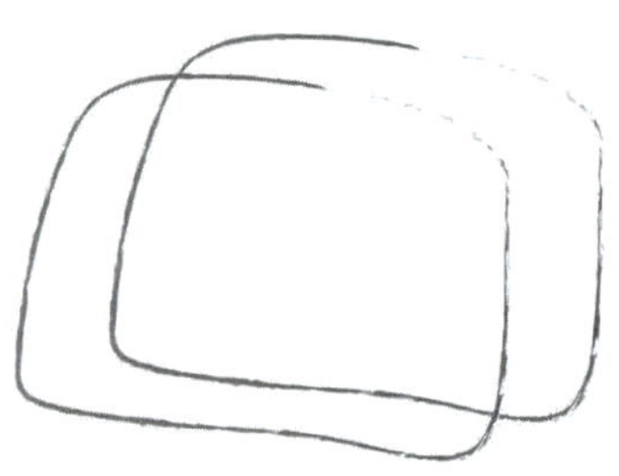

1 Sketch two slightly offset rectangles with rounded corners for your toaster.

2 Join the rectangles and sketch the toast.

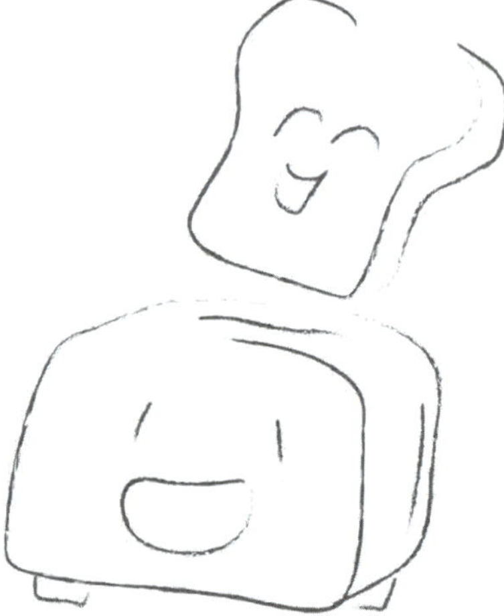

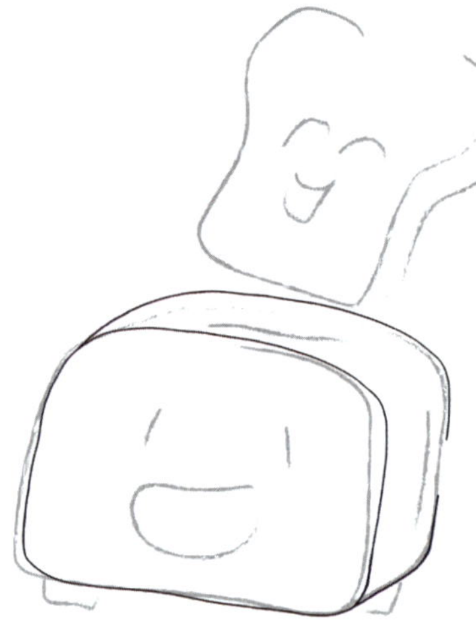

3 Use a fineliner to draw the outline of the toaster.

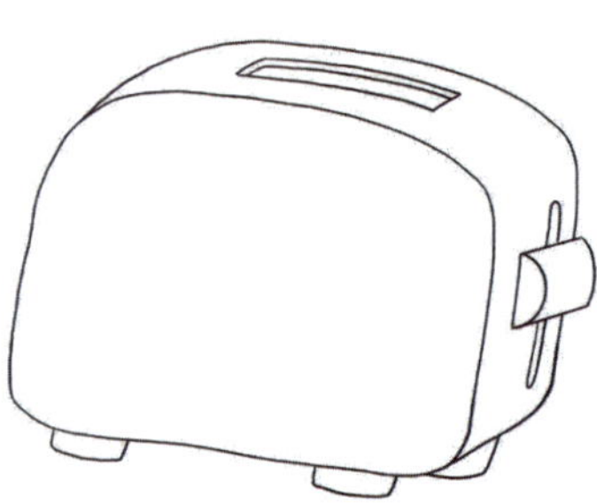

4 Add a couple of details, like the opening and the press handle.

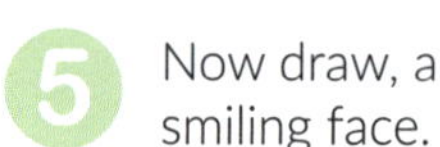

5 Now draw, a smiling face.

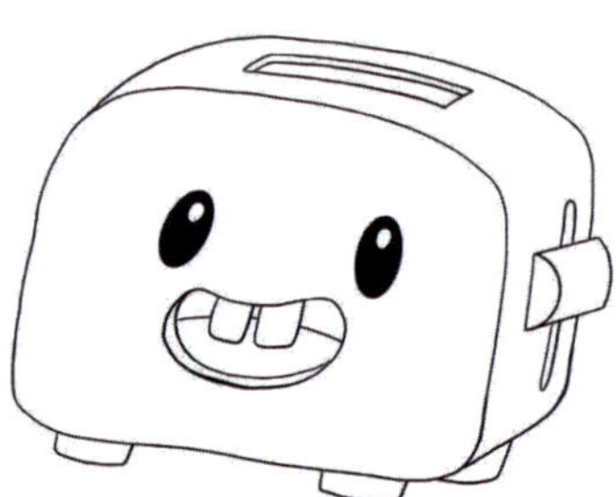

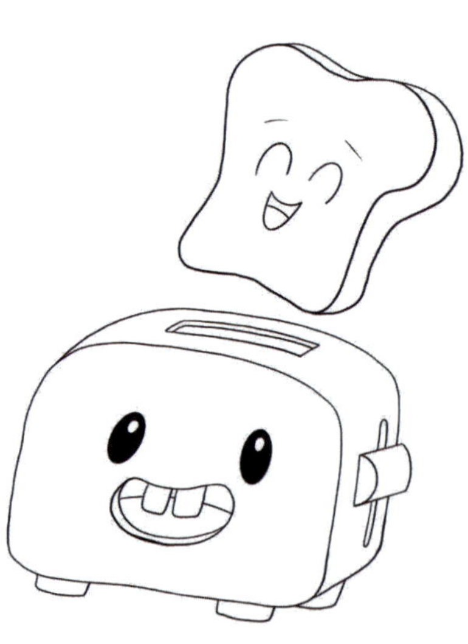

6 Draw a happy piece of toast to match.

7

Paint your funny toast buddies and voilà the illustration is finished.

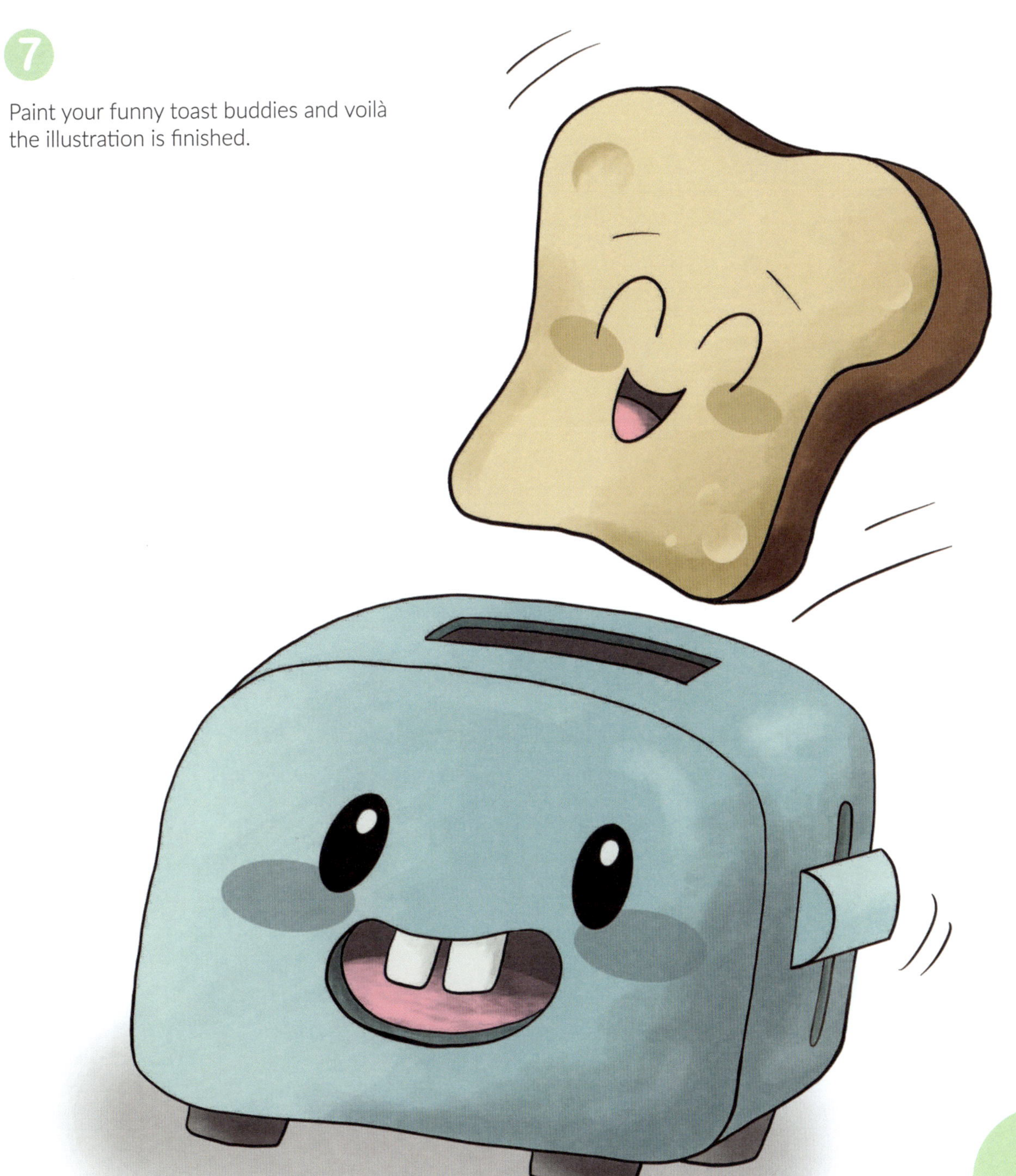

Hot Banditos

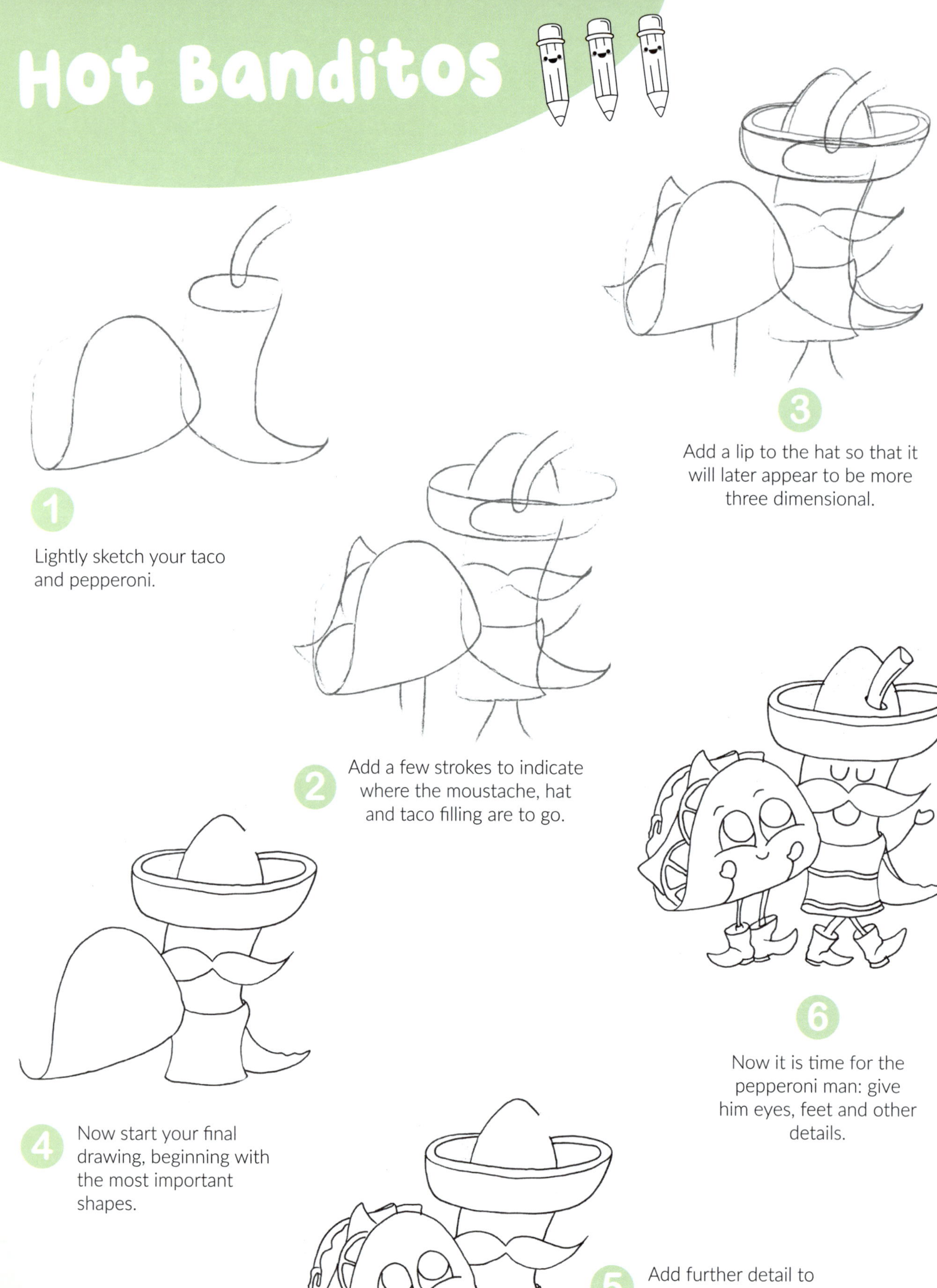

1

Lightly sketch your taco and pepperoni.

2 Add a few strokes to indicate where the moustache, hat and taco filling are to go.

3

Add a lip to the hat so that it will later appear to be more three dimensional.

4 Now start your final drawing, beginning with the most important shapes.

5 Add further detail to your taco and draw the ingredients that it is filled with, such as lettuce, cheese and tomato.

6

Now it is time for the pepperoni man: give him eyes, feet and other details.

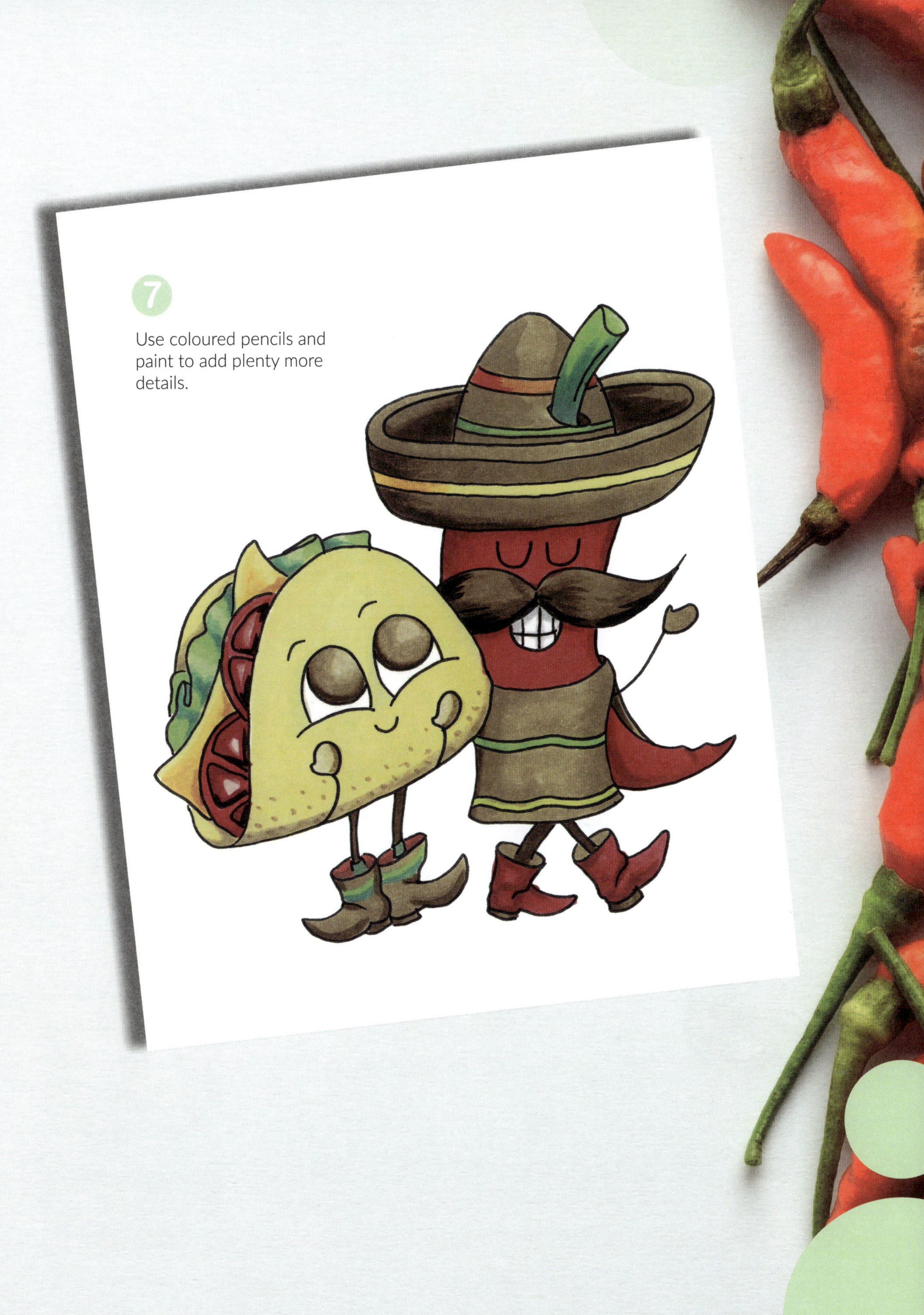
7
Use coloured pencils and
paint to add plenty more
details.

Sweet Doughnuts

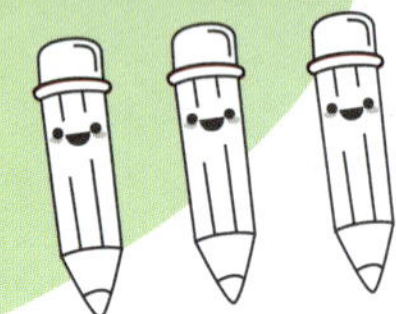

1

Sketch two slightly offset ellipses and a smaller ellipse at the top for your first doughnut.

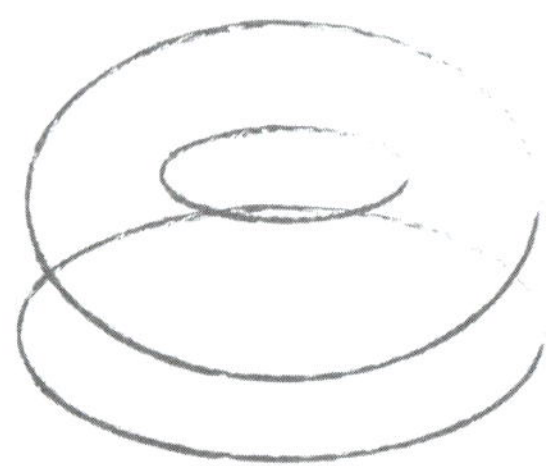

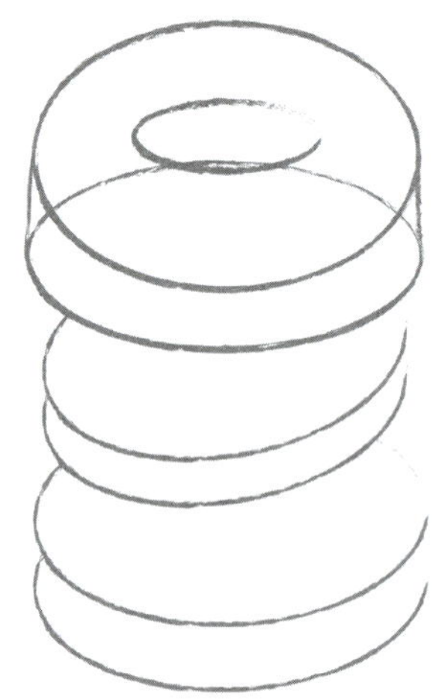

2 Then sketch your other two doughnuts.

3

Paint the icing pink and the doughnut in brown.

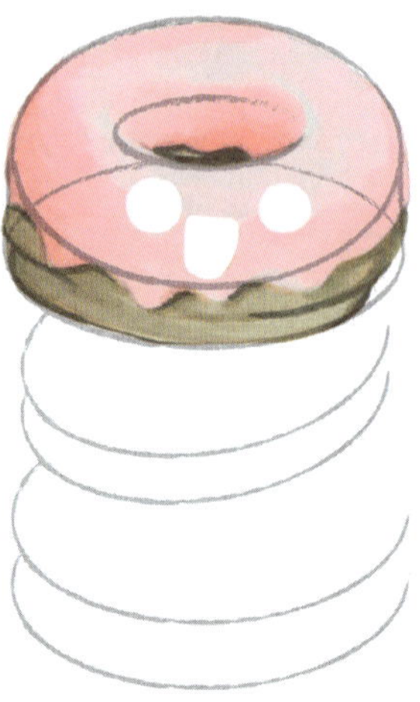

4 Now you can paint the second doughnut. Remember to leave the mouth and sugar decoration blank.

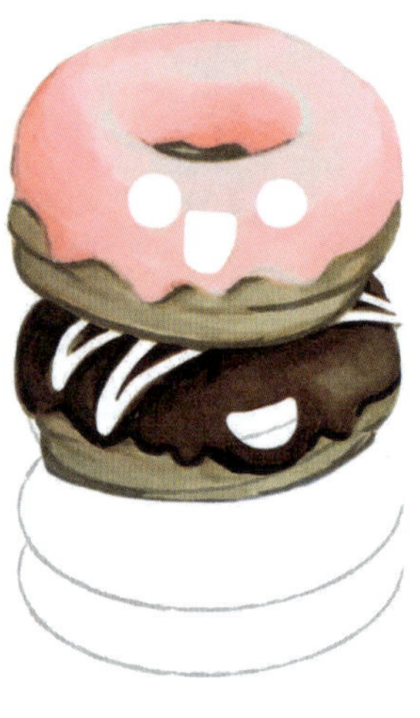

5 Now paint the third doughnut. Ensure that the shade from the overhanging doughnuts is darker.

6 Now you can paint the details, such as eyes, mouth and sugar pearls.

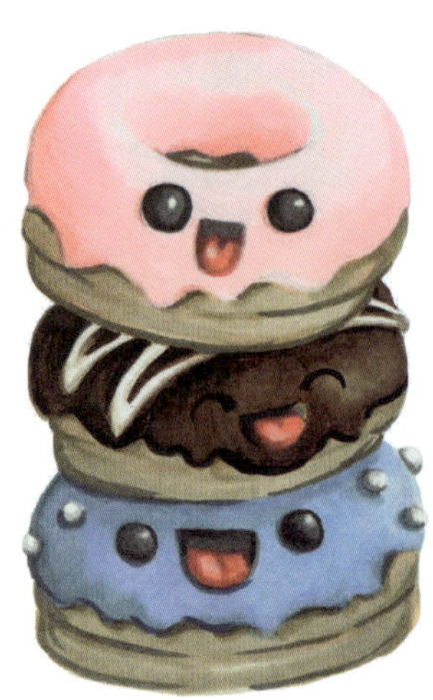

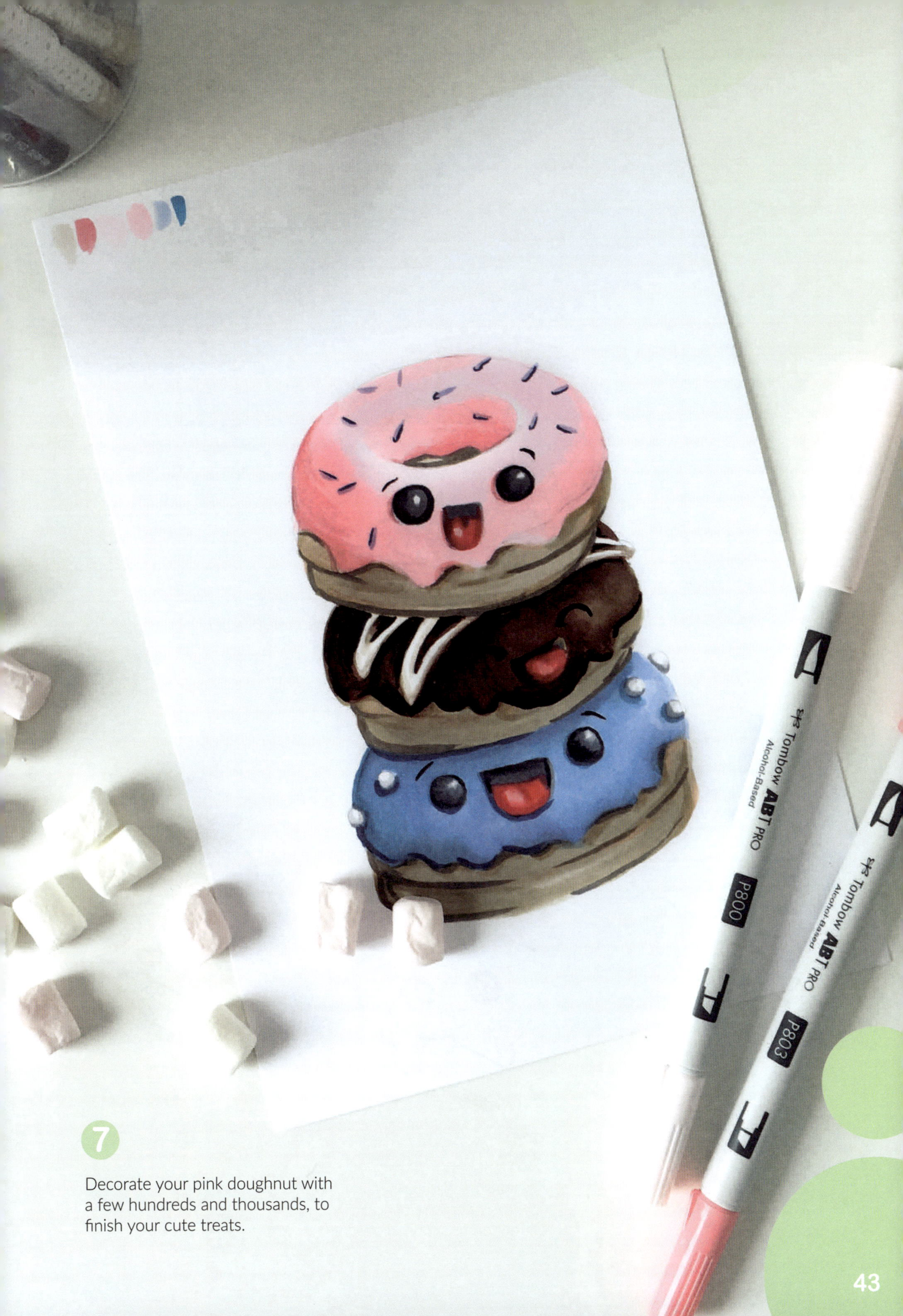

7

Decorate your pink doughnut with a few hundreds and thousands, to finish your cute treats.

Pizza

Lightly sketch your heart-shaped pizza.

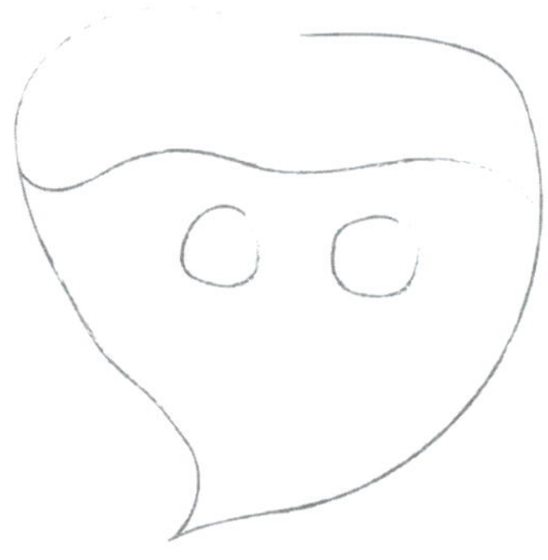

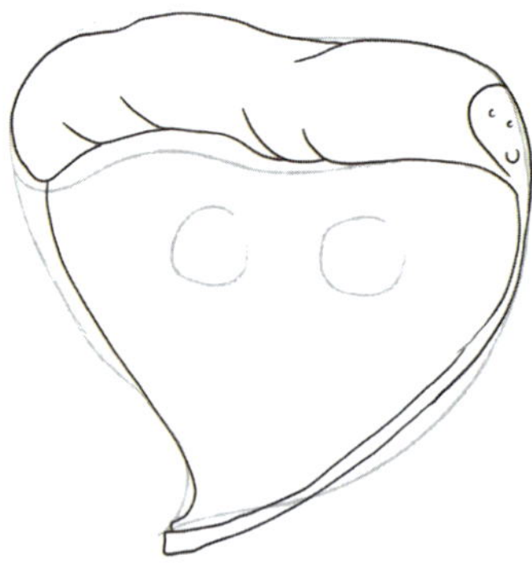

2 Use a fineliner to draw round the outlines - ensure that the base has a double line, so that it looks three dimensional.

Draw the face of the pizza with a smiling mouth.

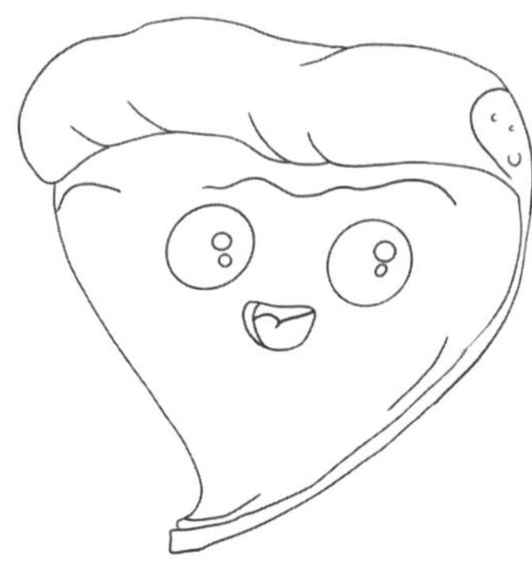

Add slices of salami and hands forming the shape of a heart.

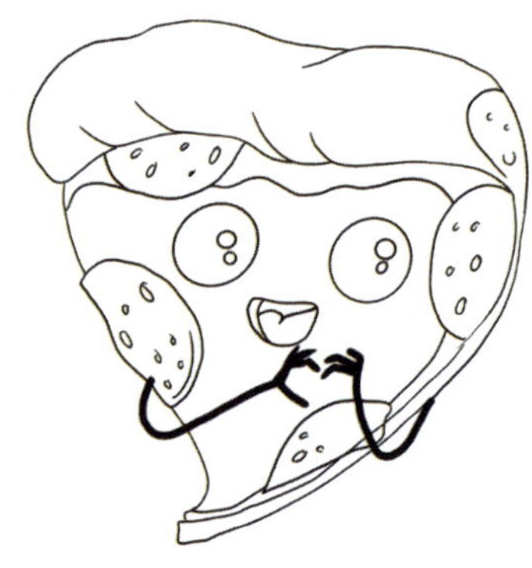

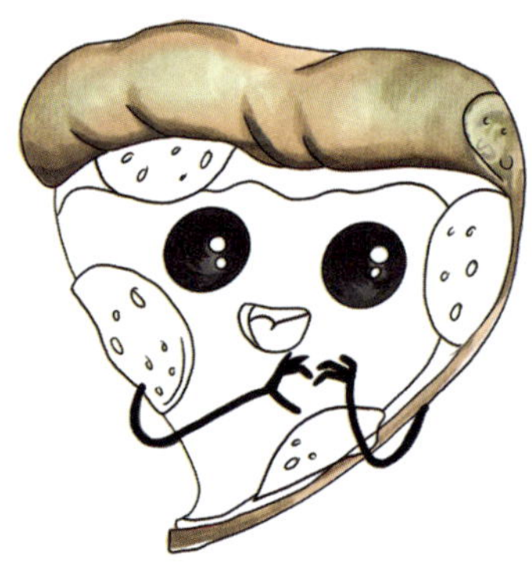

5

Colour the pizza crust in shades of brown, paying attention to light and shade.

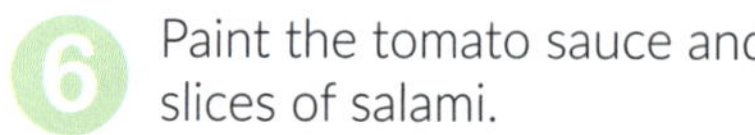

Paint the tomato sauce and slices of salami.

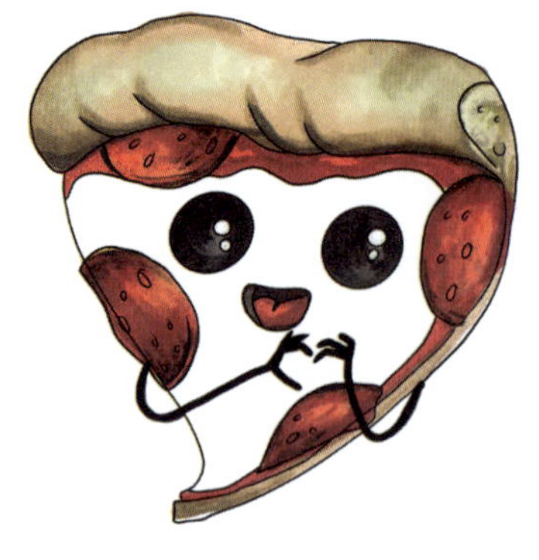

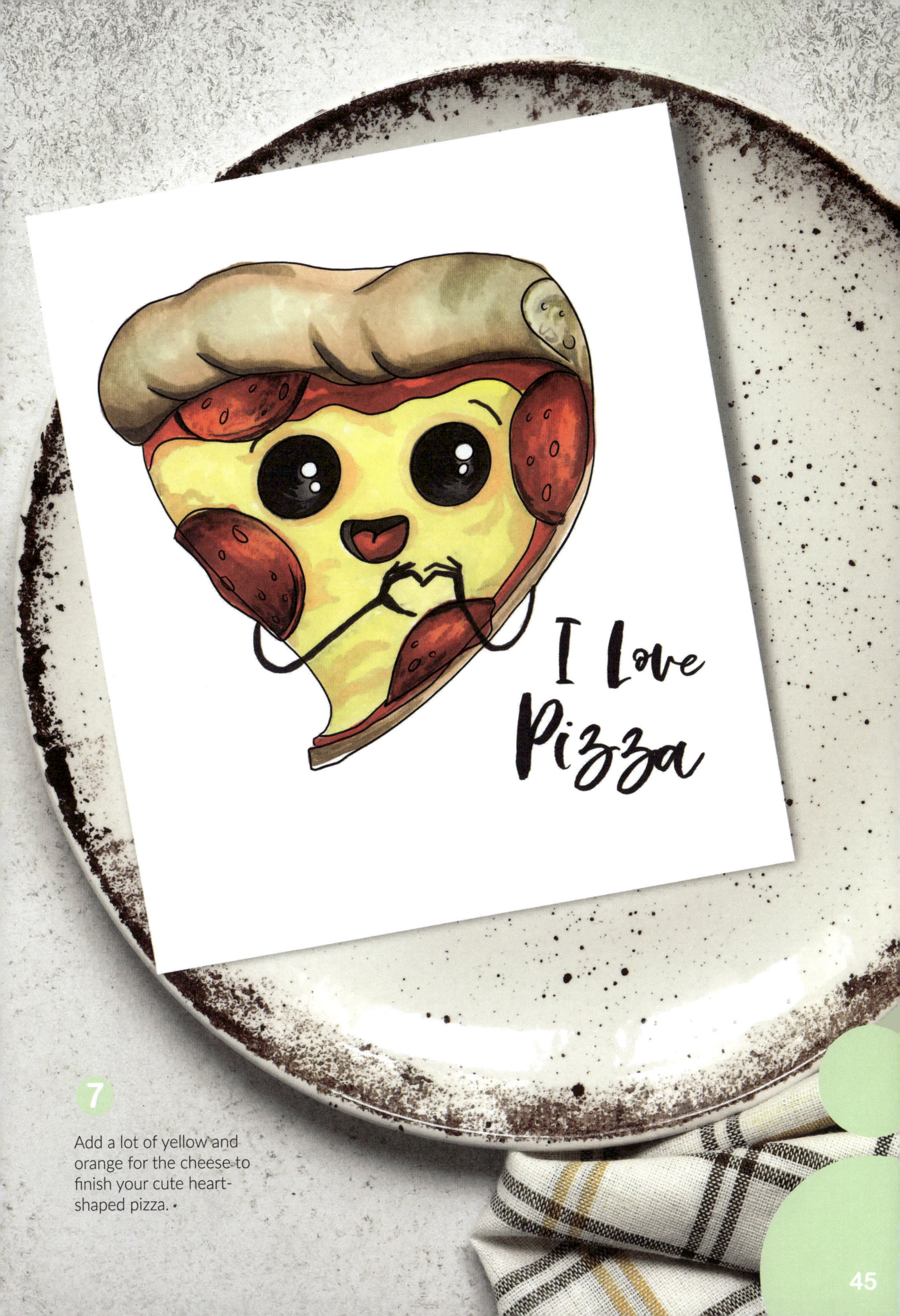

7

Add a lot of yellow and orange for the cheese to finish your cute heart-shaped pizza.

Sweet Cherries

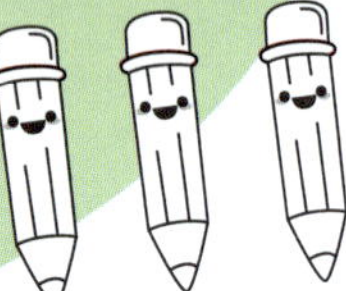

1

Sketch your cherries with the help of three circles.

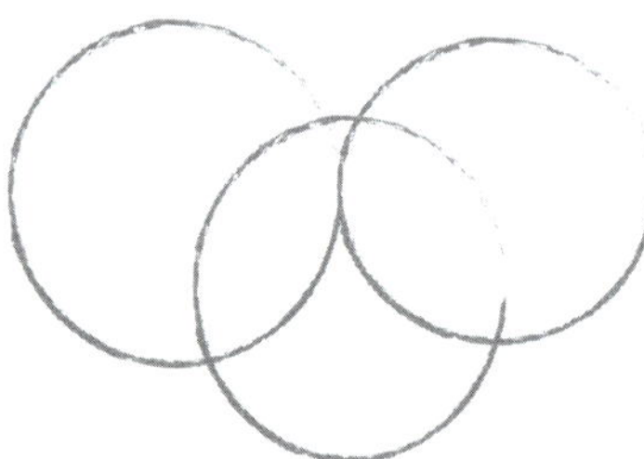

Add the stalks and a leaf to the sketch.

3

Start on the centre cherry. The strokes should follow its shape.

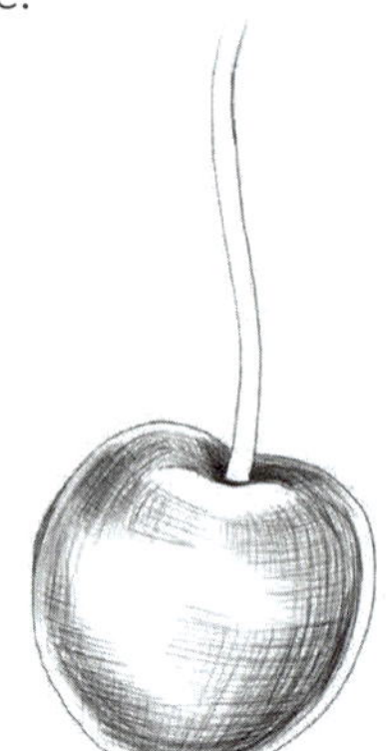

Sketch the second cherry.

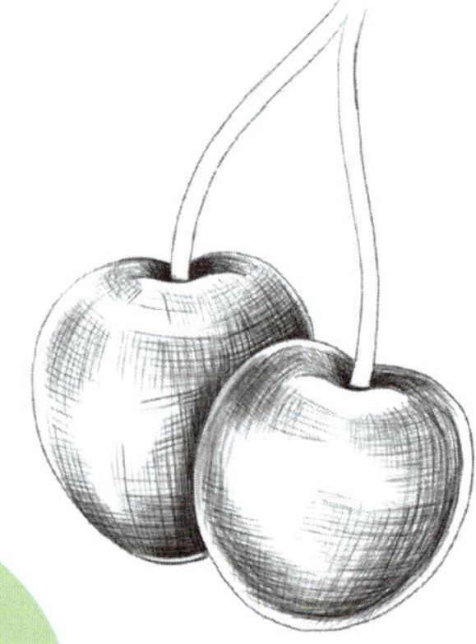

5

Sketch the third cherry and add shade to stalks.

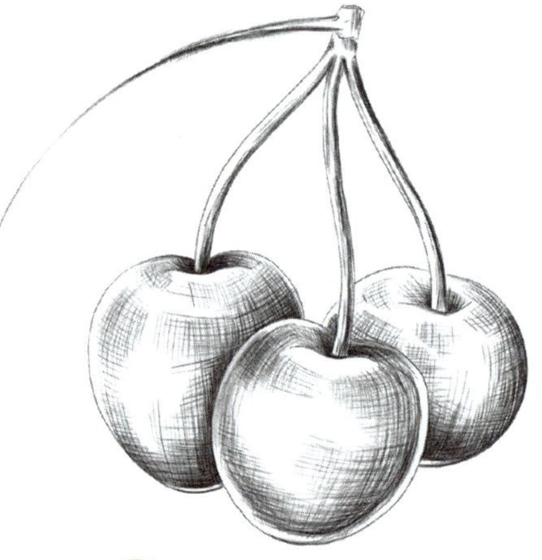

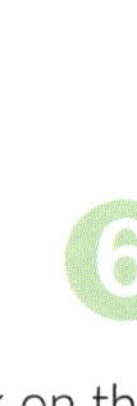

Now work on the leaf.

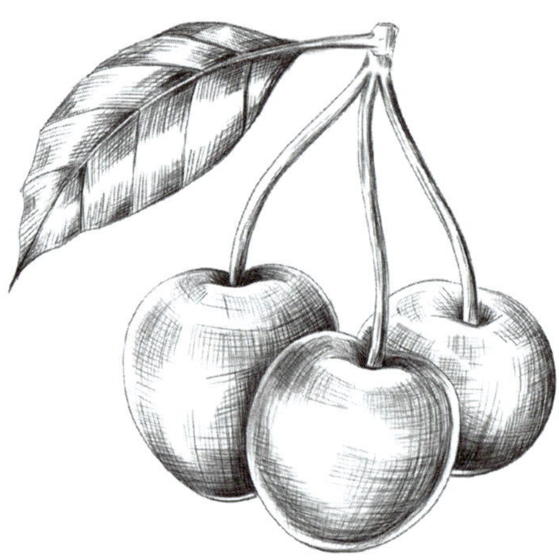

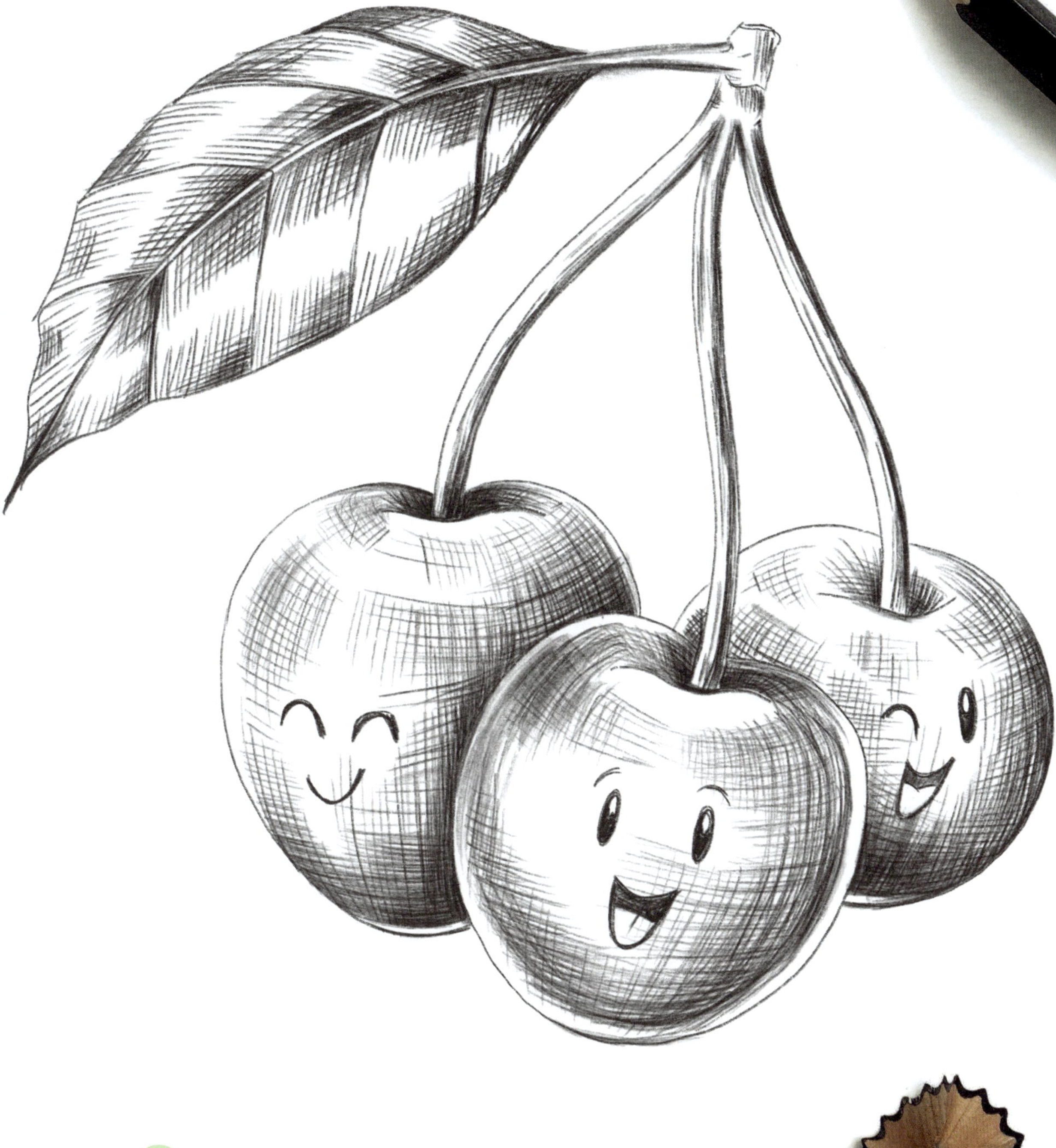

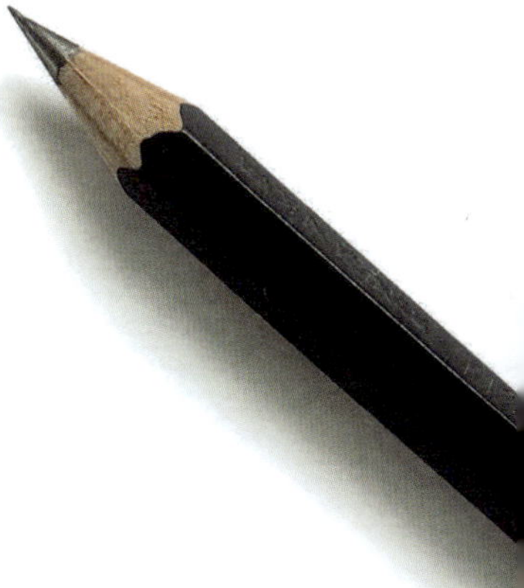

7

Add funny faces to your cherries - it makes them even sweeter.

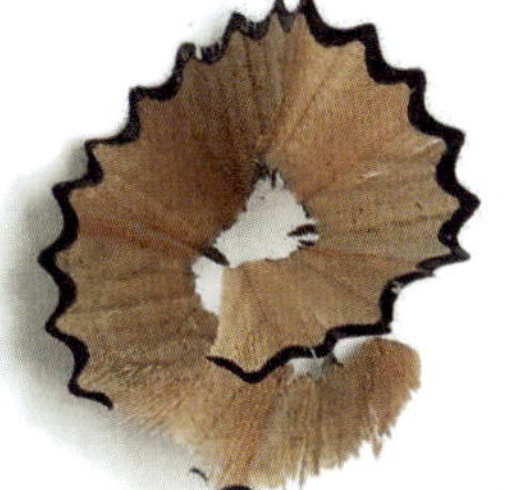

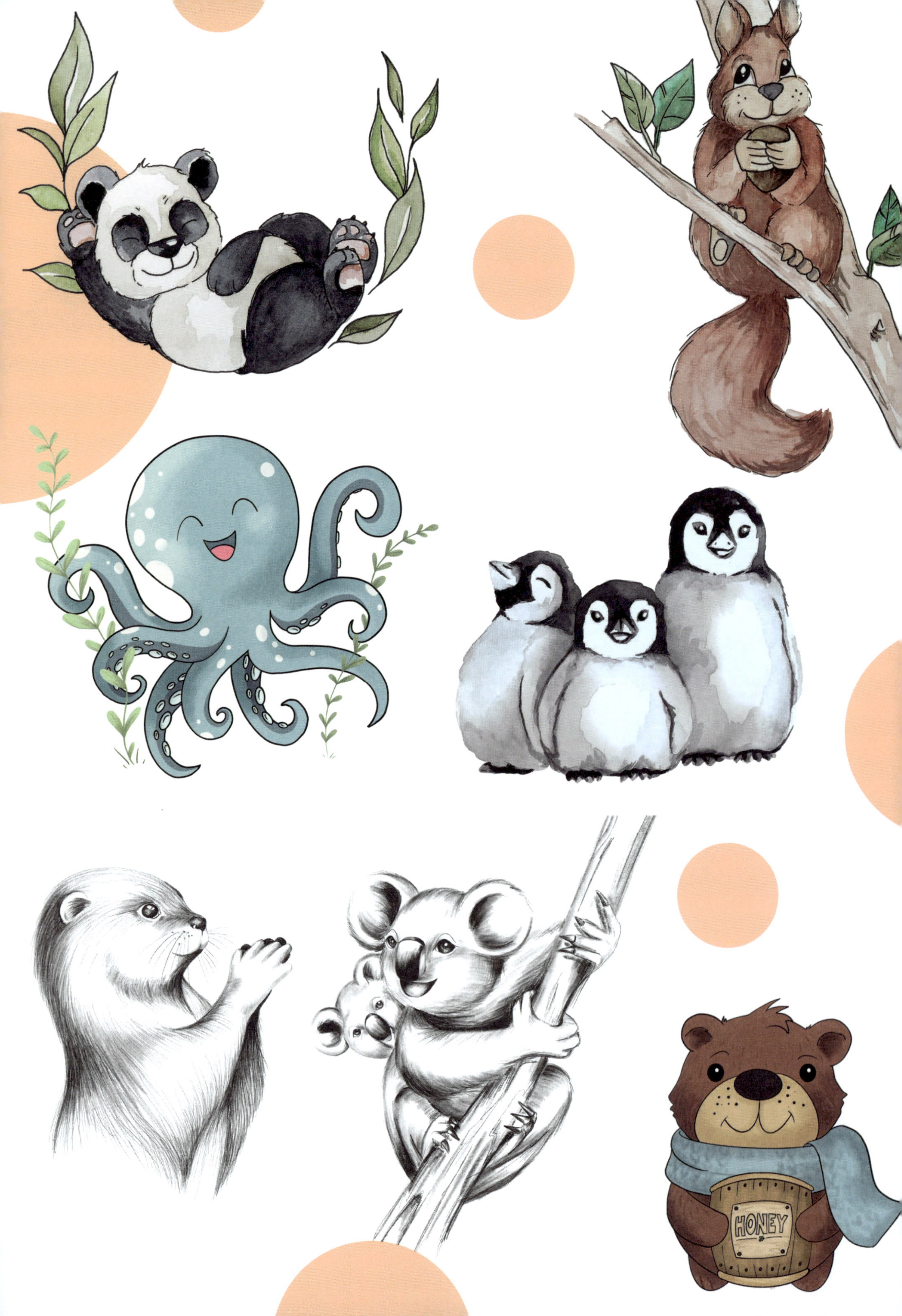
HONEY

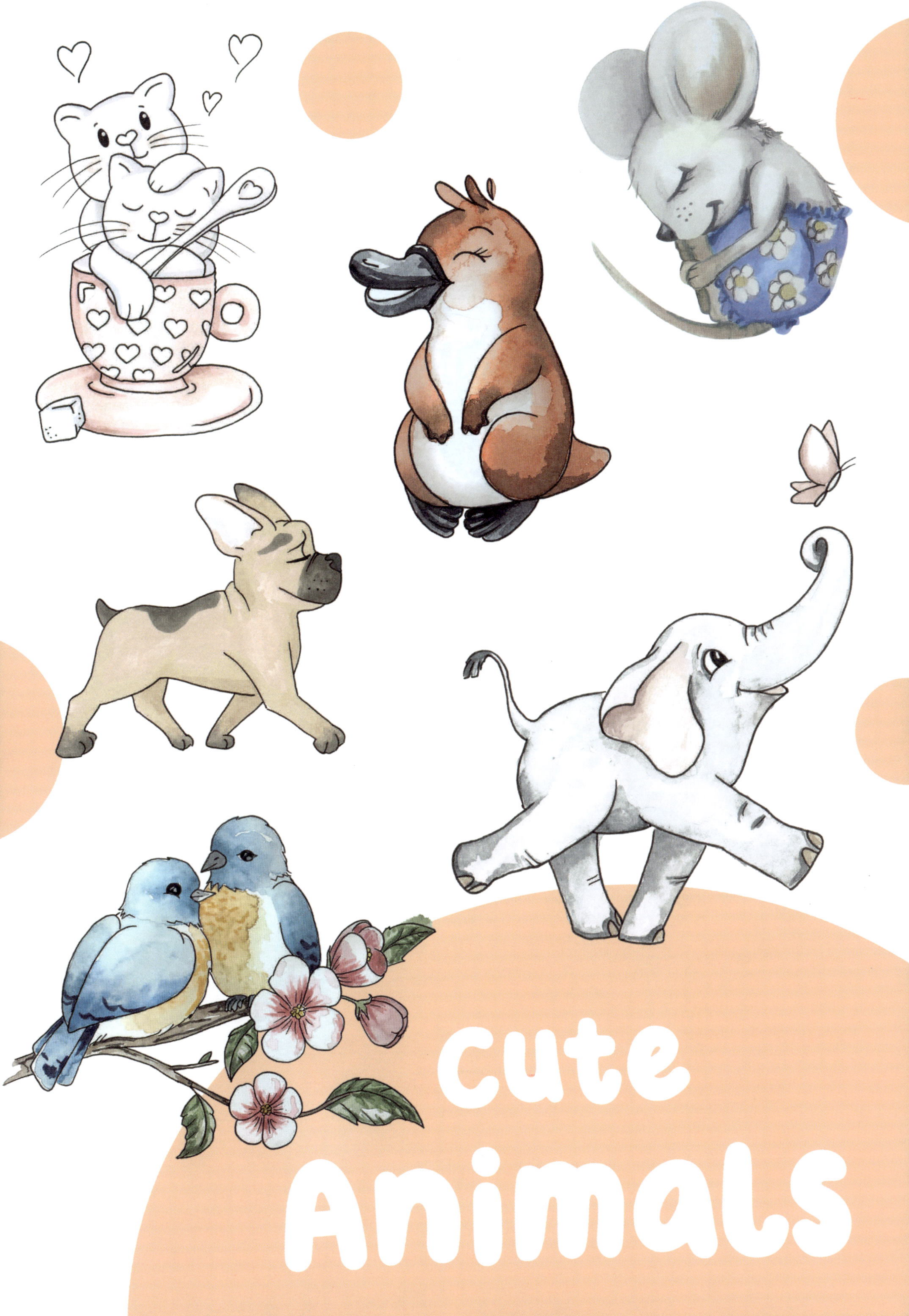
Cute
Animals

Drills

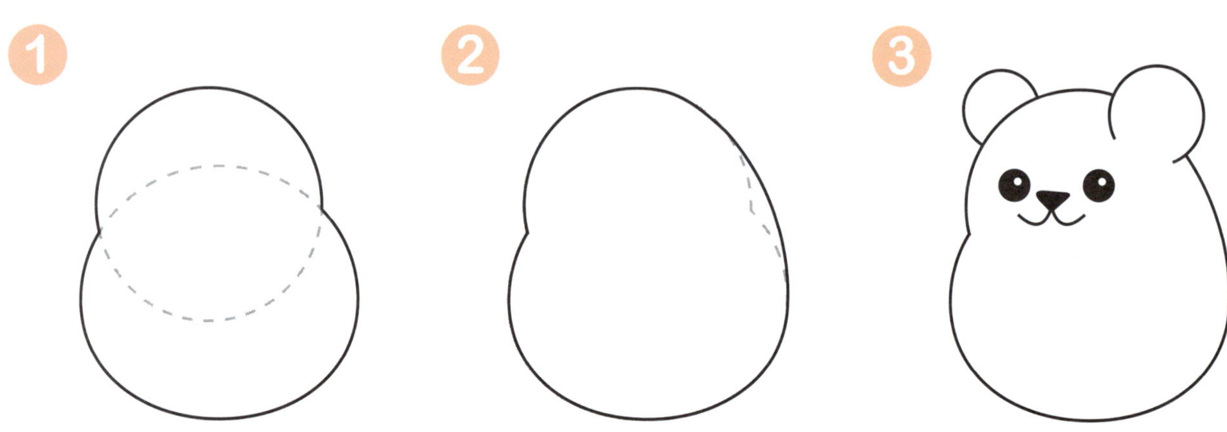

4

DRAW YOUR HAMSTER HERE.

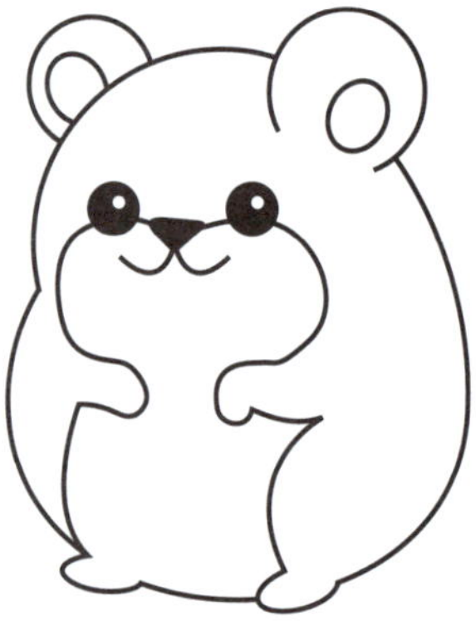

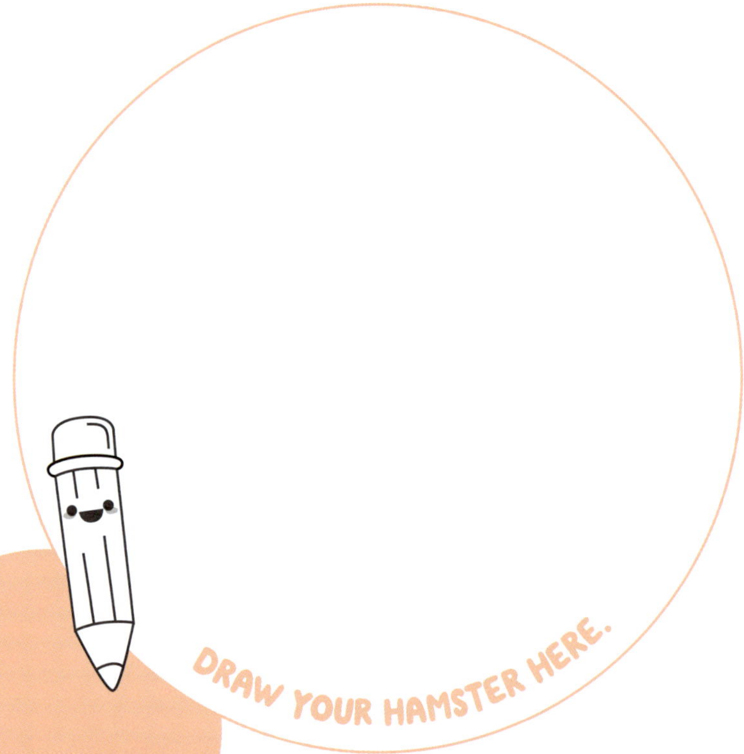

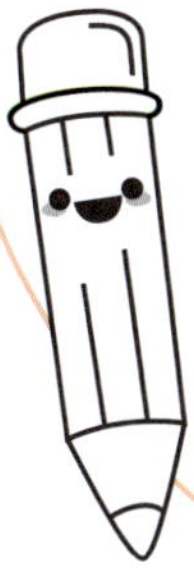

DRAW YOUR NARWHAL HERE.

1

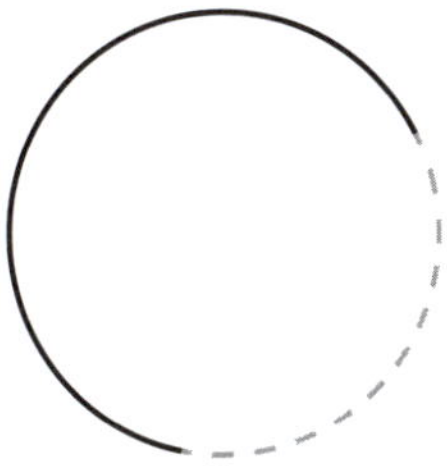

2

3

4

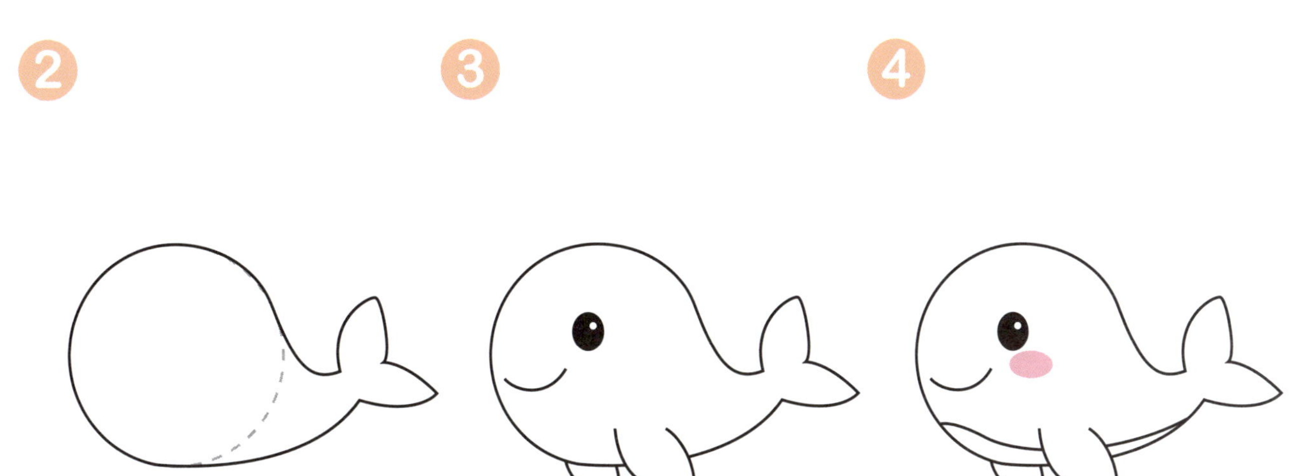

Drills

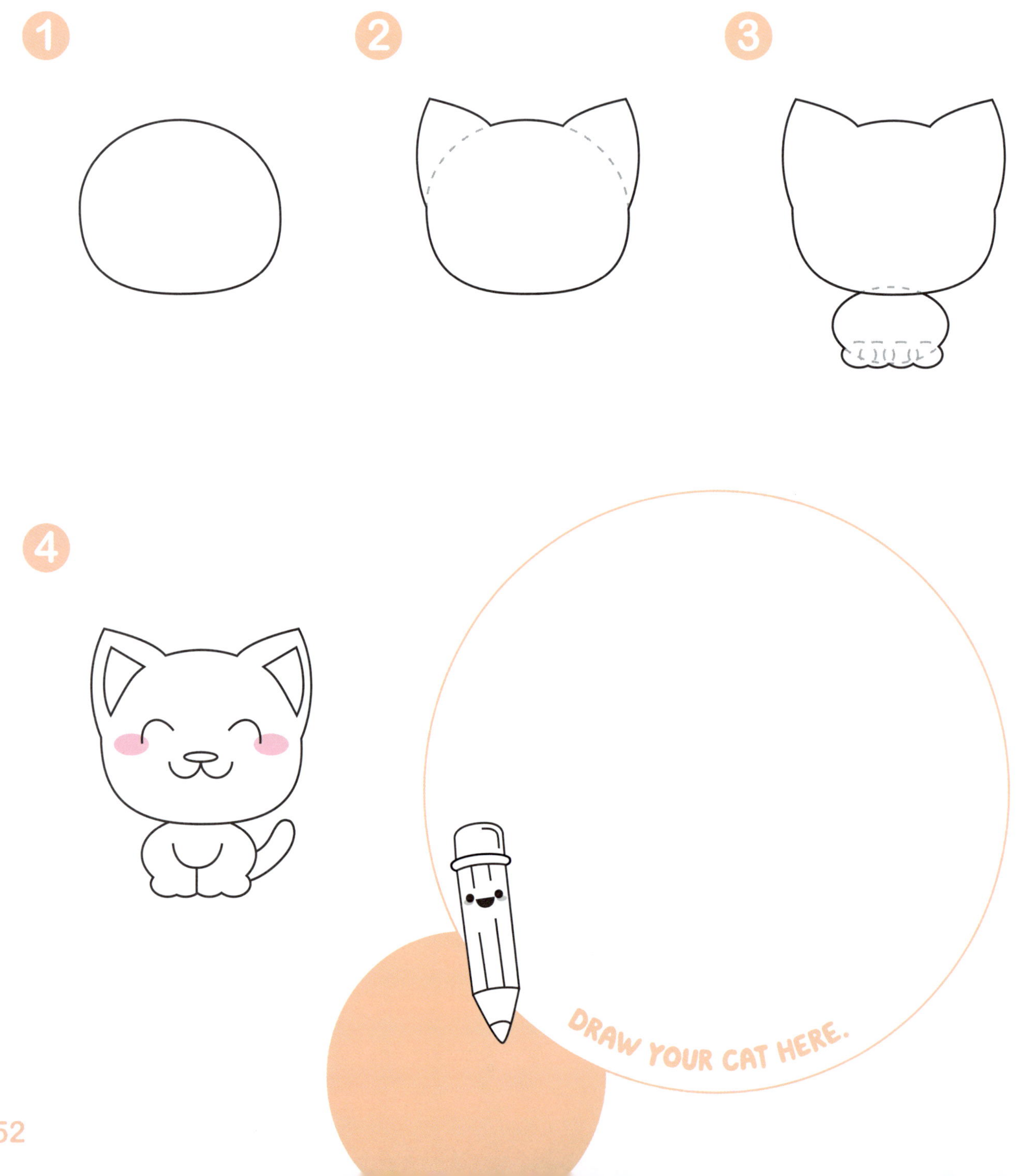

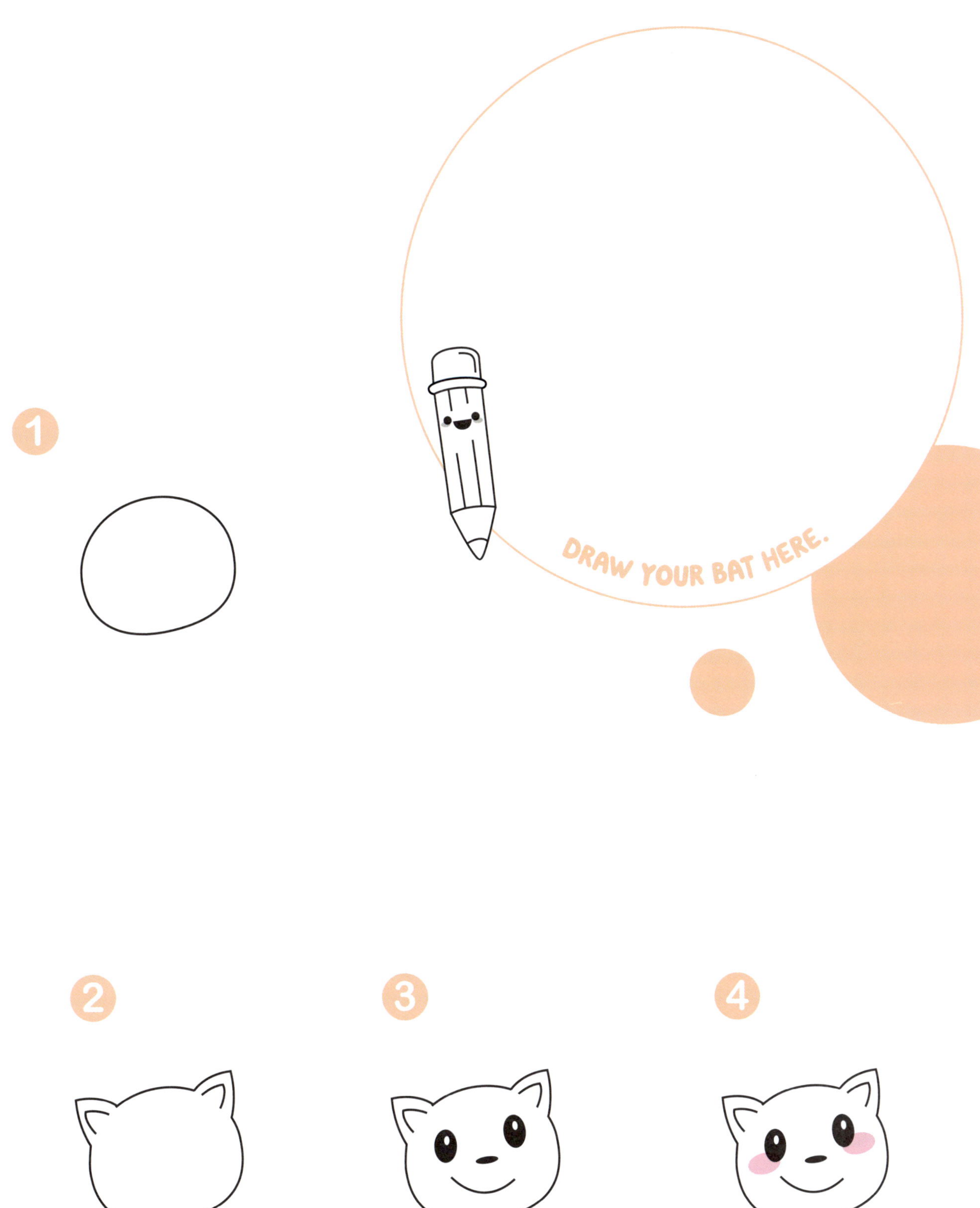
1
DRAW YOUR BAT HERE.
2
3
4

Drills

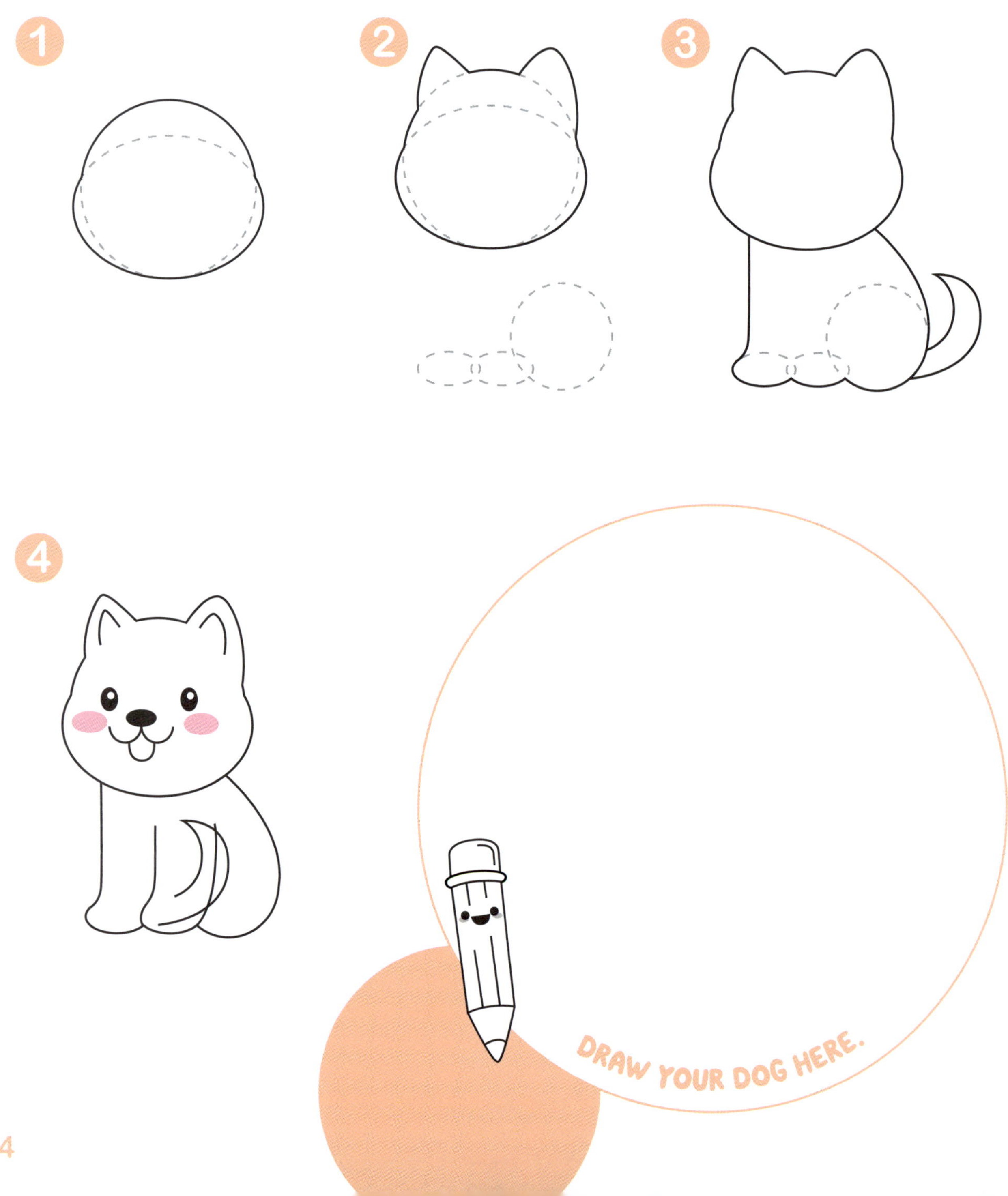

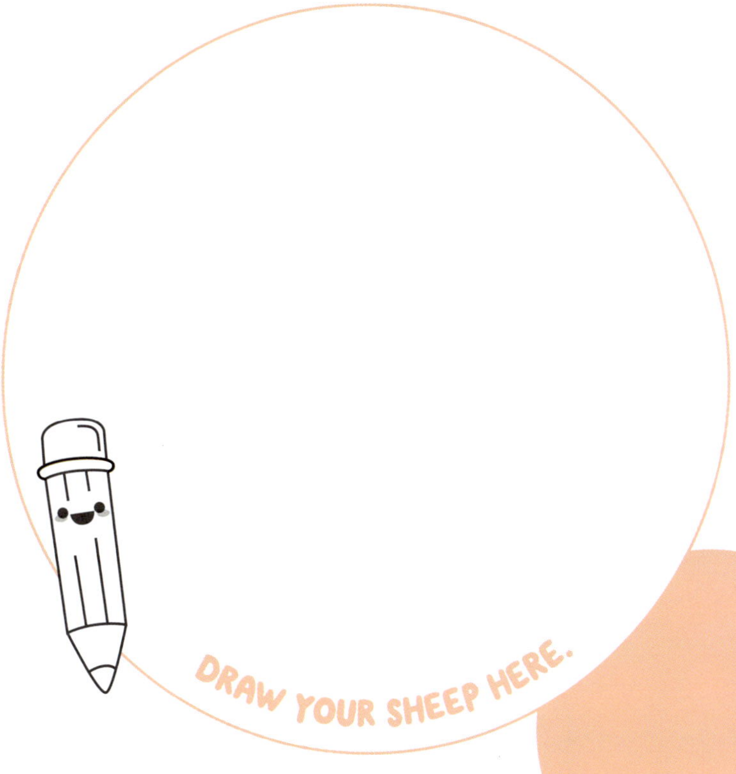

DRAW YOUR SHEEP HERE.

1

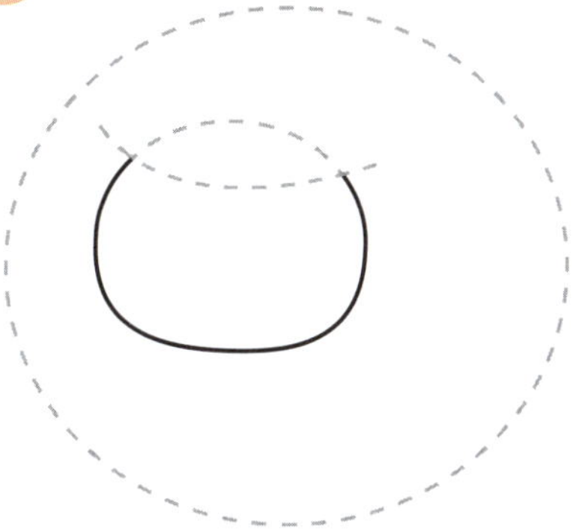

2

3

4

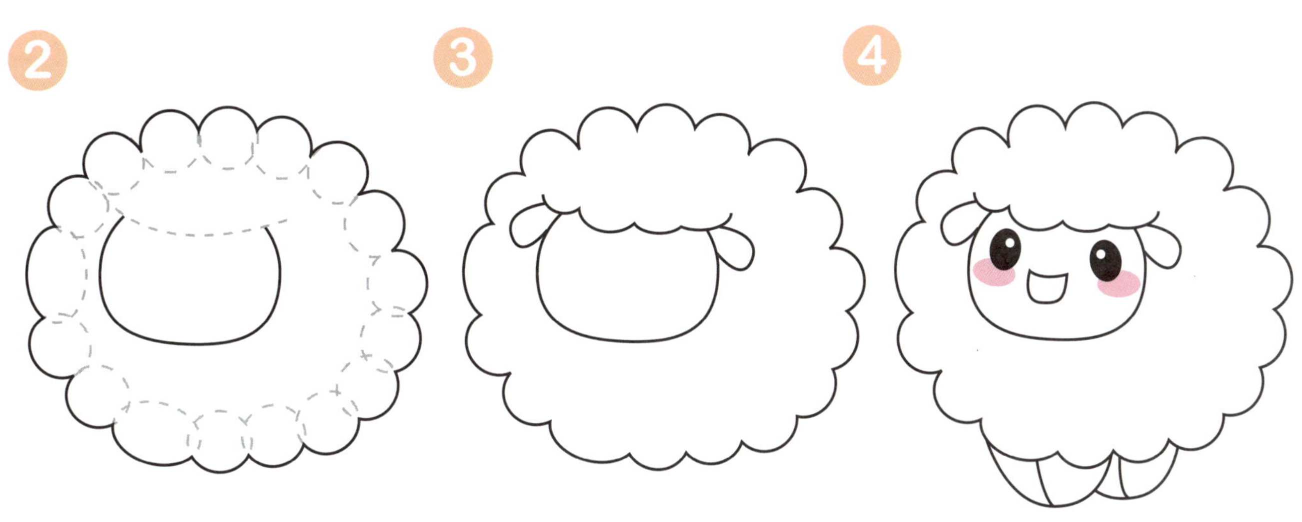

Happy Elephant

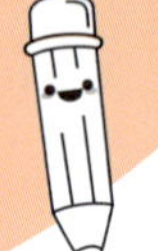

Sketch three circles, starting with the head.

Add the trunk and legs to your sketch.

3

Now plan the ear and also the legs in the background.

Use a fineliner to draw the outline and carefully erase your sketch.

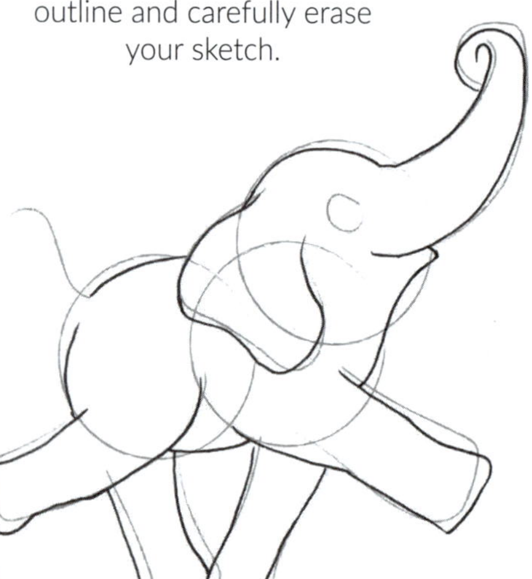

In the next step, draw the eye and the tail.

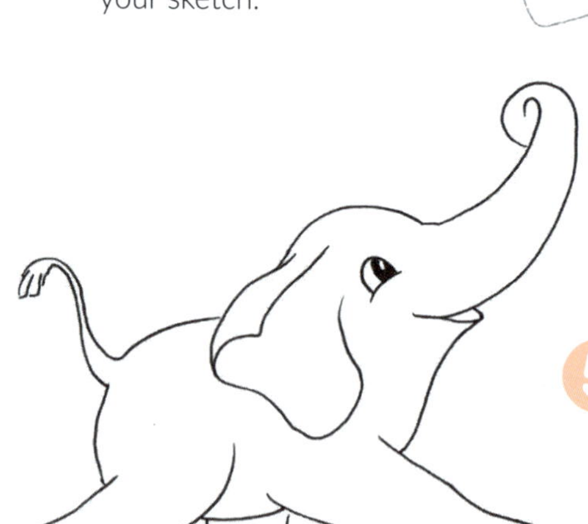

Add a couple of wrinkles and details, and if you feel like it, add a butterfly too.

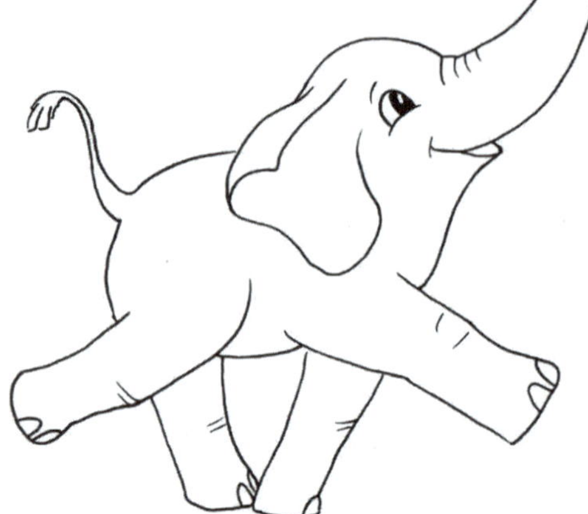

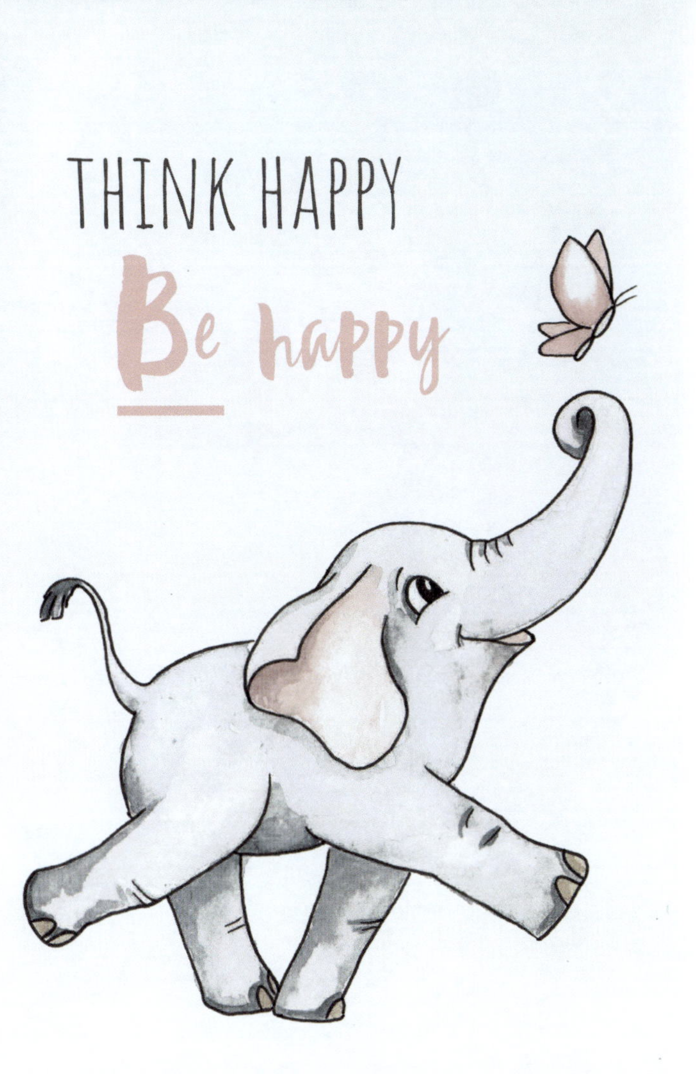

Refine your elephant with colours, adding light and shadow.

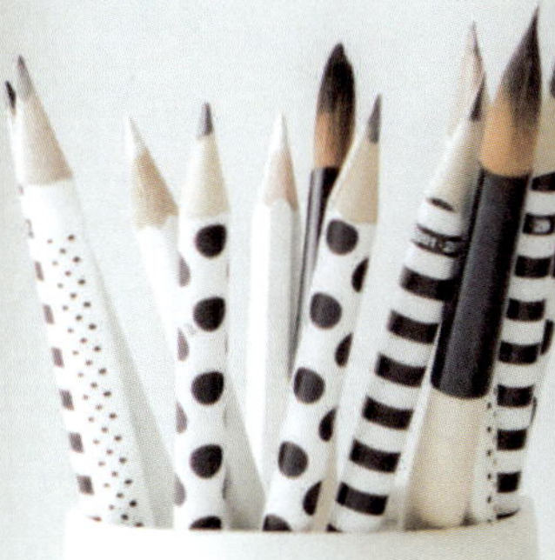

Platypus 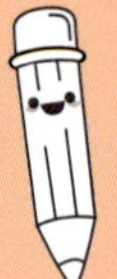

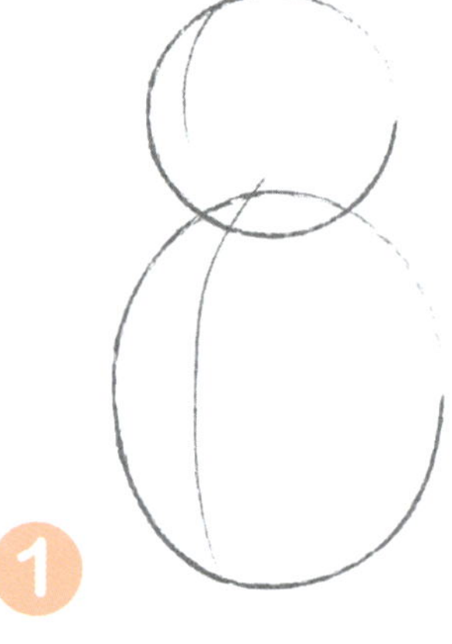

1

Start by sketching two circles for your platypus. Add a guideline in order to indicate where the platypus is looking.

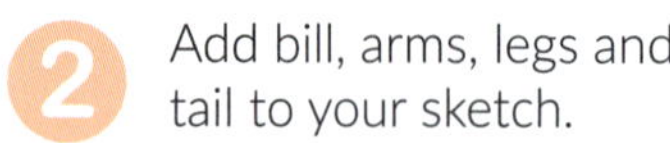

2 Add bill, arms, legs and tail to your sketch.

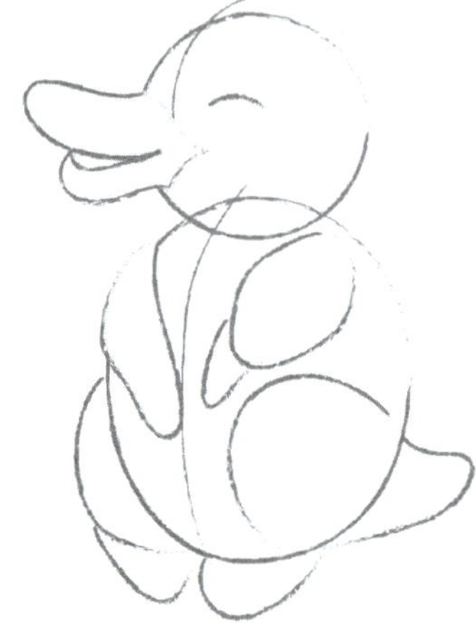

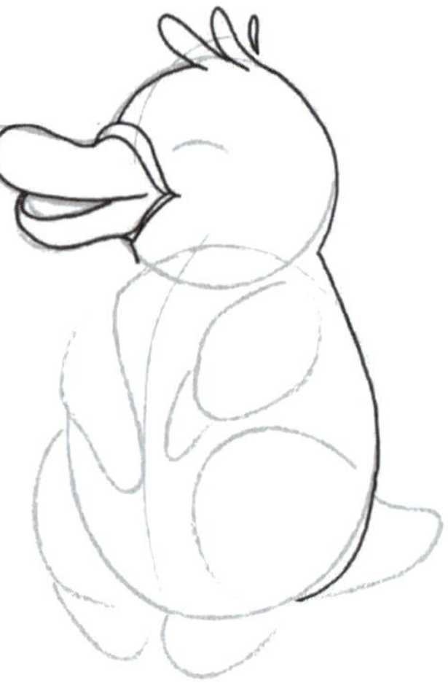

3 Start to go over the outlines with a fineliner.

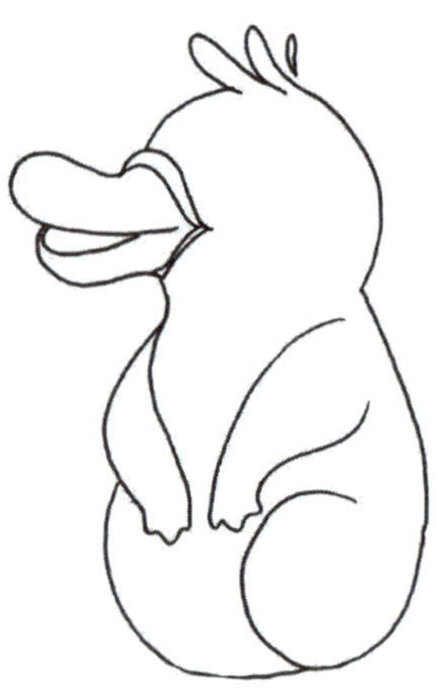

4 Draw the arms and the right thigh.

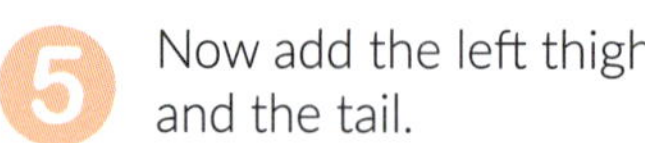

5 Now add the left thigh and the tail.

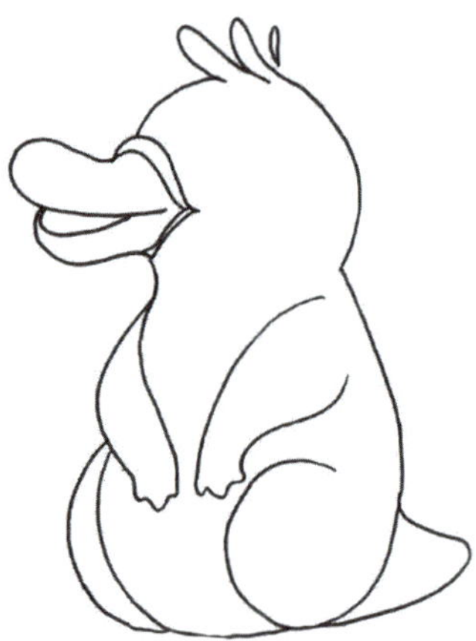

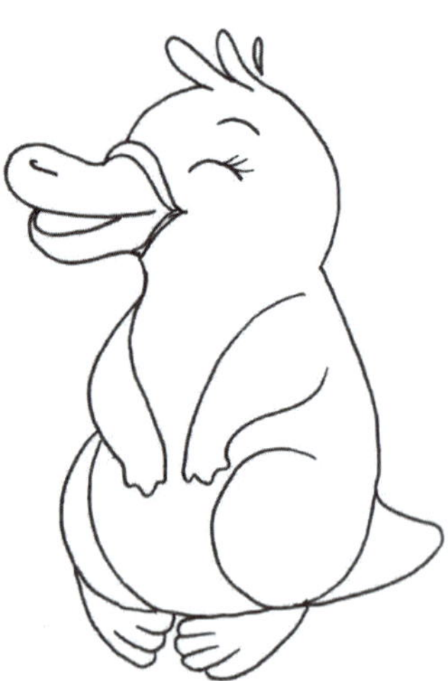

6 Add the feet and details, such as eyes and eyebrows.

It´s a good DAY to be HAPPY

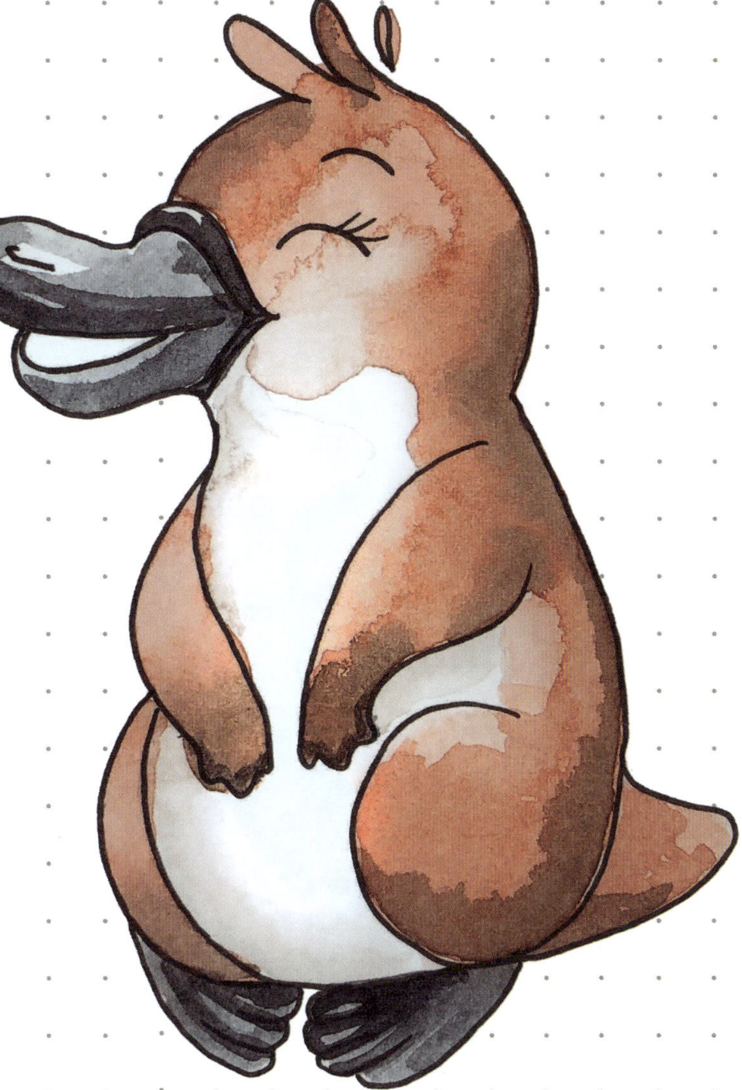

7 Paint your platypus in pretty colours.

Penguins

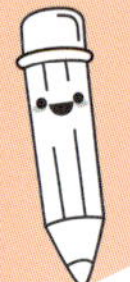

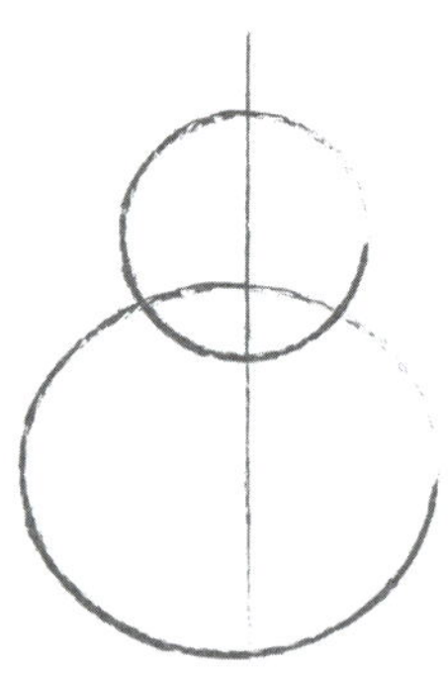

Start by drawing two circles for the central penguin.

Add the two other penguins on the left and the right.

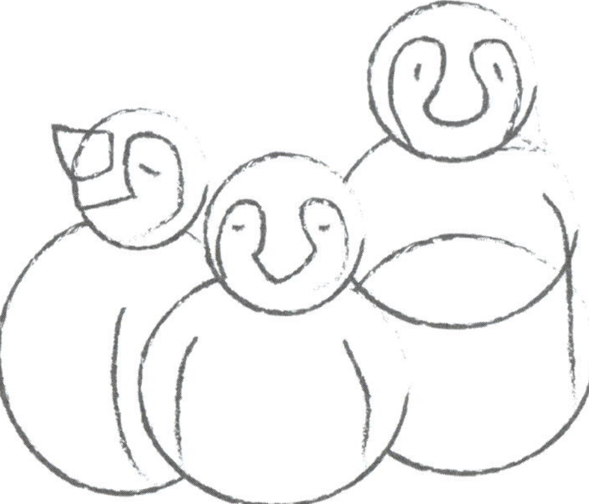

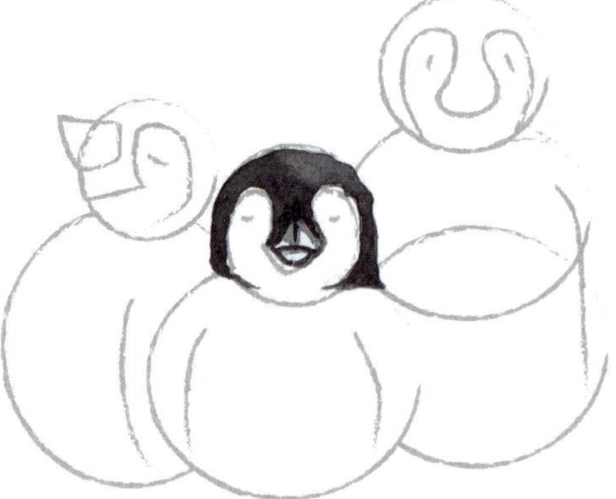

3 Paint the head of the first penguin black and leave it to dry.

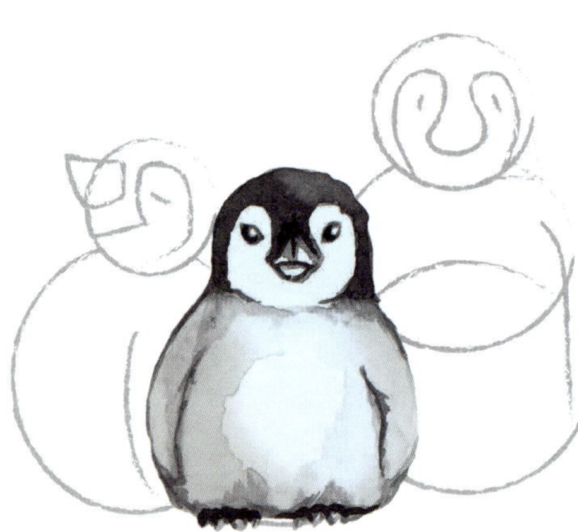

Paint the rest of the first penguin using shades of light grey.

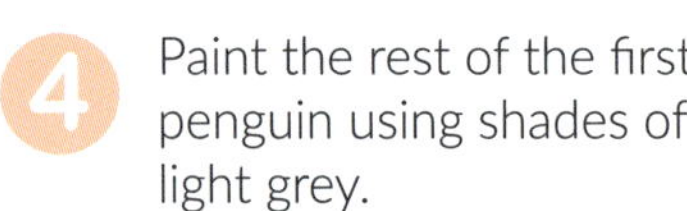

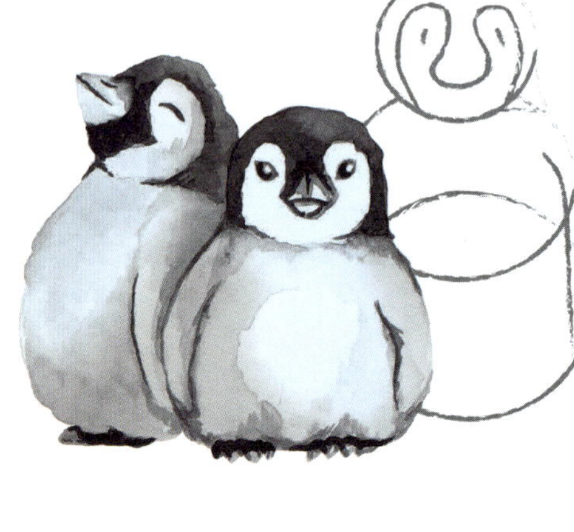

Repeat steps 3 and 4 for the second penguin.

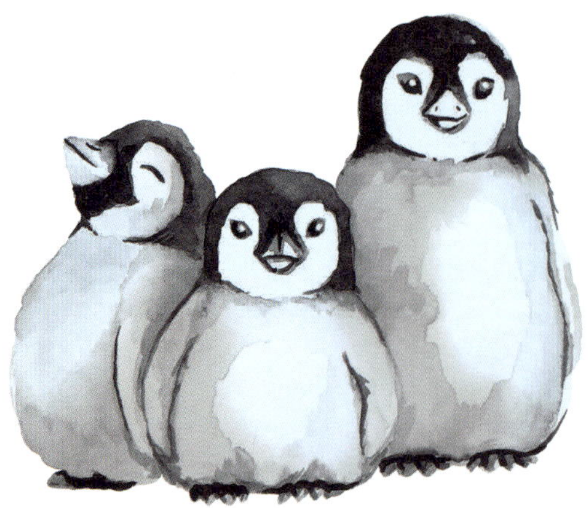

Do the same for penguin number three.

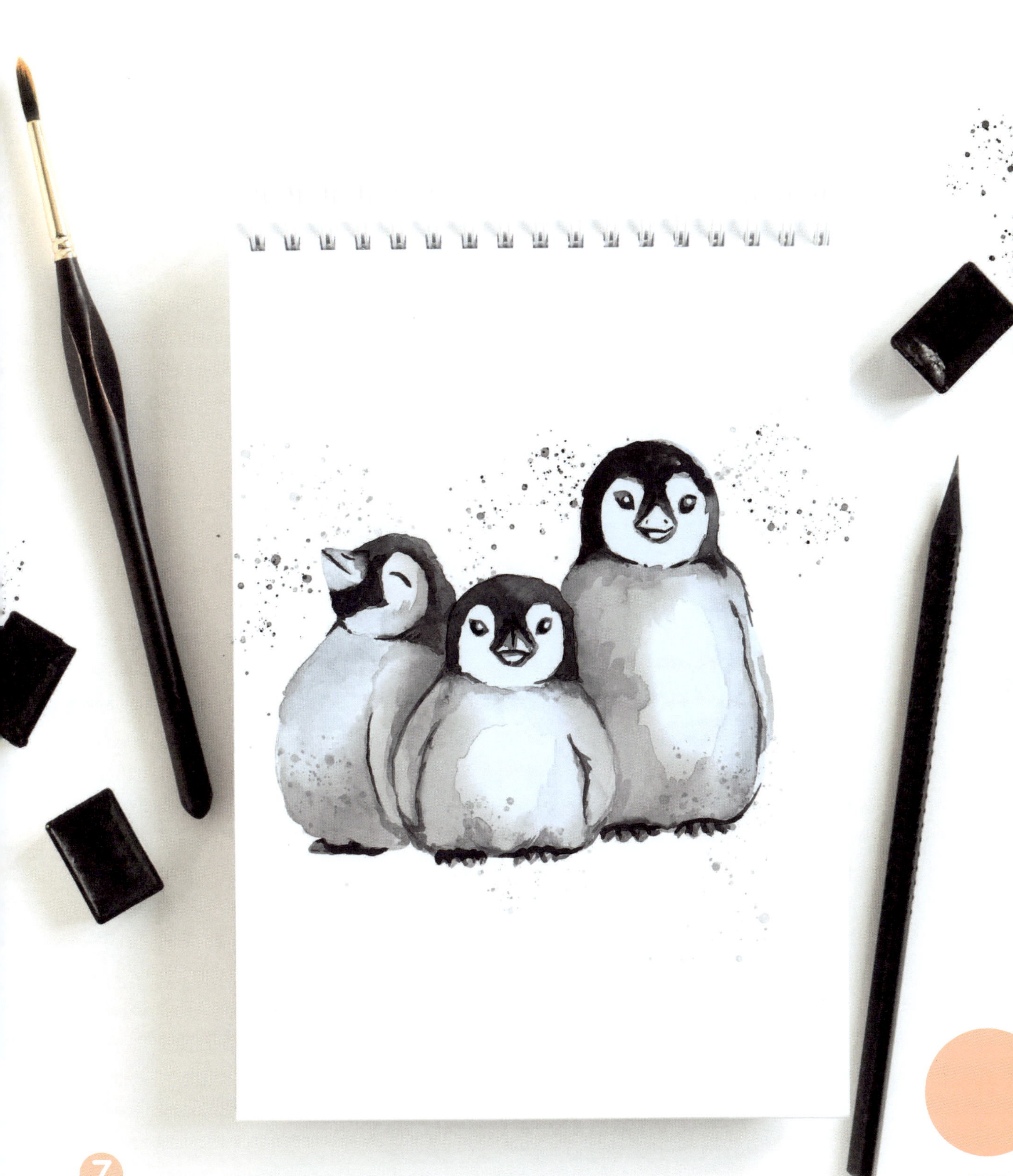

7

Add a few splats of paint to bring the illustration to life.

Frenchie

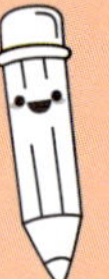

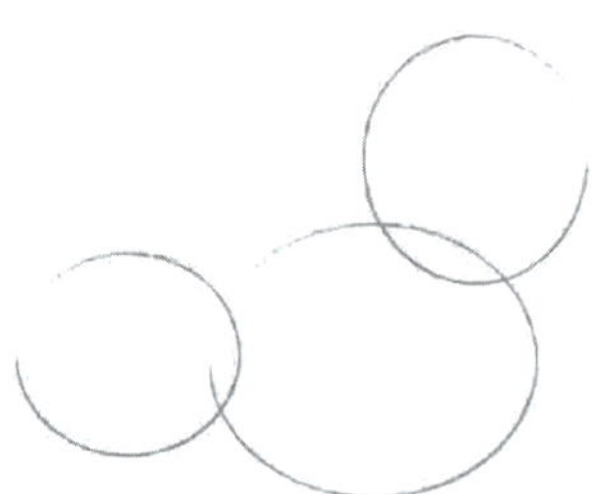

1 Start by drawing three circles for the head, body and behind of your French bulldog.

Use ovals to plan in your dog's legs and paws.

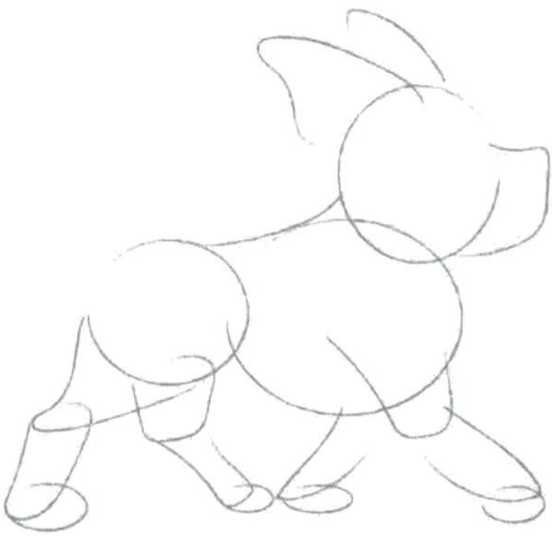

3 Lightly sketch the snout and ears.

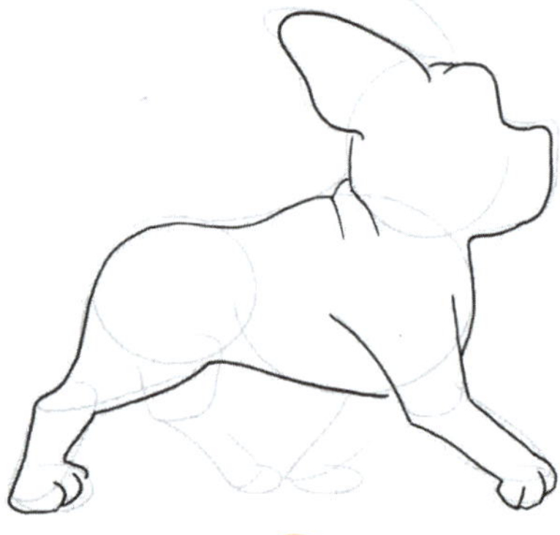

4 Use a fineliner to draw the outline of your dog's body.

Add your dog's paws, ears and tail.

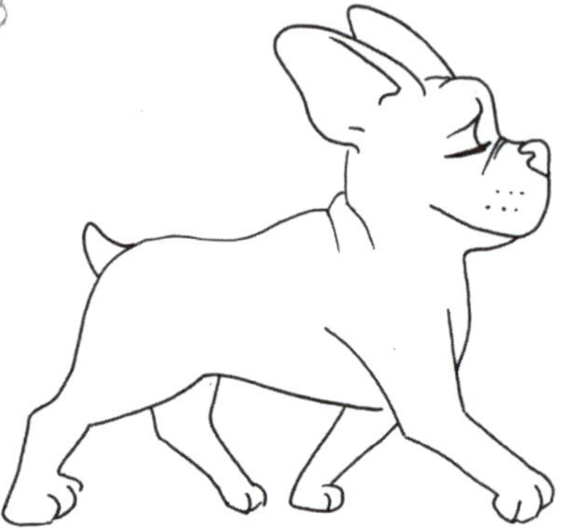

6 Now add details, such as wrinkles, eyes, nose and ears to your Frenchie.

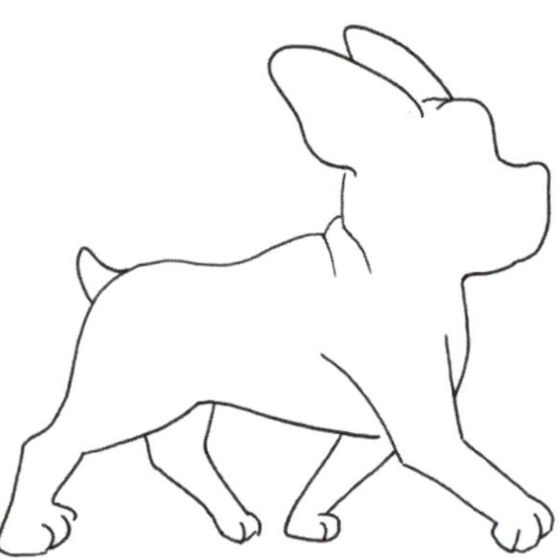

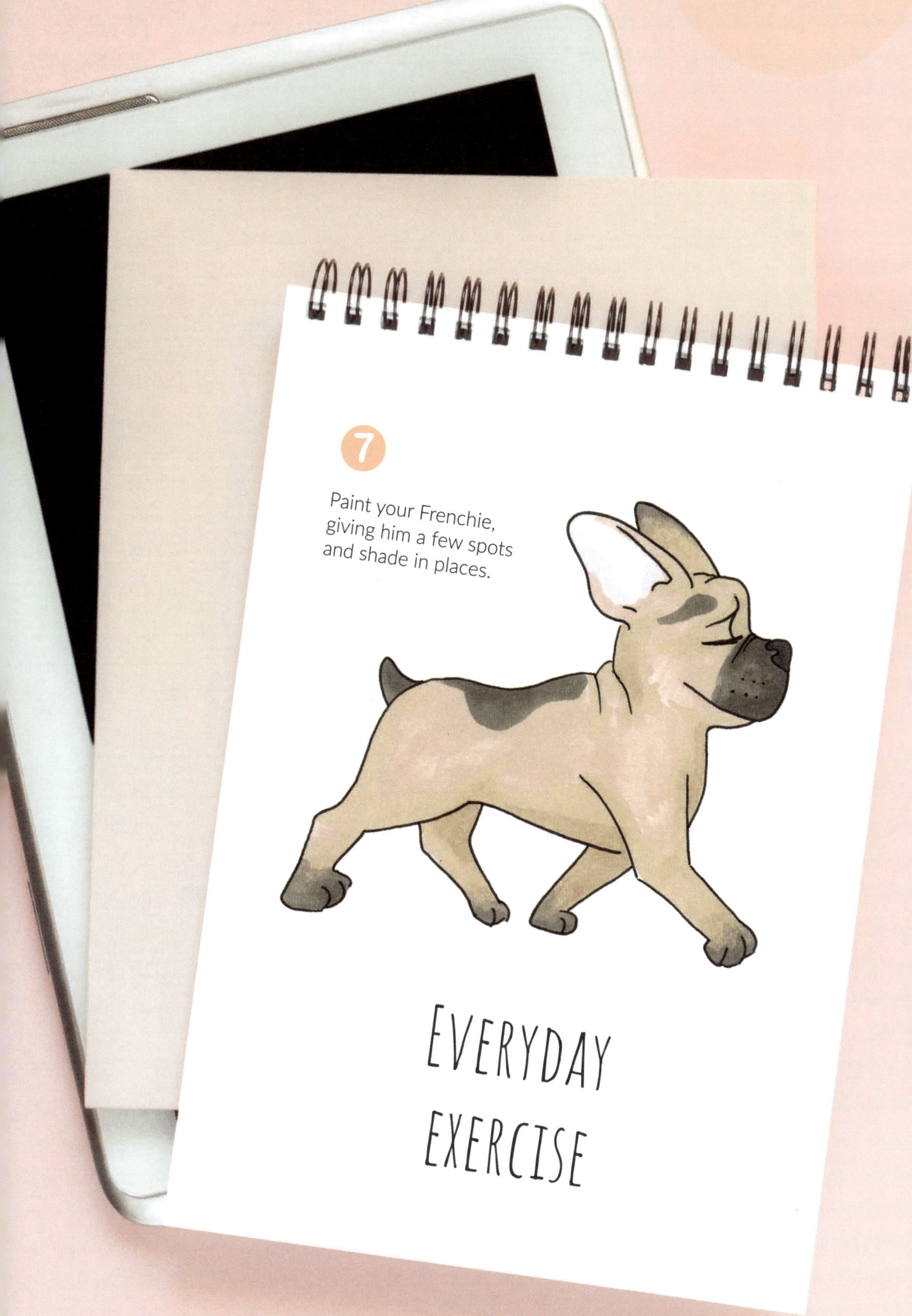
7
Paint your Frenchie,
giving him a few spots
and shade in places.
EVERYDAY
EXERCISE

Party Hedgehog

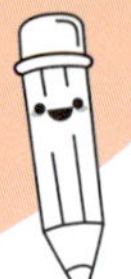

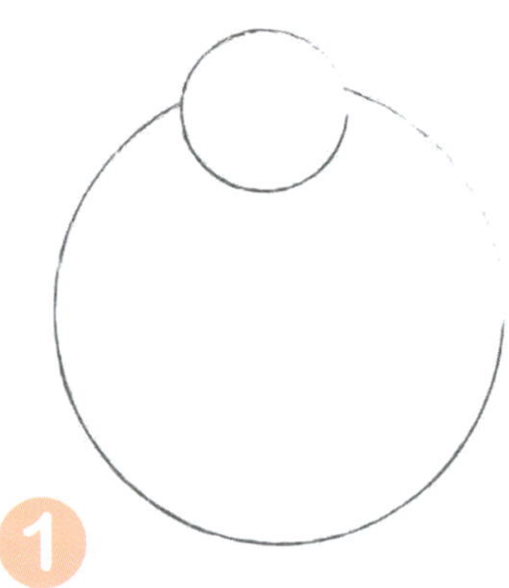

1

Sketch two circles; a small one for the head and a large one for the body.

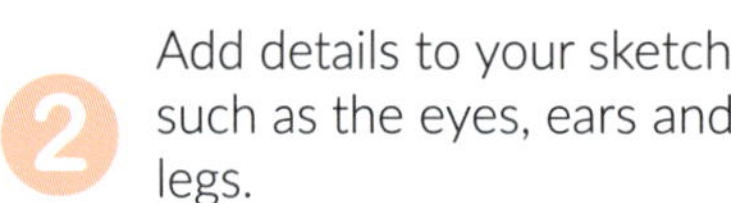

2 Add details to your sketch, such as the eyes, ears and legs.

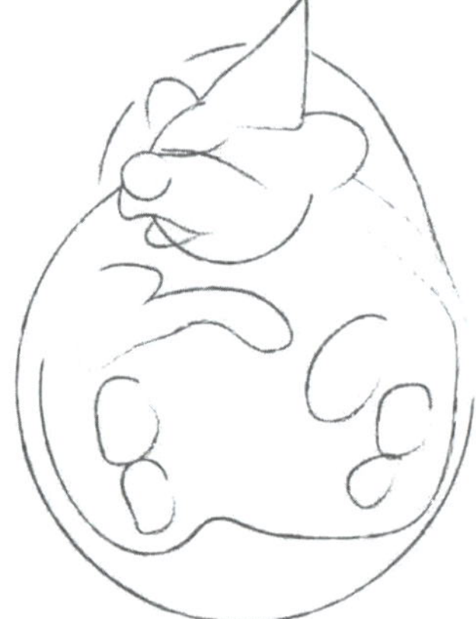

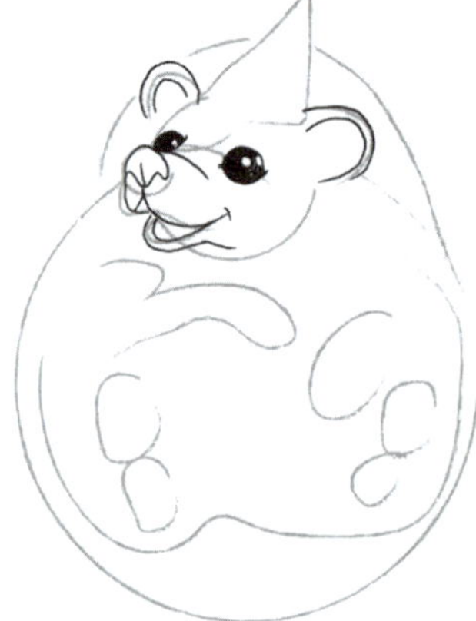

3 Use a fineliner to draw in the first details, starting with the face.

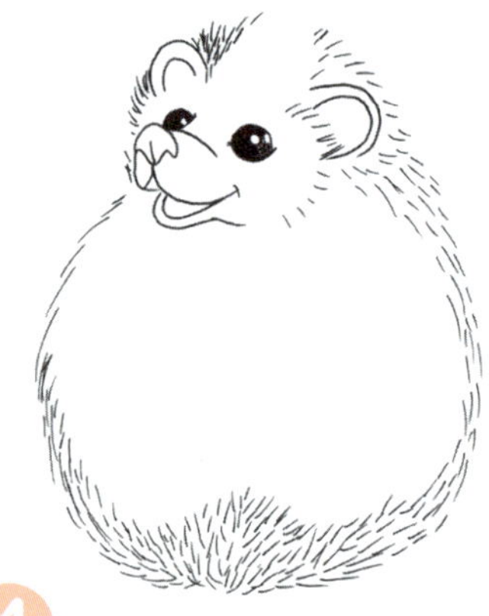

4

Indicate the spikes of the hedgehog with just a few pen strokes.

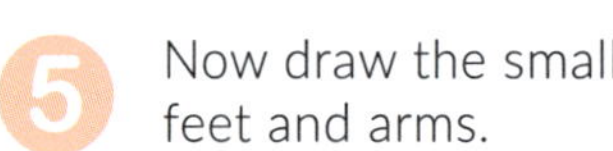

5 Now draw the small feet and arms.

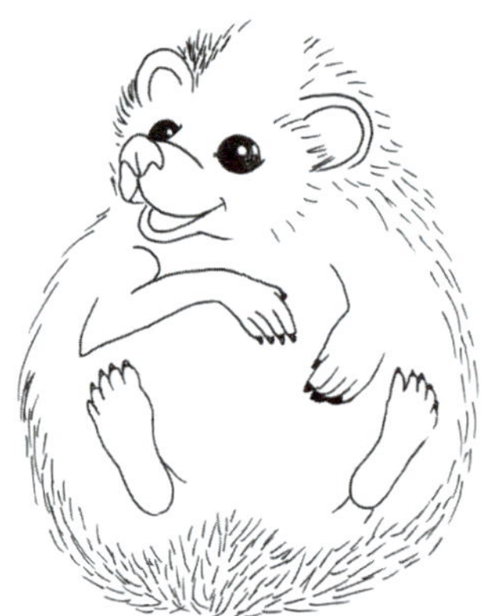

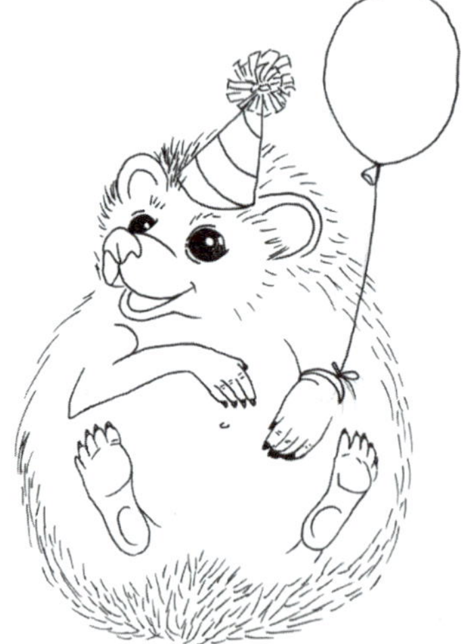

6 Before adding colour to your illustration, add a few further details that make it even more beautiful.

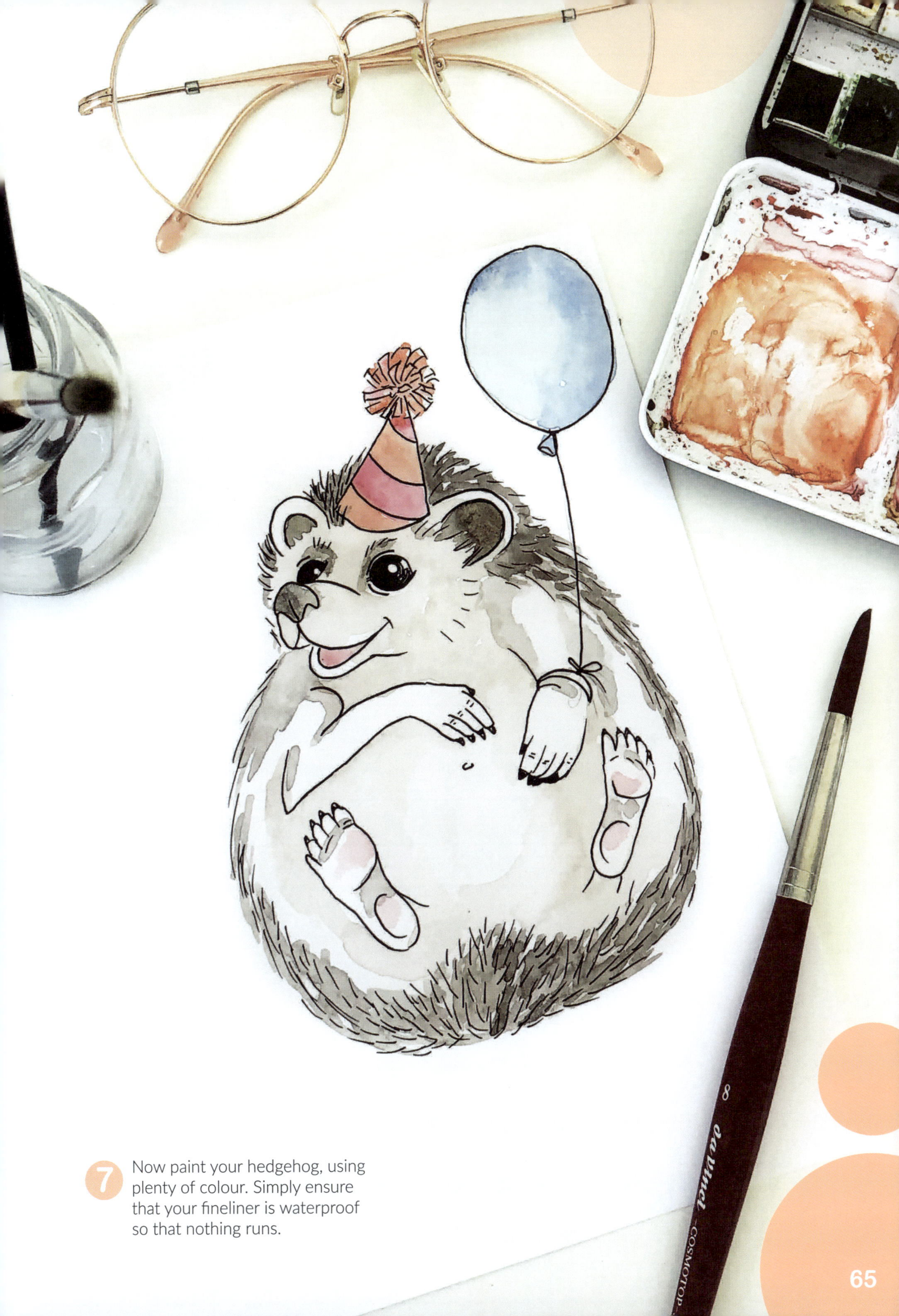

7 Now paint your hedgehog, using plenty of colour. Simply ensure that your fineliner is waterproof so that nothing runs.

Honey Bear

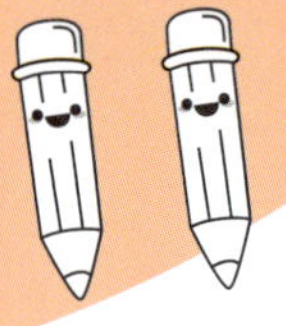

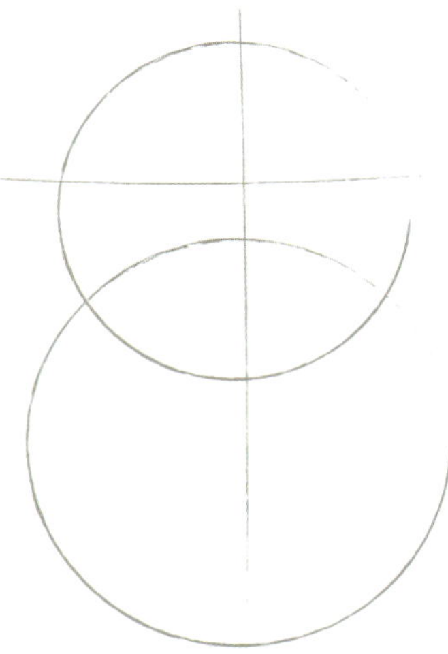

1 Start by drawing two circles for your bear.

2 Add more details to your sketch, such as arms, legs, scarf and a honey pot.

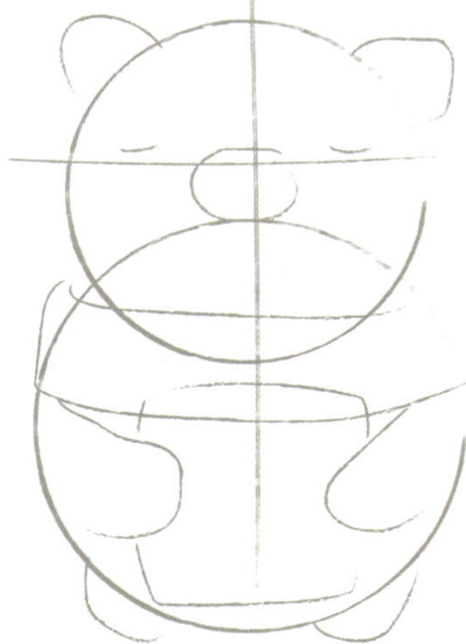

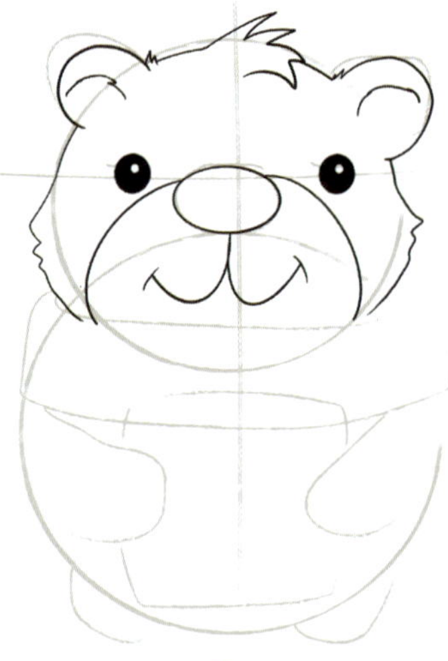

3 Now draw the outlines with a fineliner. Always start with the head.

4 Draw the scarf that the bear is wearing around his neck, making sure that the lines are curved and not straight.

5 Draw the body and the honey pot. Carefully erase your sketch.

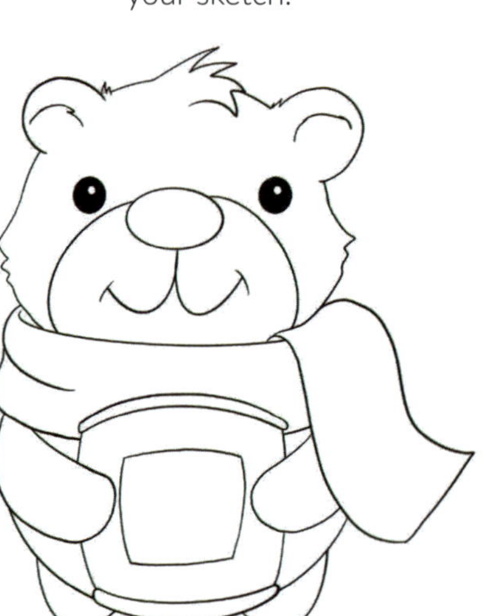

6 Add a few more details, such as the label on the honey pot.

7

Paint your bear in pretty shades of brown so that he looks even cuter.

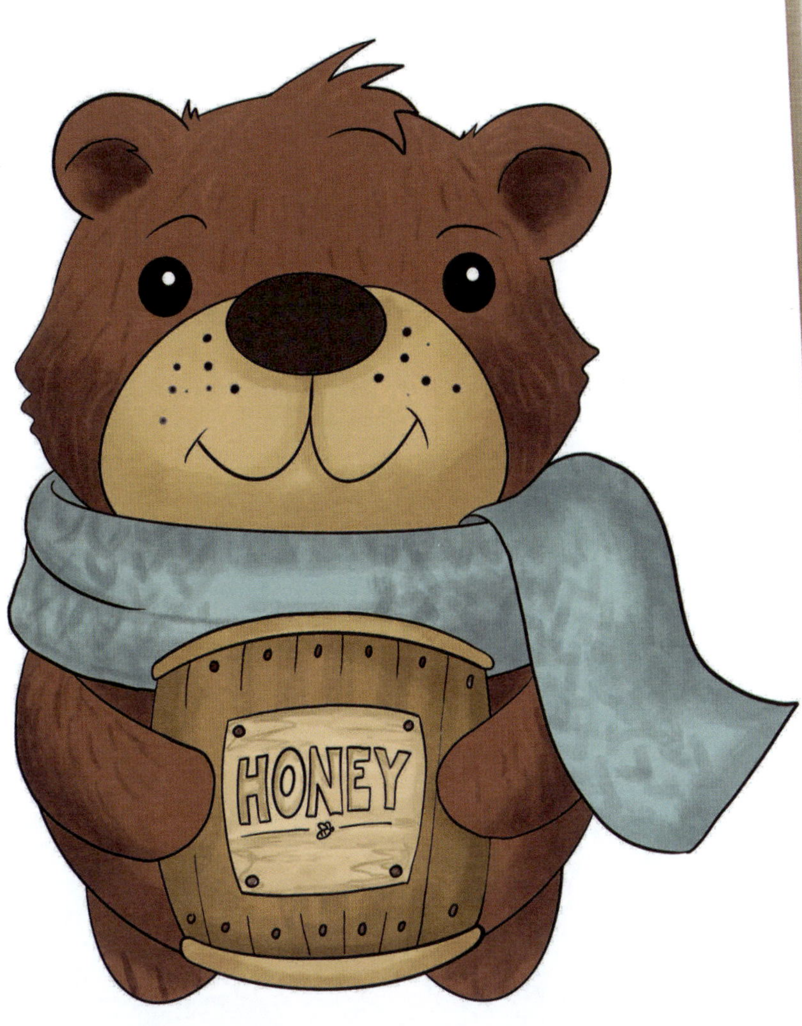

Kitty Love

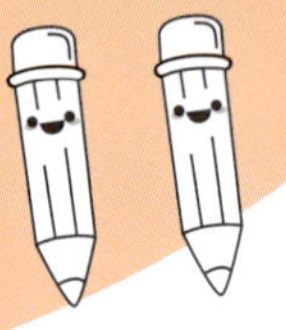

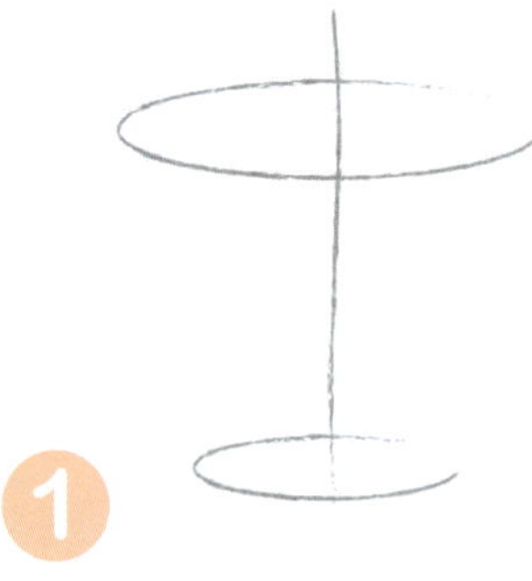

1 Start by sketching two ellipses for your cup.

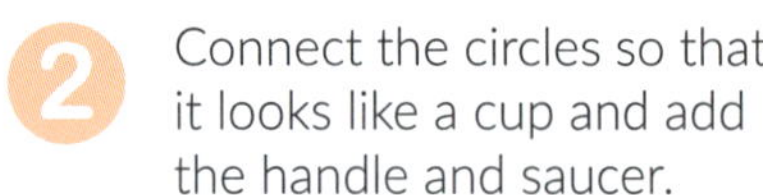

2 Connect the circles so that it looks like a cup and add the handle and saucer.

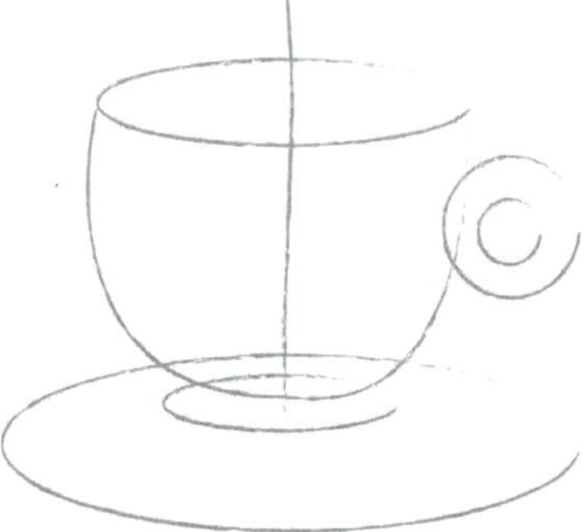

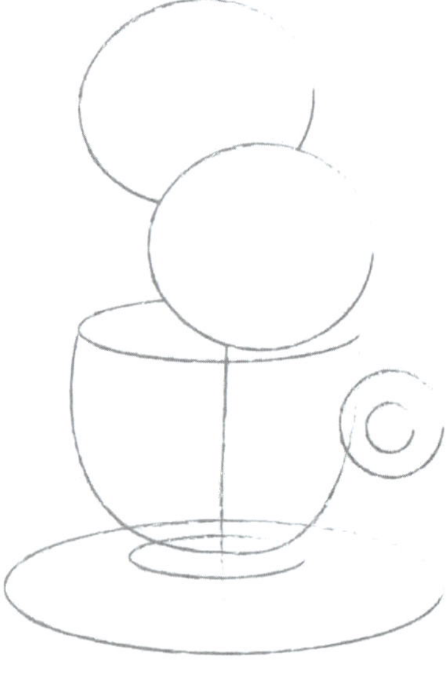

3 Plan the cats' heads with two large circles.

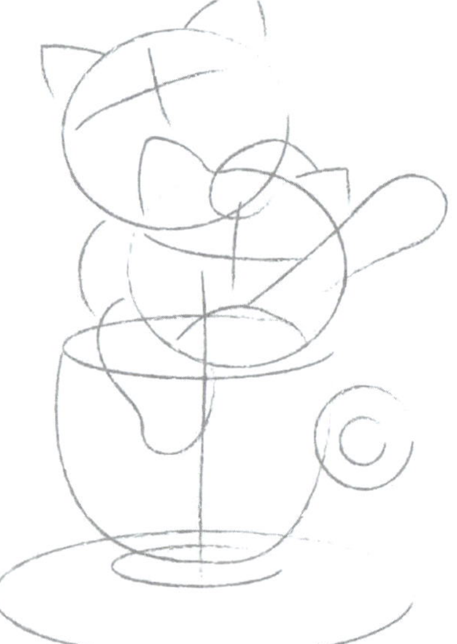

4 Lightly sketch where the cats' ears, eyes and paws will go.

5 Use a fineliner to go over the outline of your cats.

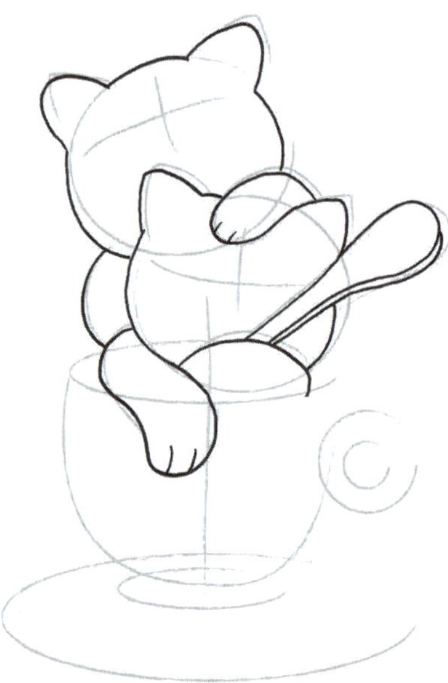

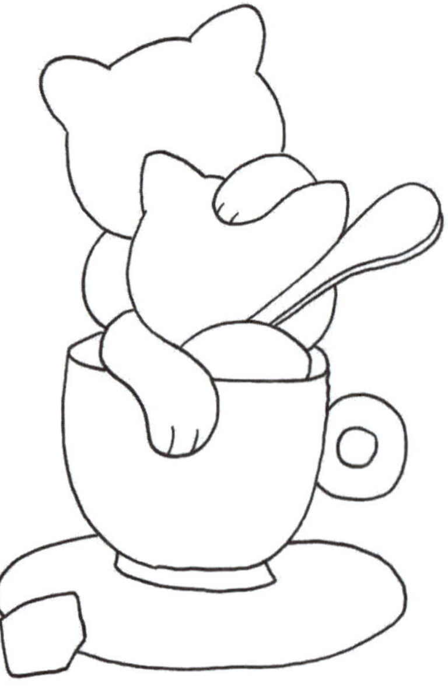

6 In the next step, work on the cup and maybe add a sugar cube.

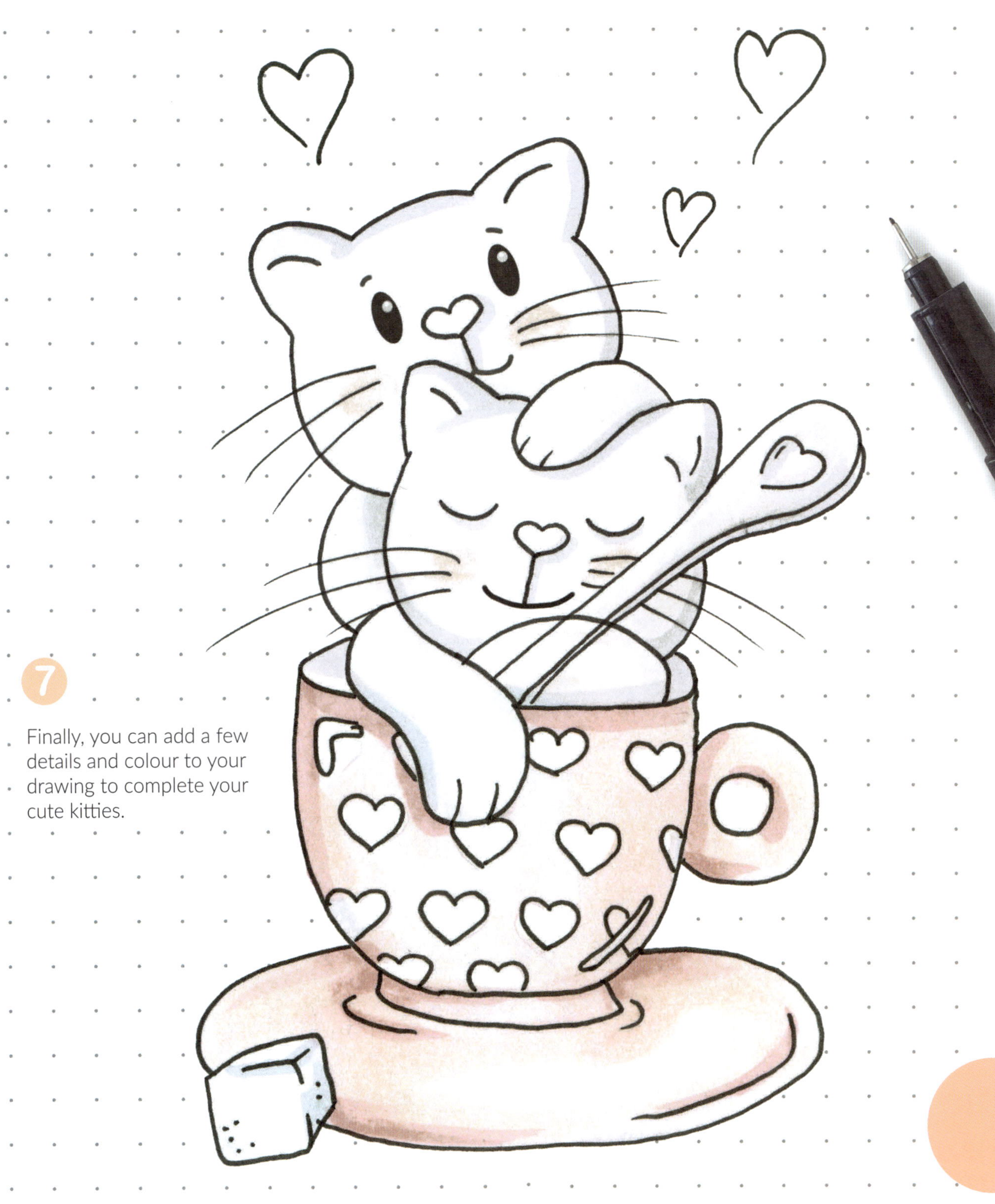

7

Finally, you can add a few details and colour to your drawing to complete your cute kitties.

squirrel

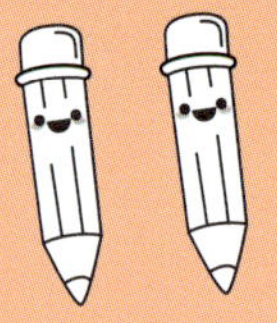

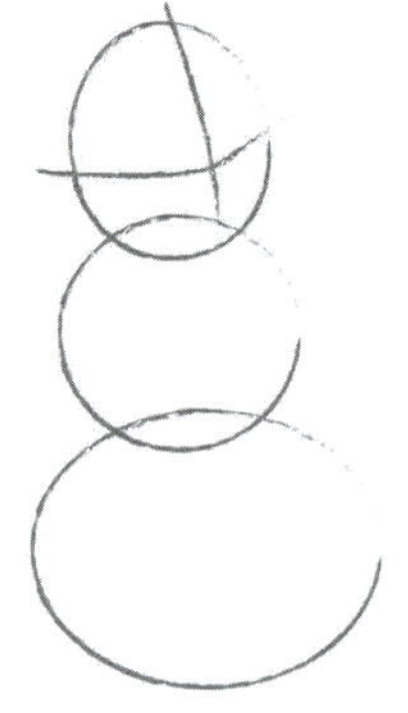

1

Start your sketch with three circles and use a cross to indicate the direction your squirrel will look.

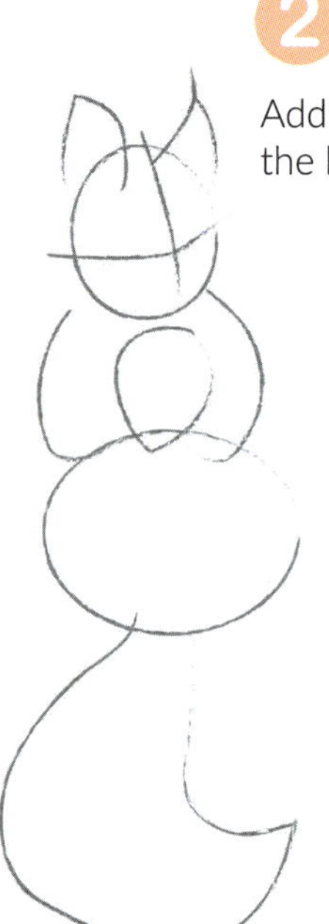

2

Add ears, arms and the bushy tail.

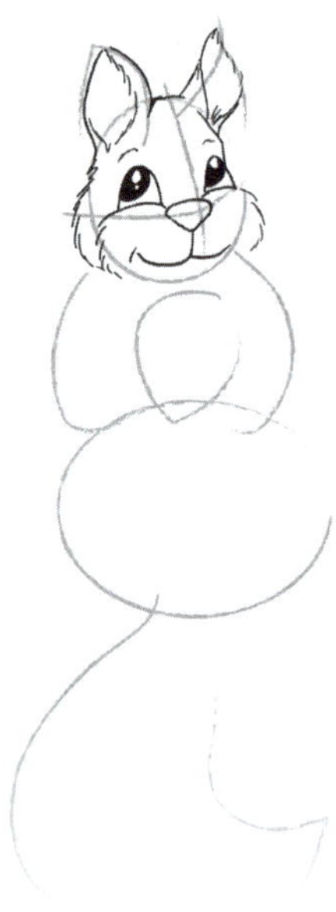

3

Use a fineliner to draw the outline of the head, starting with the eyes and nose followed by the head and ears.

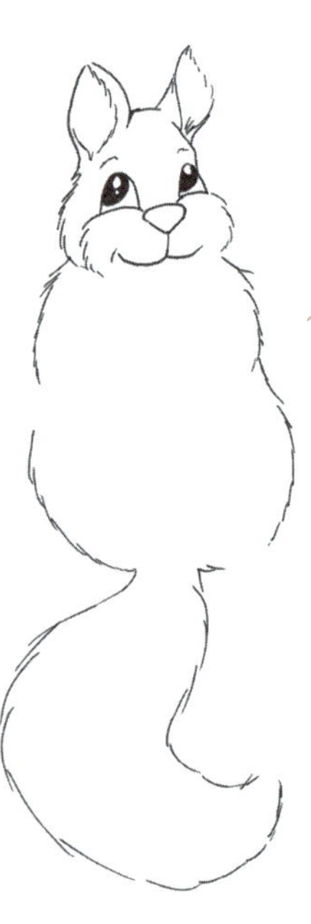

4

Now draw the outline of the body, ensure that your squirrel appears a little fluffy and the lines are not too straight.

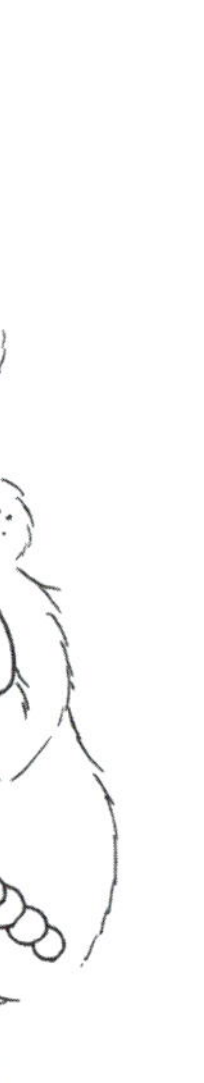

5

Now add the arms, nut and feet.

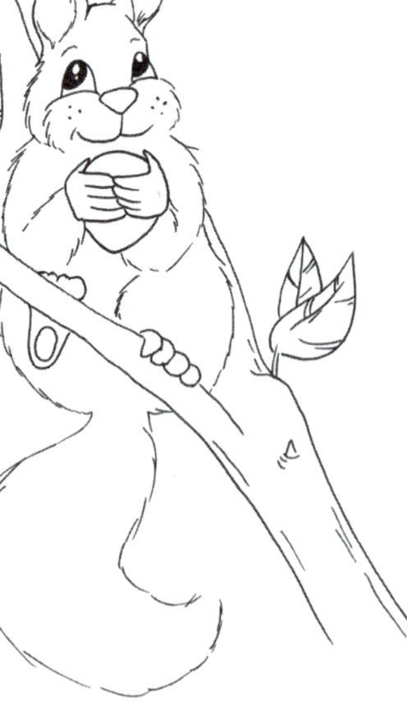

6

In the final step, draw the branch where the squirrel is sitting.

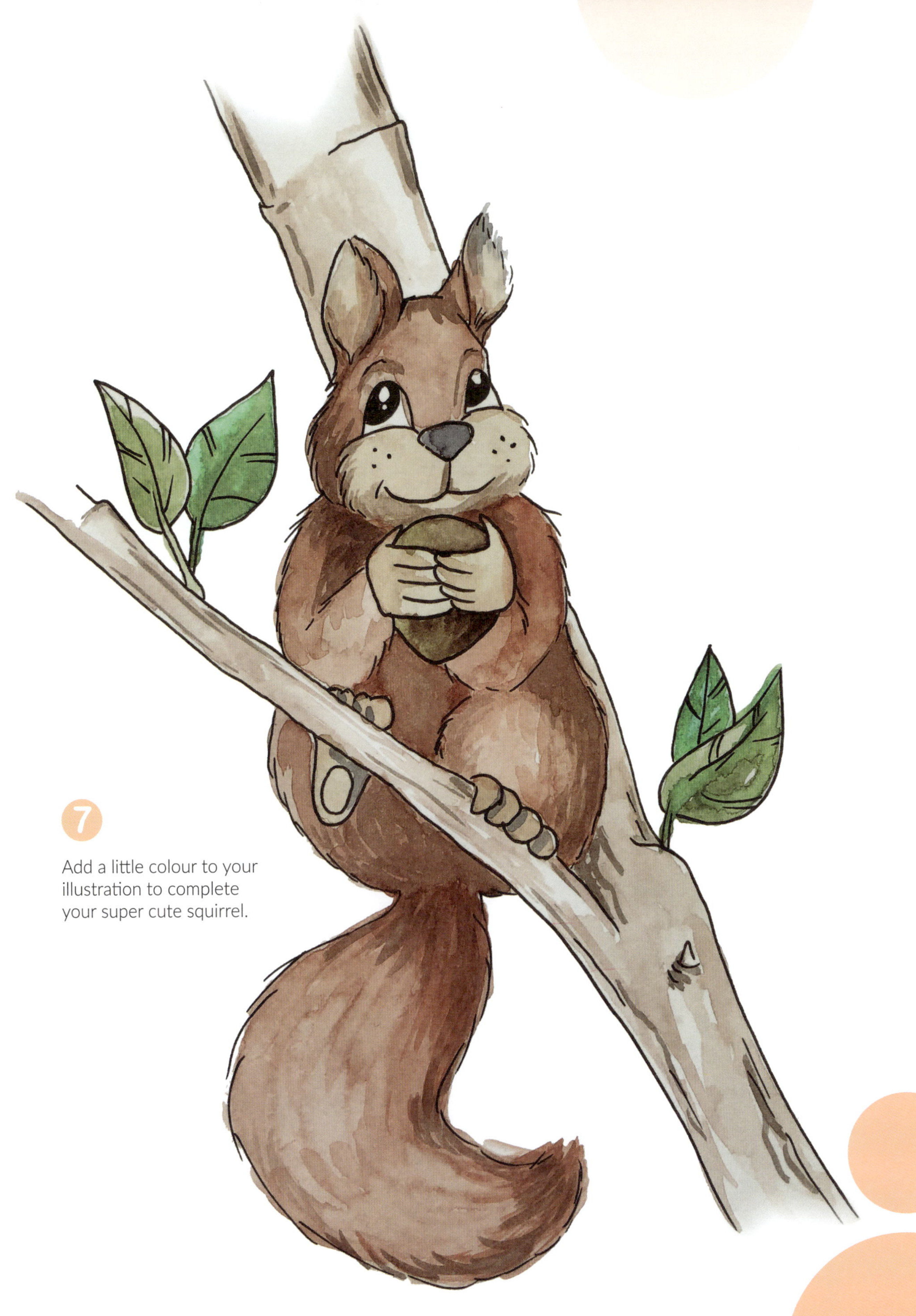

7

Add a little colour to your illustration to complete your super cute squirrel.

Happy Tentacles

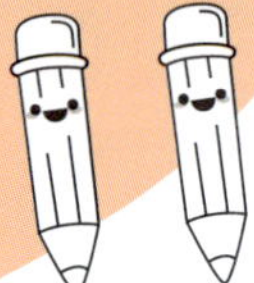

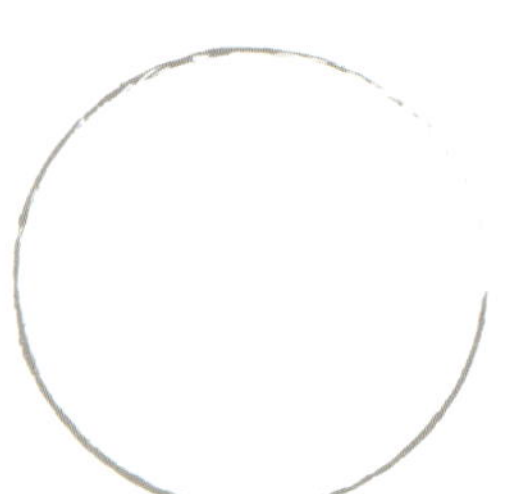

1

Start by sketching a circle for your octopus.

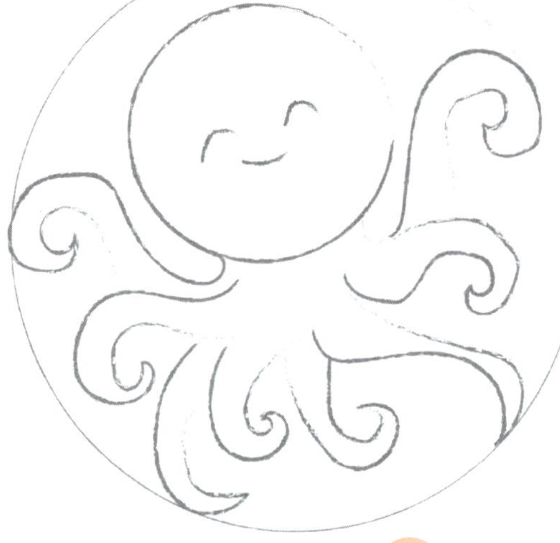

2

Lightly sketch a bigger circle, that you will use for the tentacles.

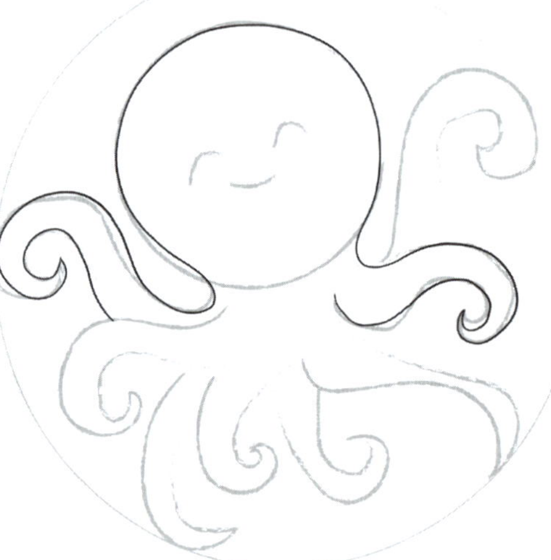

3

Use a fineliner to start drawing the outline of the head and the first tentacles.

4

Draw six legs on your octopus and carefully erase the sketch.

5

Draw two more legs in the background.

6

Add a few more details, such as suckers, eyes and mouth.

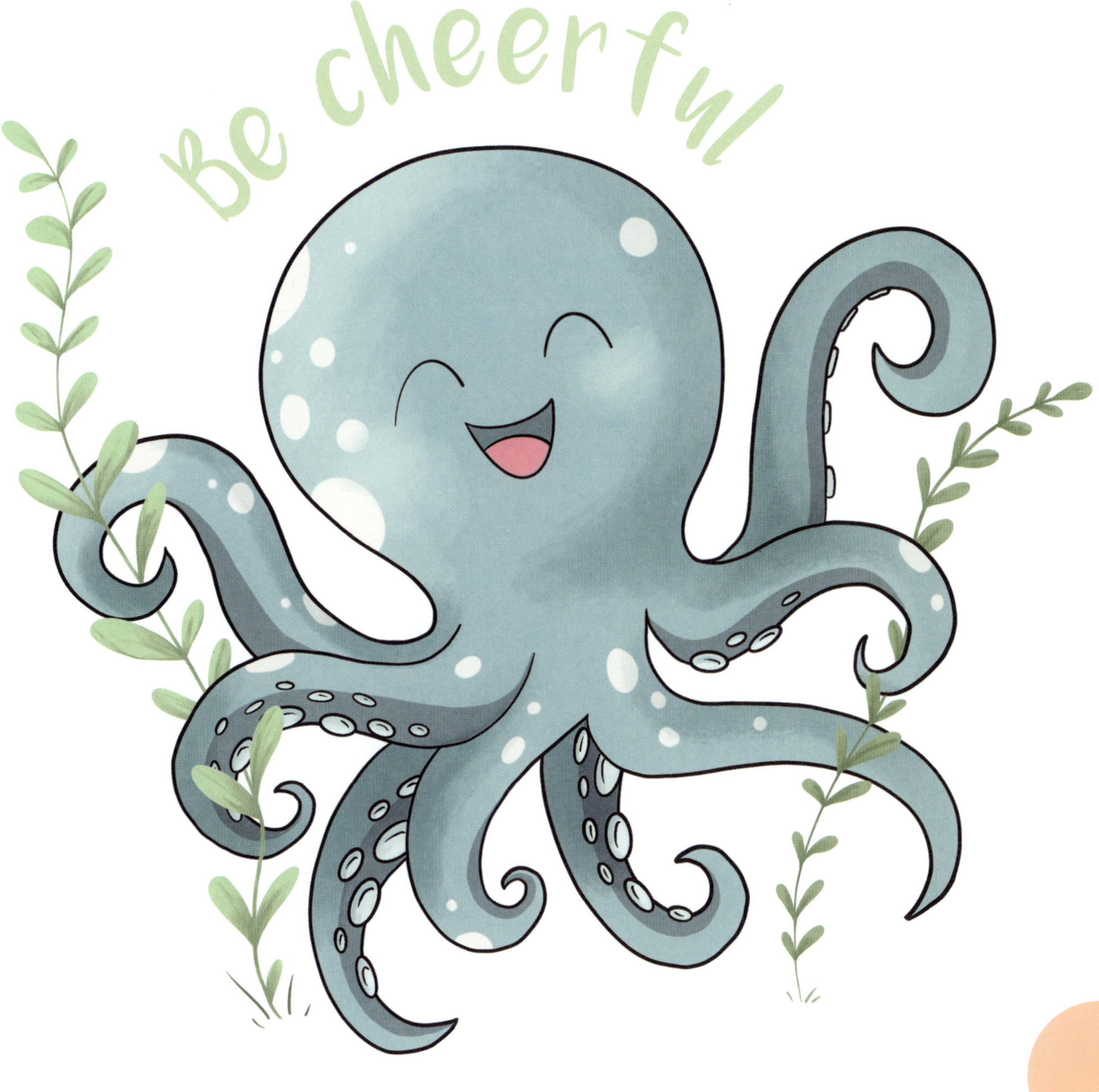

Be cheerful

With a little colour as well as water plants here and there, the octopus looks even happier.

Little Birds

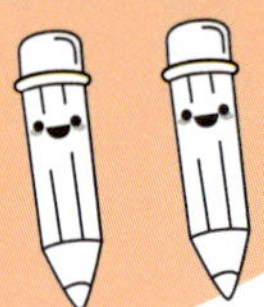

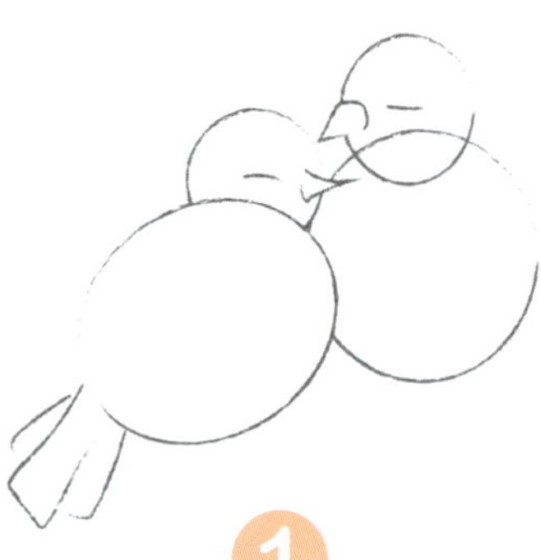

1

Lightly sketch the two birds, using circles to help you.

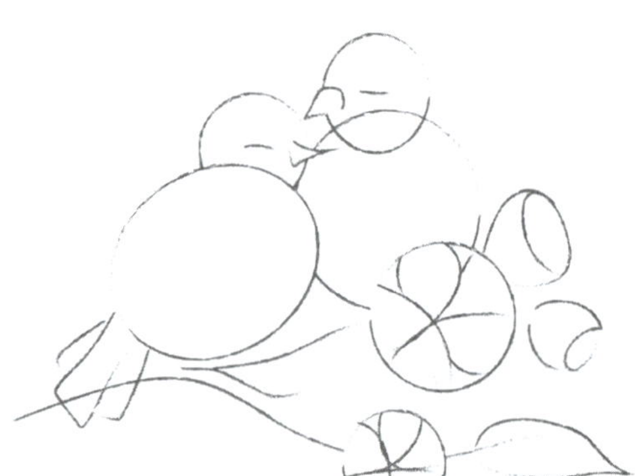

2

Draw guidelines for the branch and circles where the larger flowers will be later.

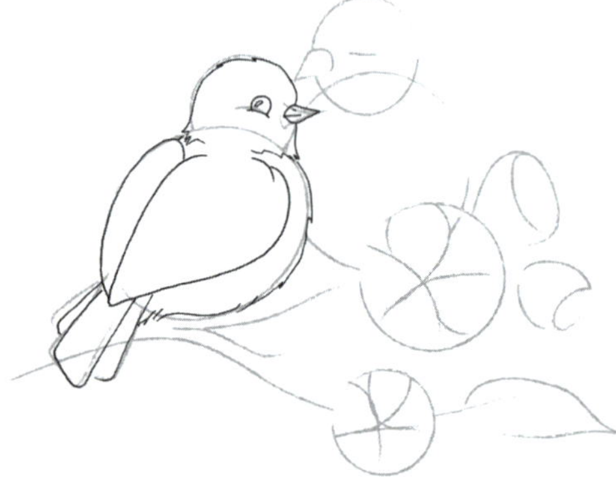

3

Use a fineliner to draw the outlines of the first bird, starting as always with the head.

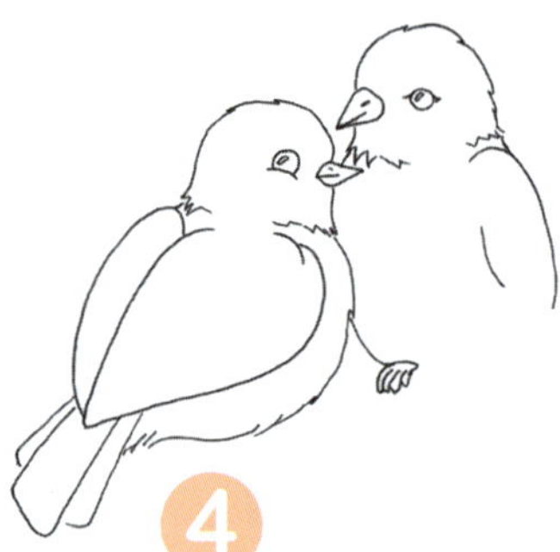

4

Then draw the second bird.

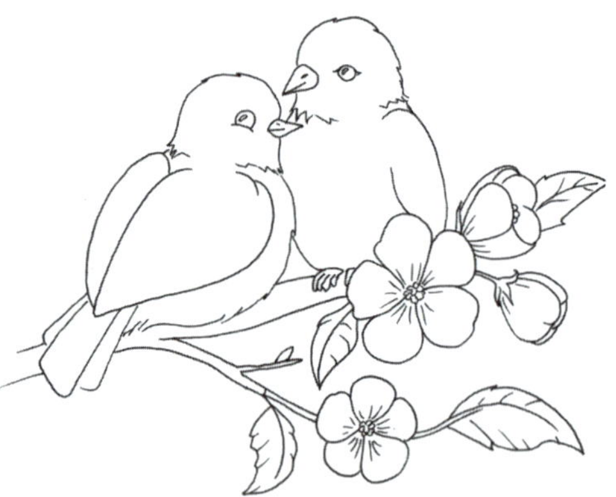

6

Once the branch is finished, add a couple of leaves.

5

Now work on the branch that they are sitting on. Start with the flowers.

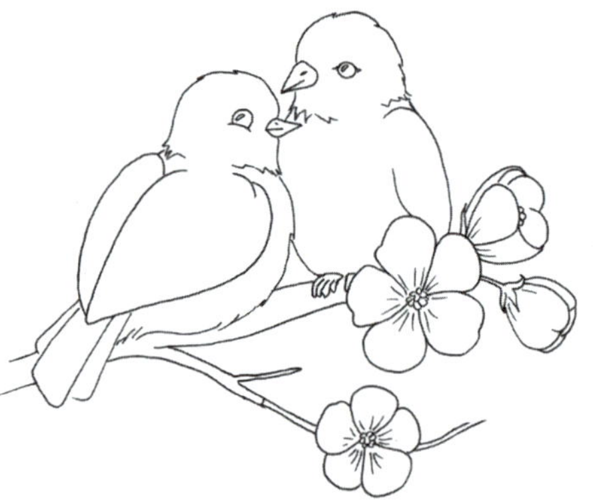

7 The birds on the spring branch look particularly beautiful when painted in bright colours.

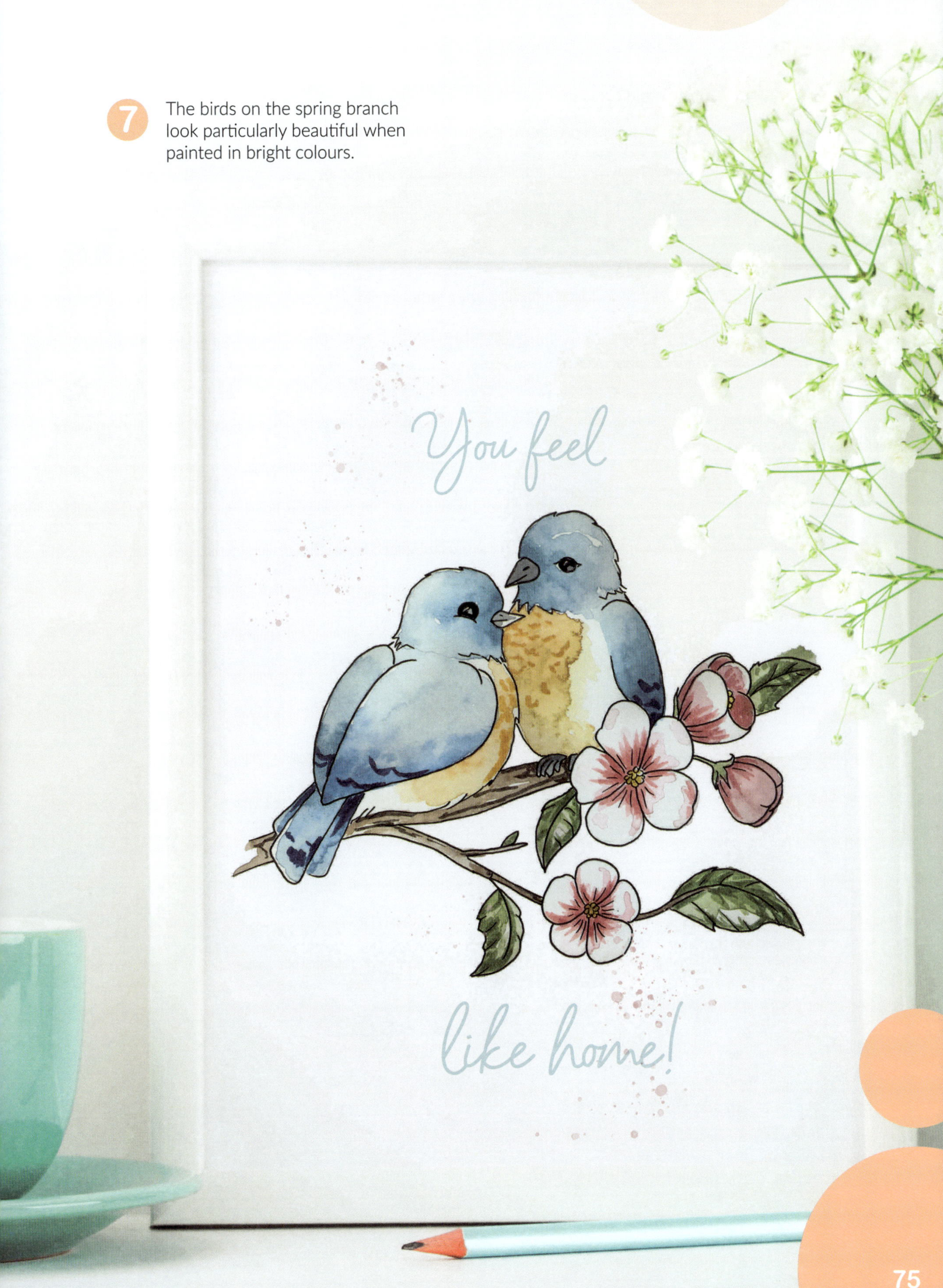

Cuddly Panda

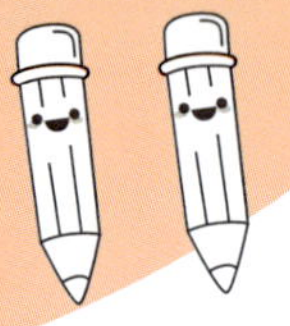

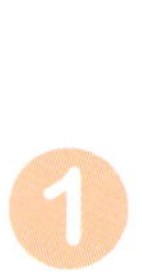

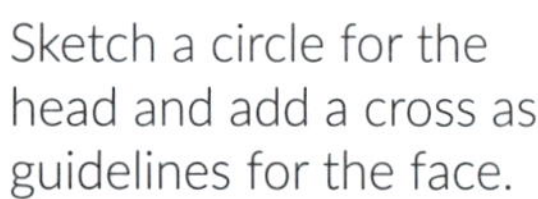

1

Sketch a circle for the head and add a cross as guidelines for the face.

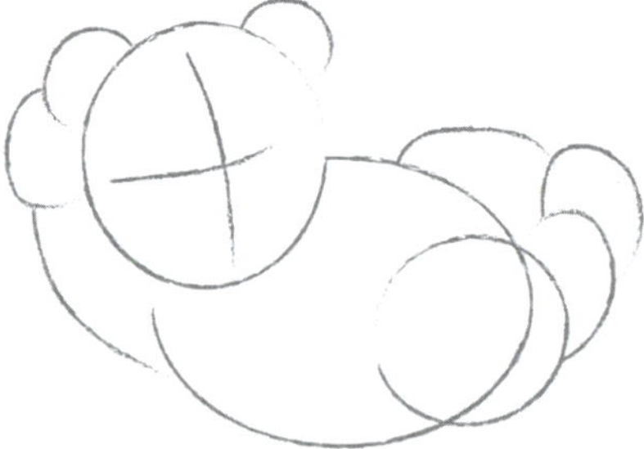

2

Sketch the body, arms and legs using a few more circles and a large ellipse.

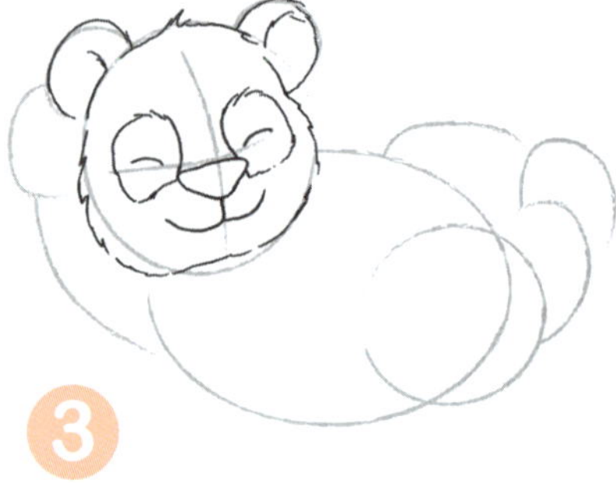

3

Now use a fineliner to draw round the head and face.

5

Add a few details to your panda, e.g., paws, claws and snout.

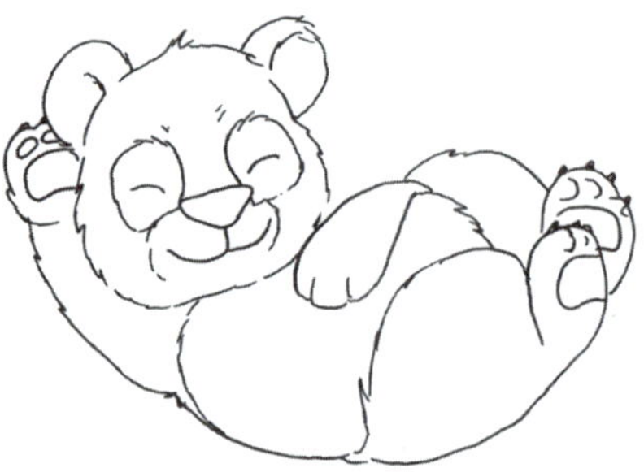

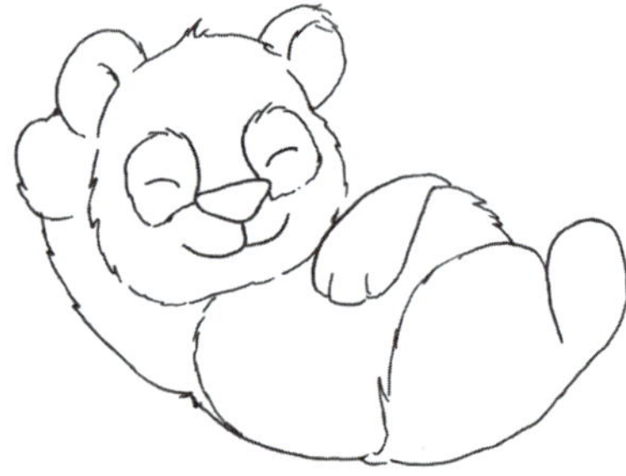

4

Draw the outline of your panda. Ensure the outline is not smooth or straight so your panda will appear furry.

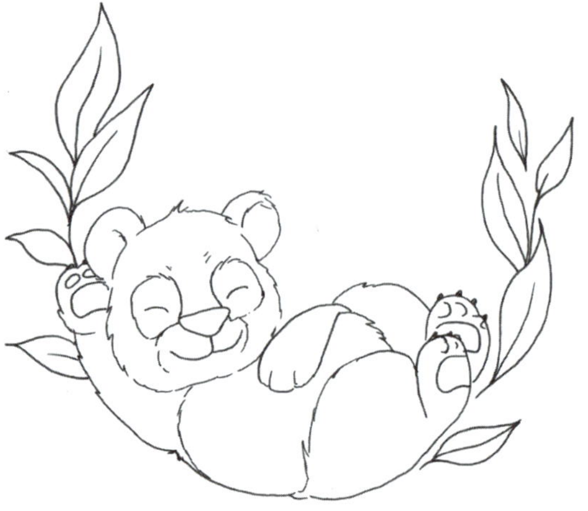

6

Draw the leaf wreath around your panda.

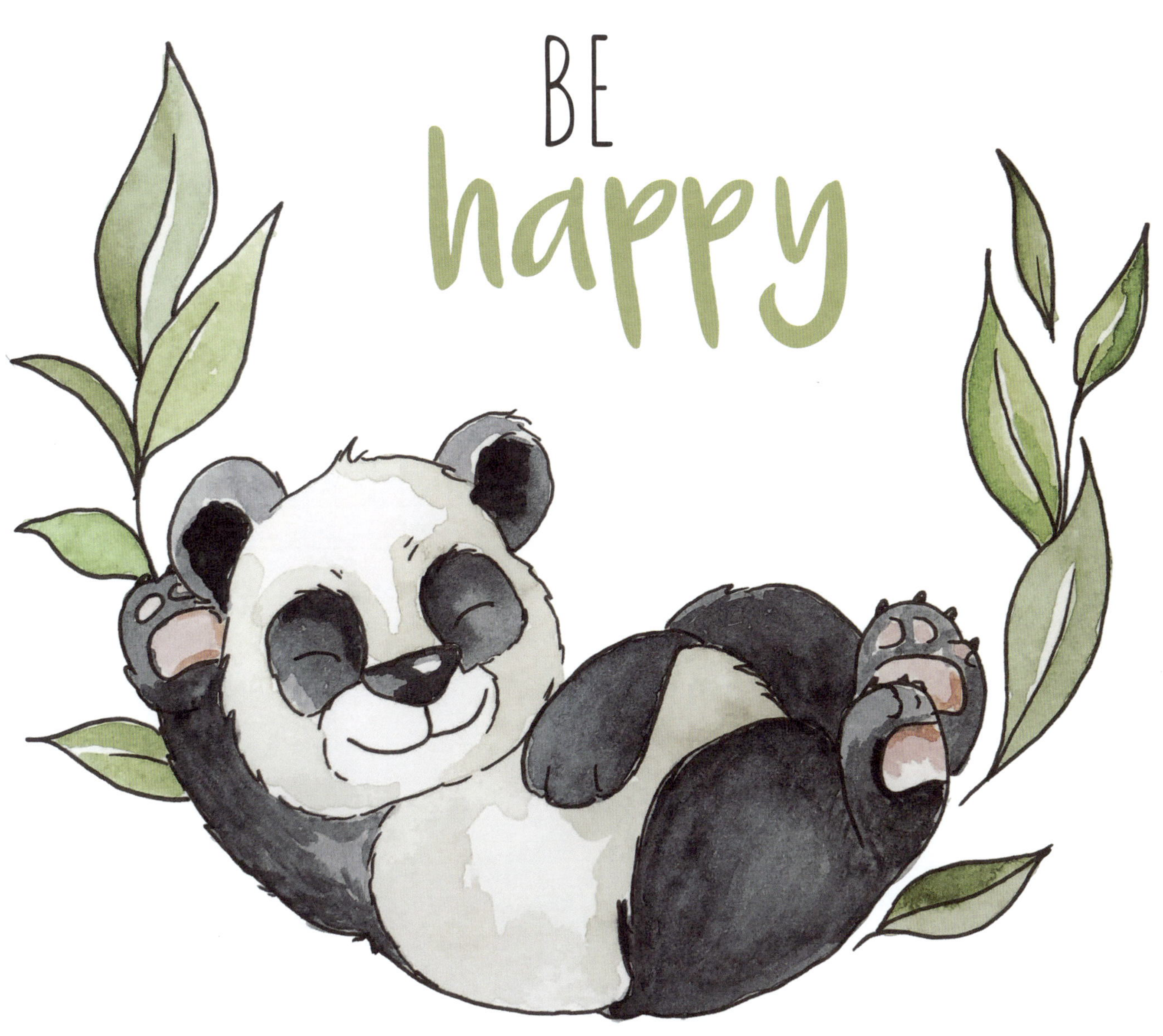

7

Add some colour to finish your wonderfully furry panda.

otter 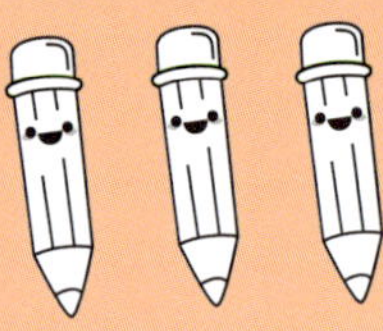

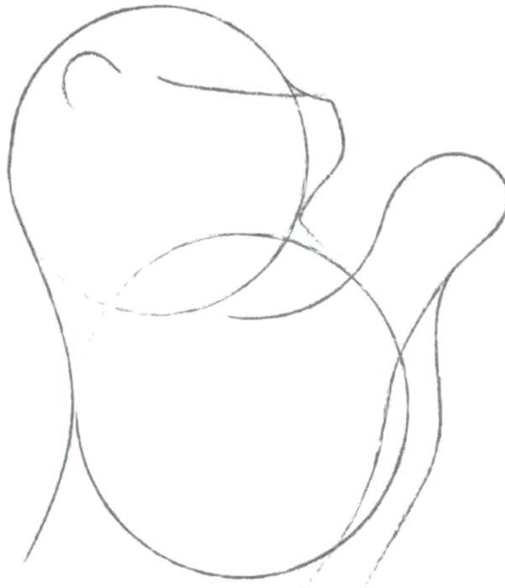

1 Two sketched circles for the head and body create the basic shape.

2 Start with the head, so that as you continue to draw you will not smudge the pencil sketch with your hand.

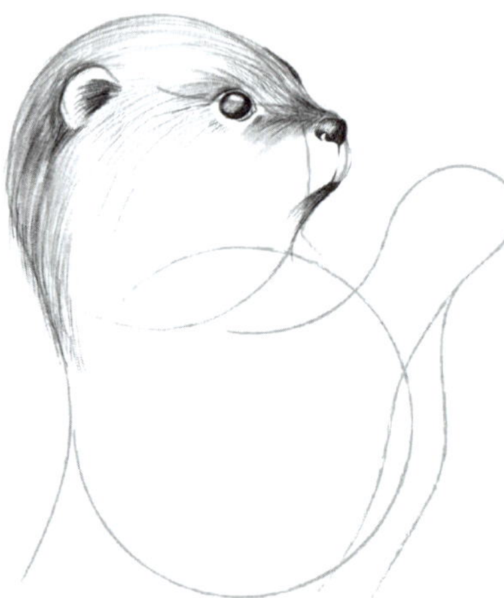

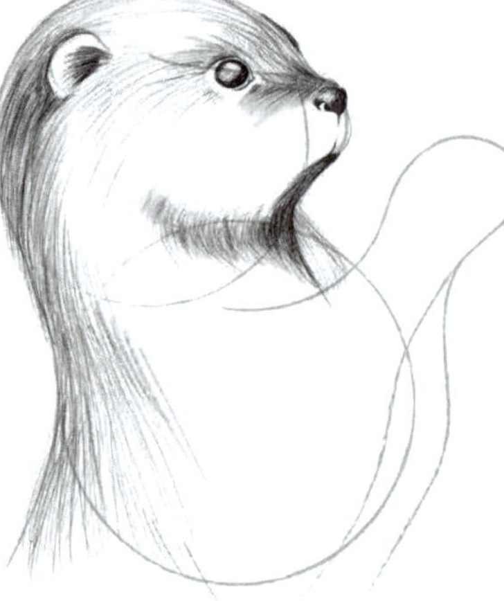

3 Only use pencil strokes for the shading so that you also create the structure of the fur.

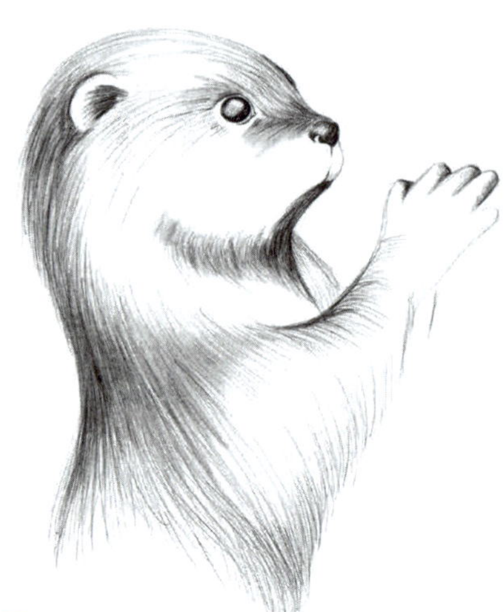

4 Draw the back and arms. The shape is created from the shaded areas where the pencil strokes are layered.

5 The paw behind the other paw is clearly darker because there is no light on it.

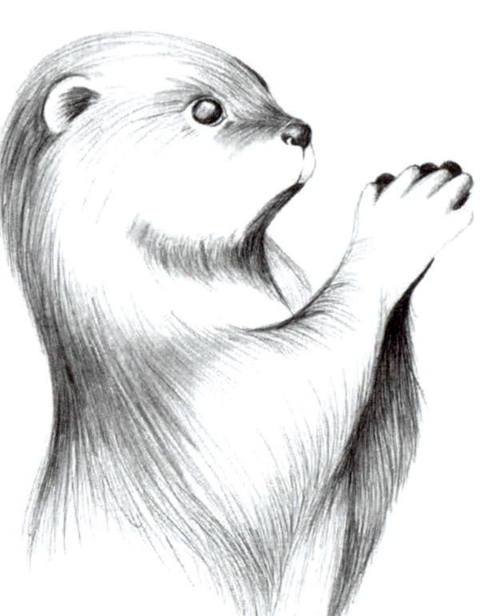

6 Continue to work more on the shading. You can use a softer pencil to do so.

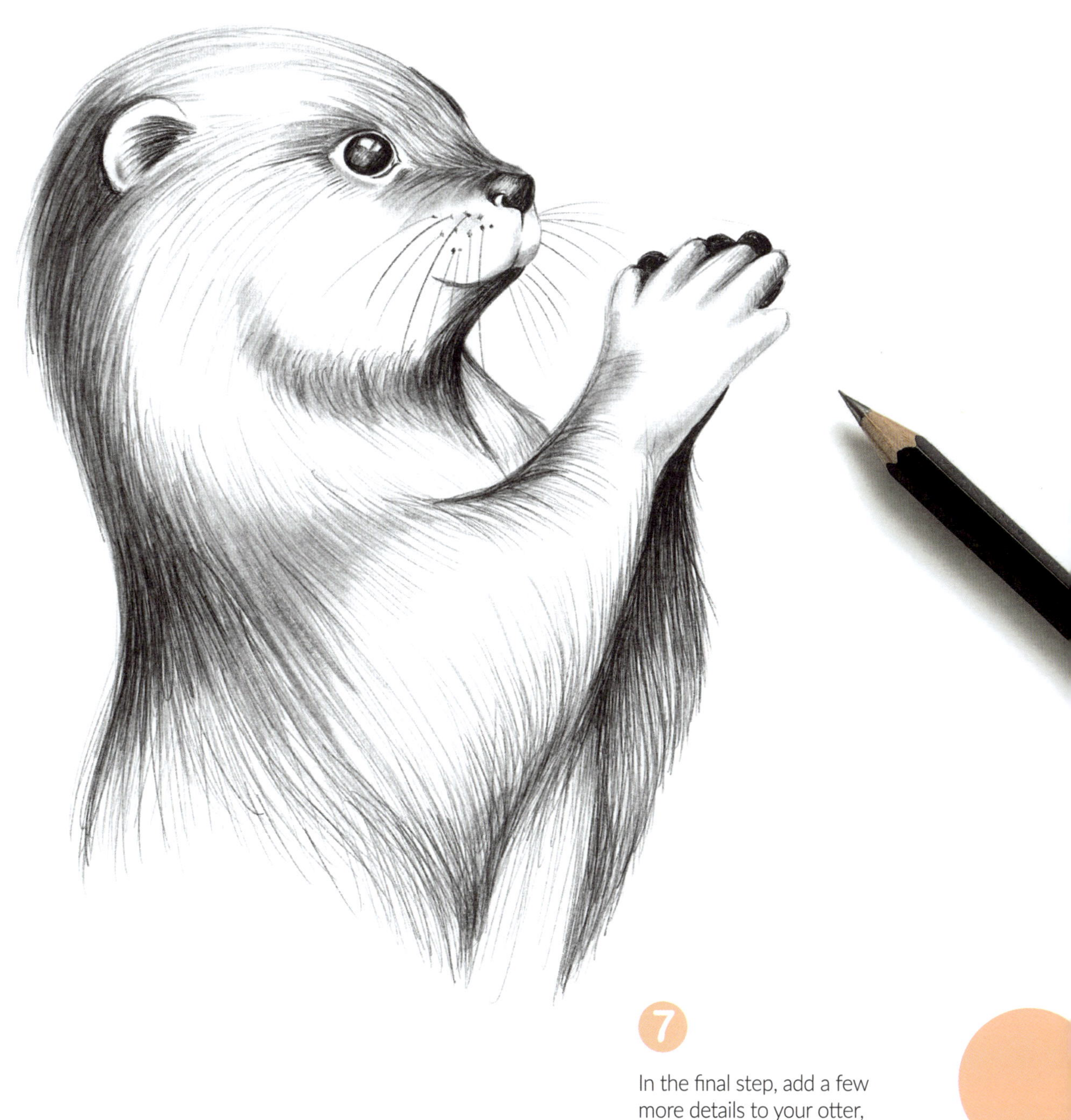

7

In the final step, add a few more details to your otter, such as whiskers.

Sleepy Mouse

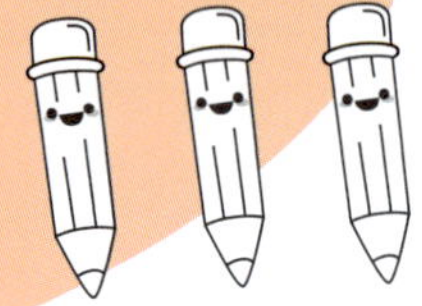

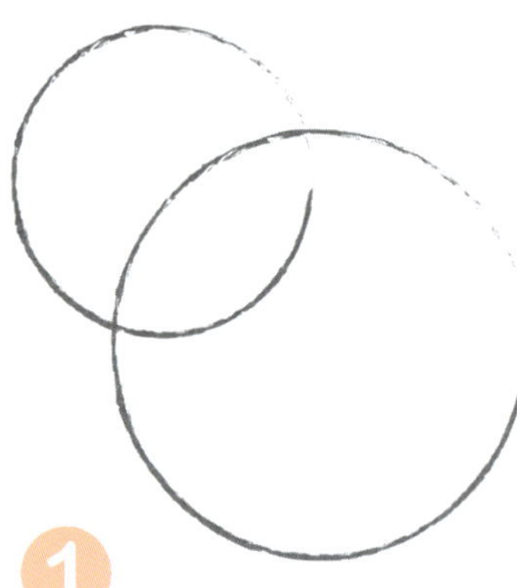

1

Draw two circles for the sketch of the mouse.

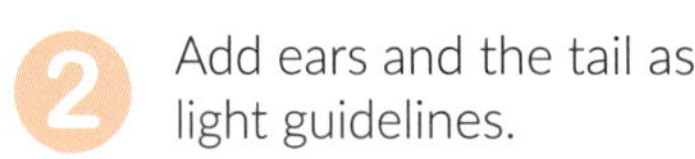

2

Add ears and the tail as light guidelines.

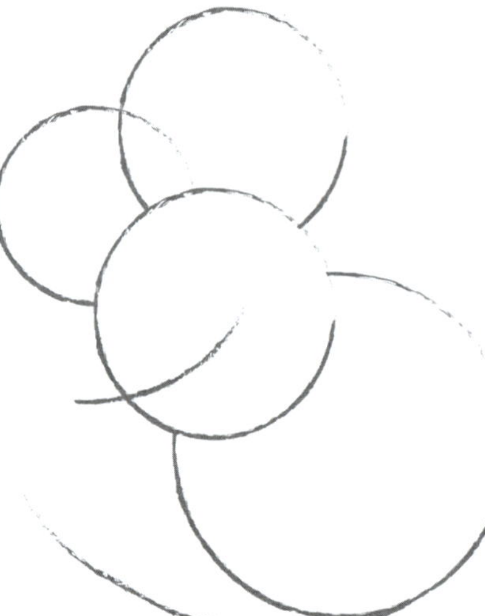

3

Now add the nose and legs. The mouse is hugging his feet with his front legs.

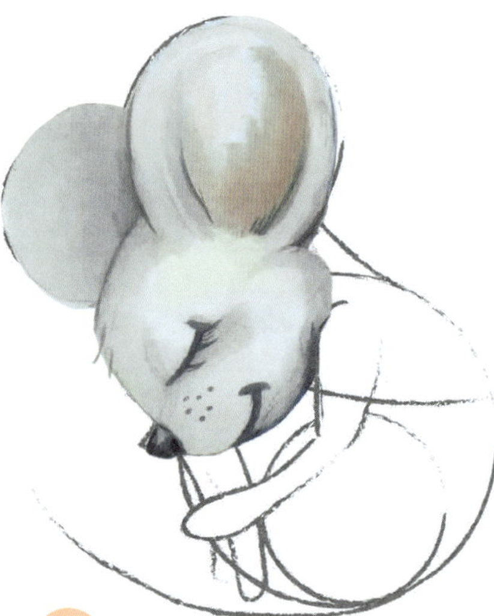

4

Start painting the head of your mouse in light grey and use darker shades for the eyes and mouth.

5

Paint the back and front legs. Play with light and shade, and use a lighter colour for the paws.

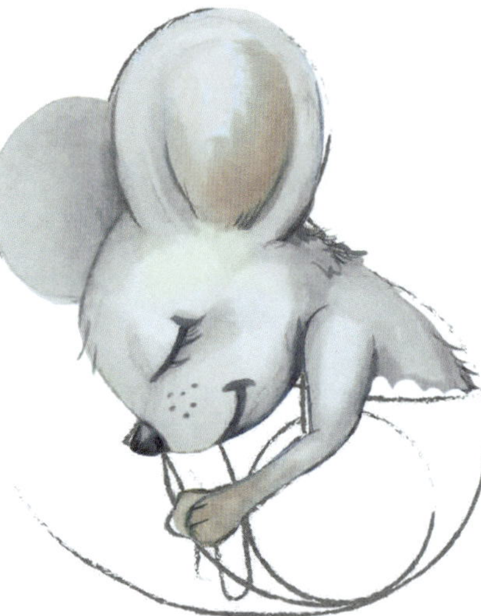

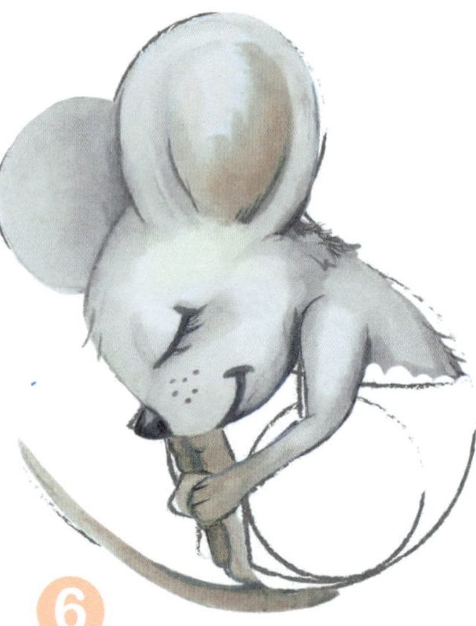

6

Give the feet and his tail the same shade as the paws and use shading to separate them optically.

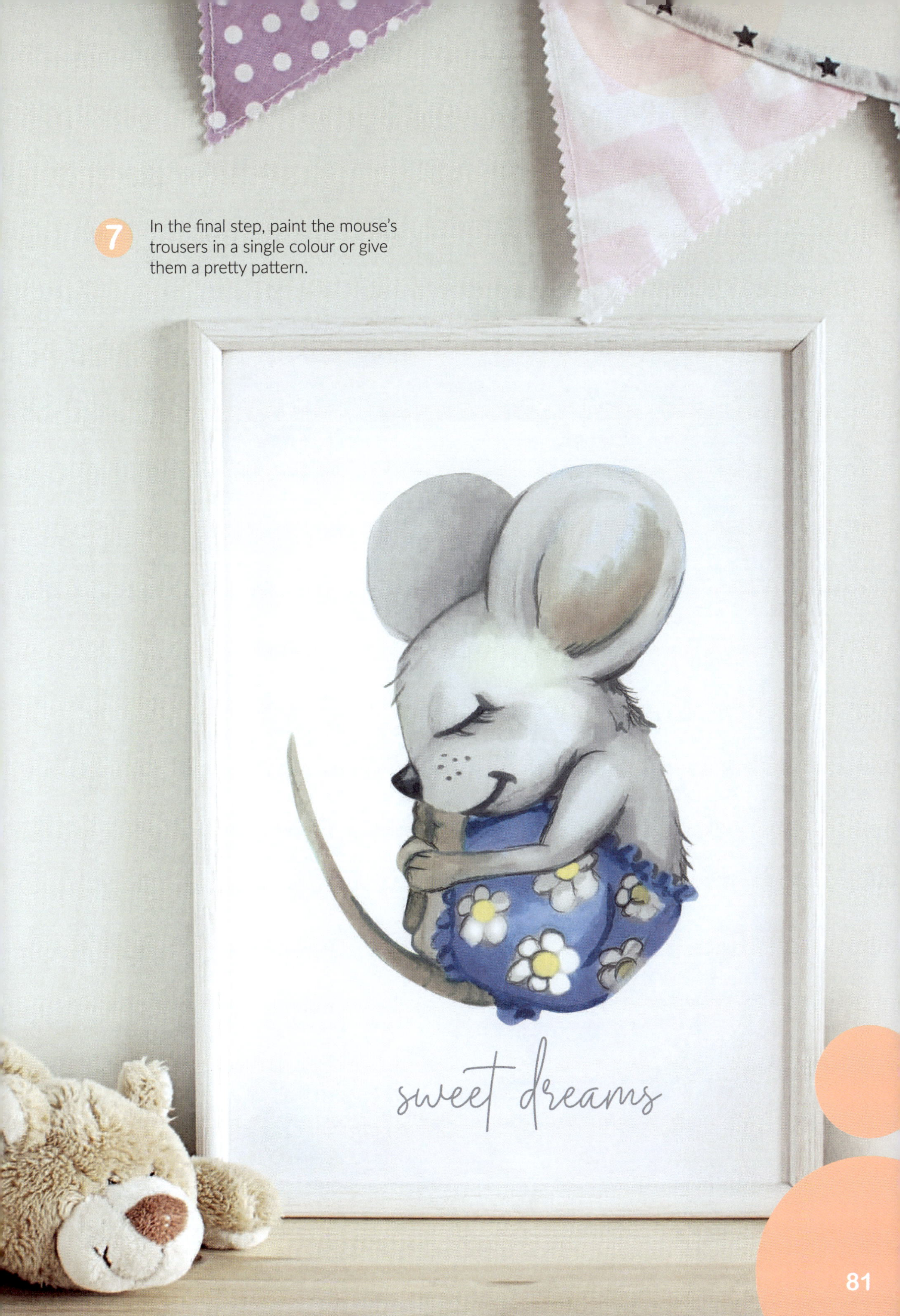

7 In the final step, paint the mouse's trousers in a single colour or give them a pretty pattern.

Koala Mother and Baby

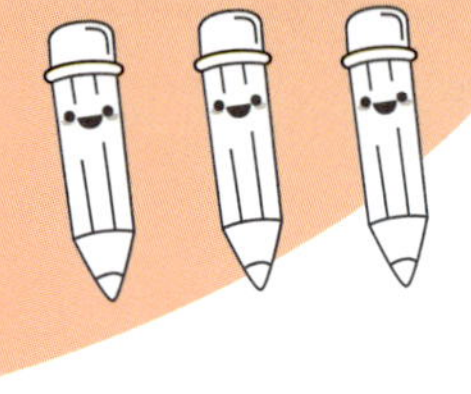

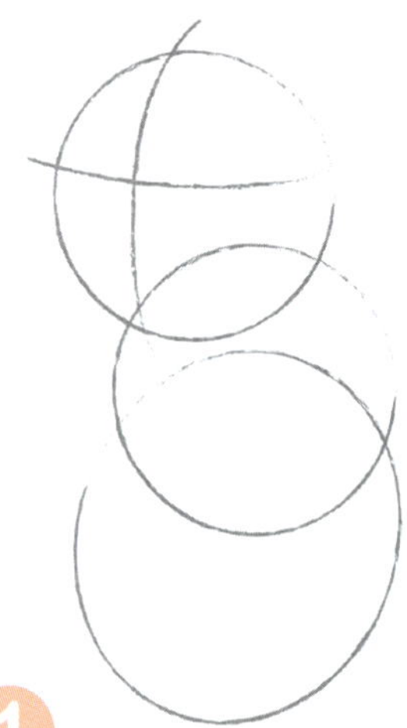

Start with the koala mother. Sketch three circles, starting with the head.

2

Add the ears, the baby and the branch that they are both perched on.

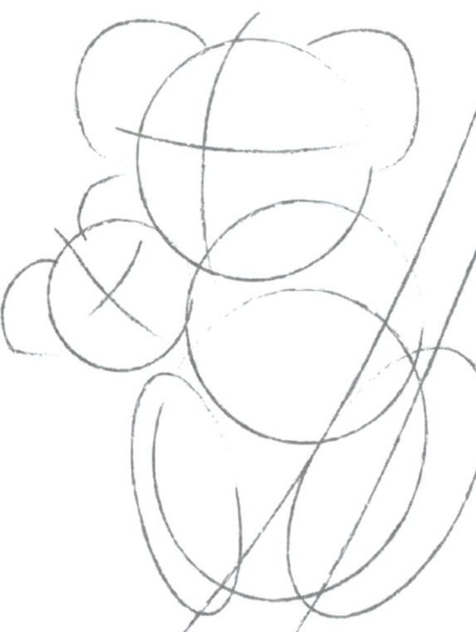

3

Start pencil shading the mother's head.

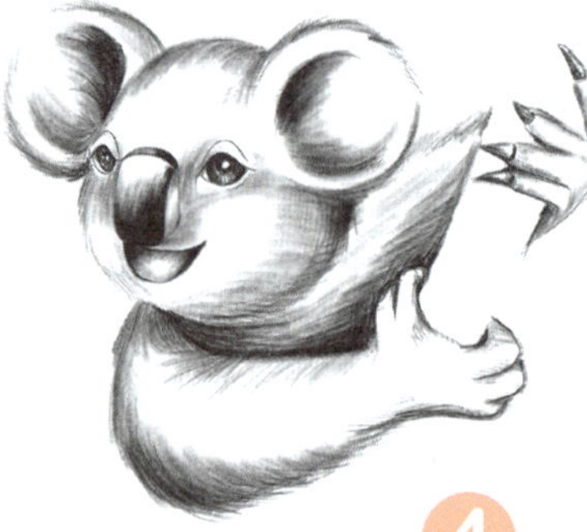

4

Continue, working from the neck to the arms ...

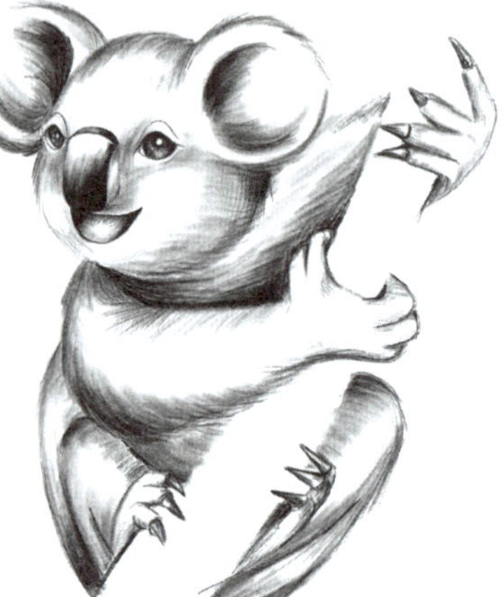

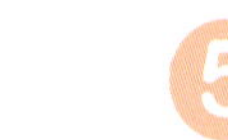

and further down to the back and legs.

6

Once the mother is finished, then you can draw and shade the baby on her back.

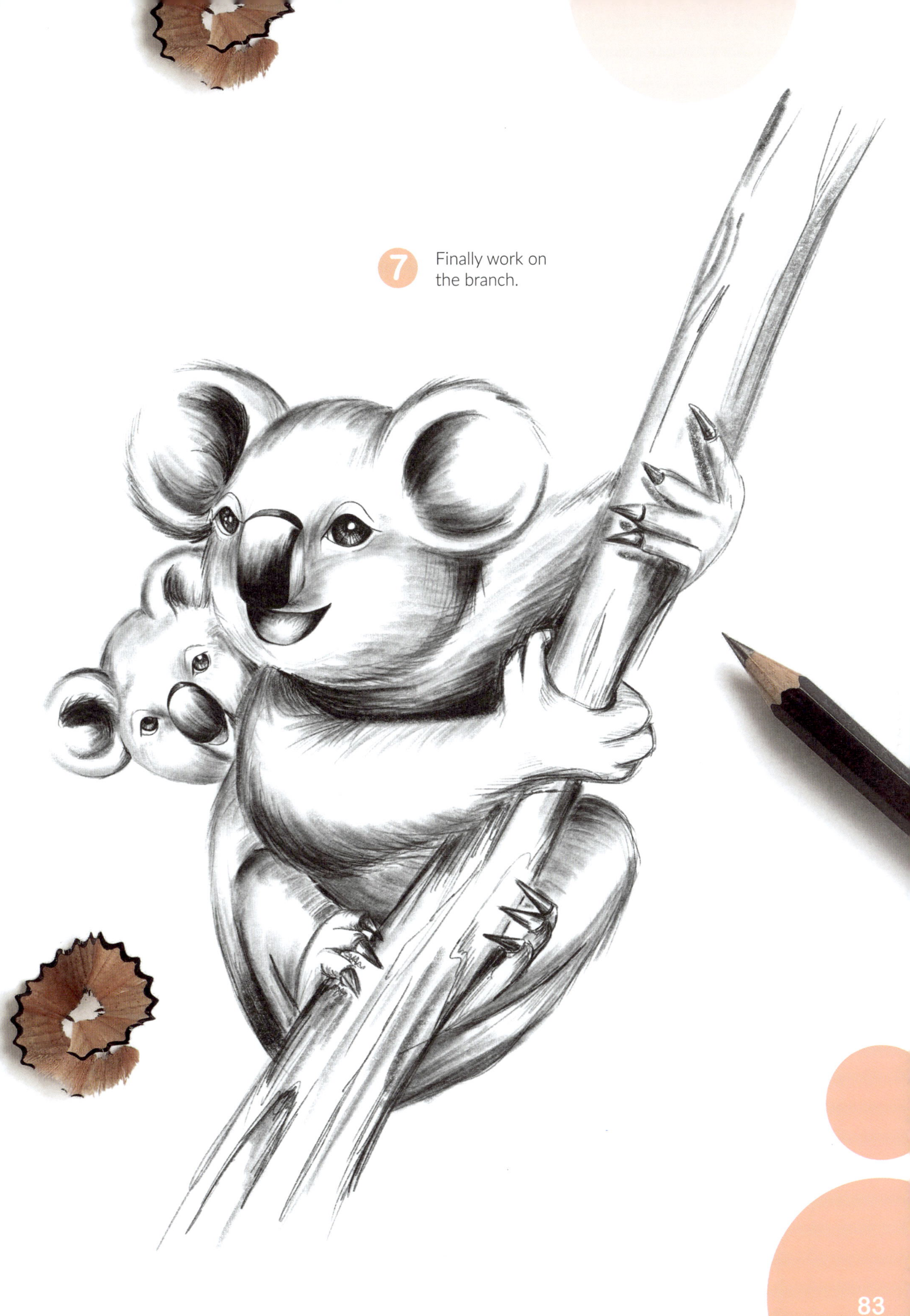

7 Finally work on the branch.

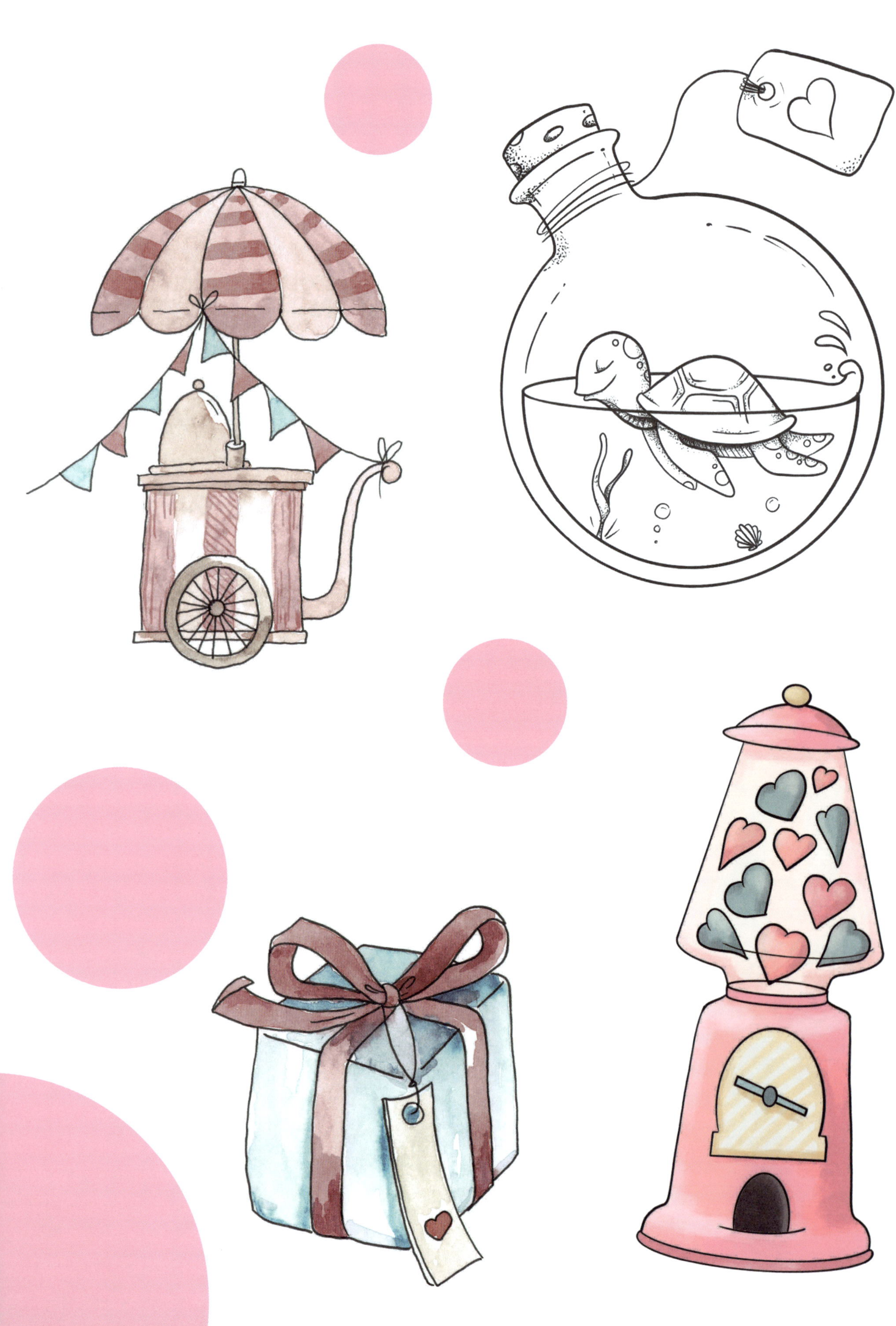

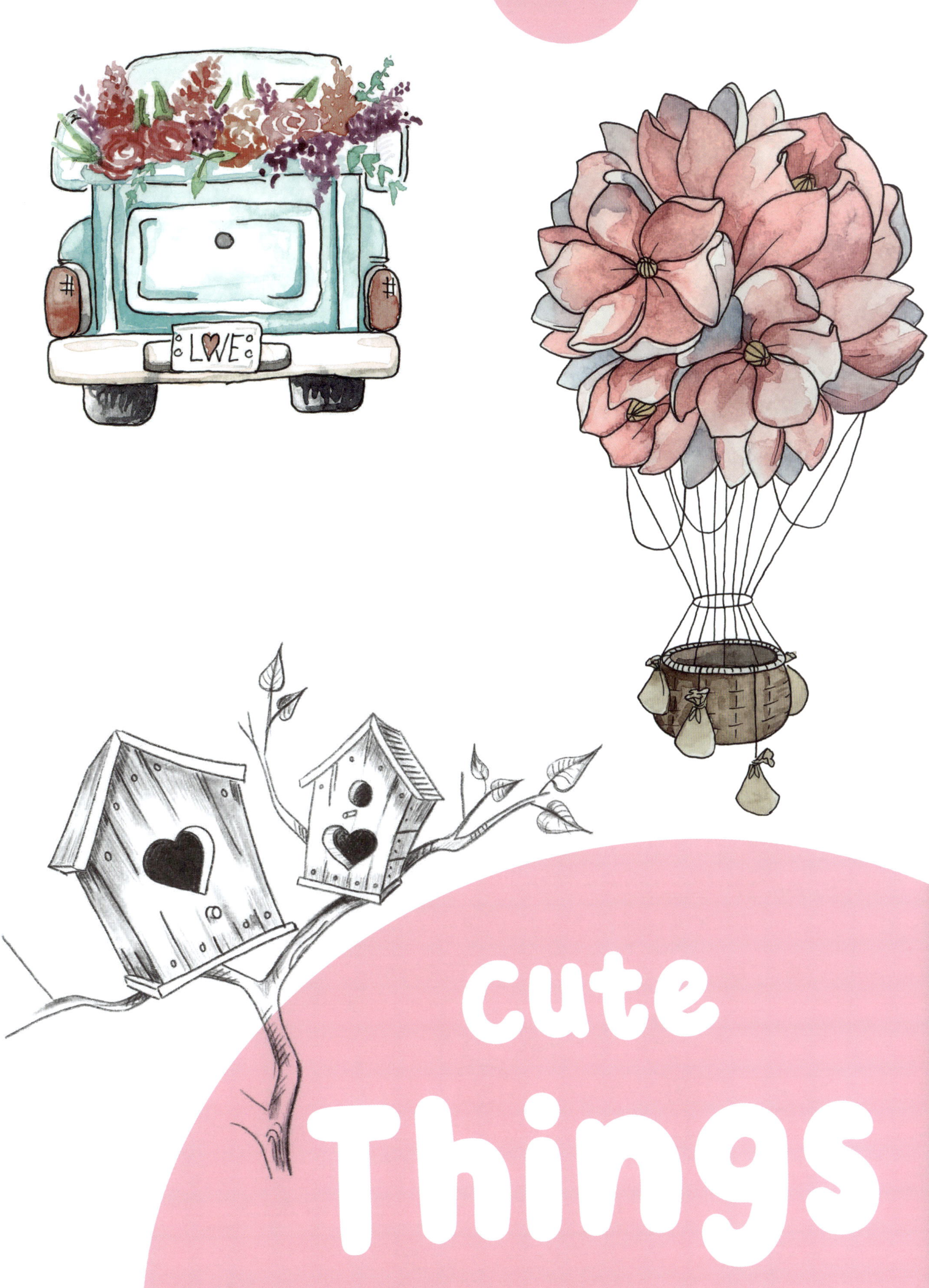
LOVE
Cute
Things

Drills

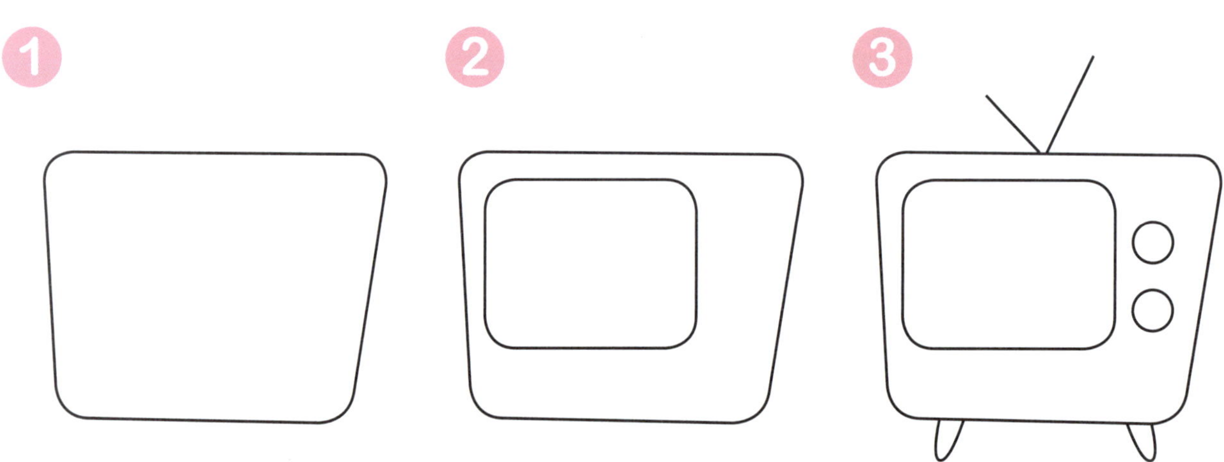

4

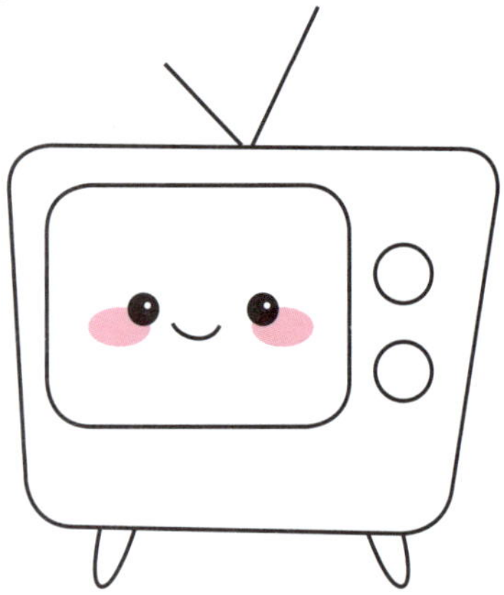

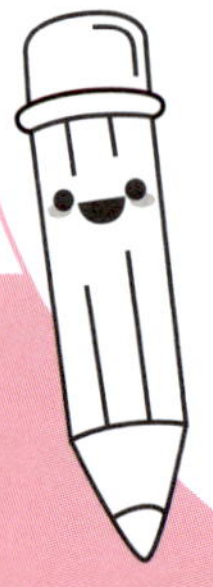

DRAW YOUR TV HERE.

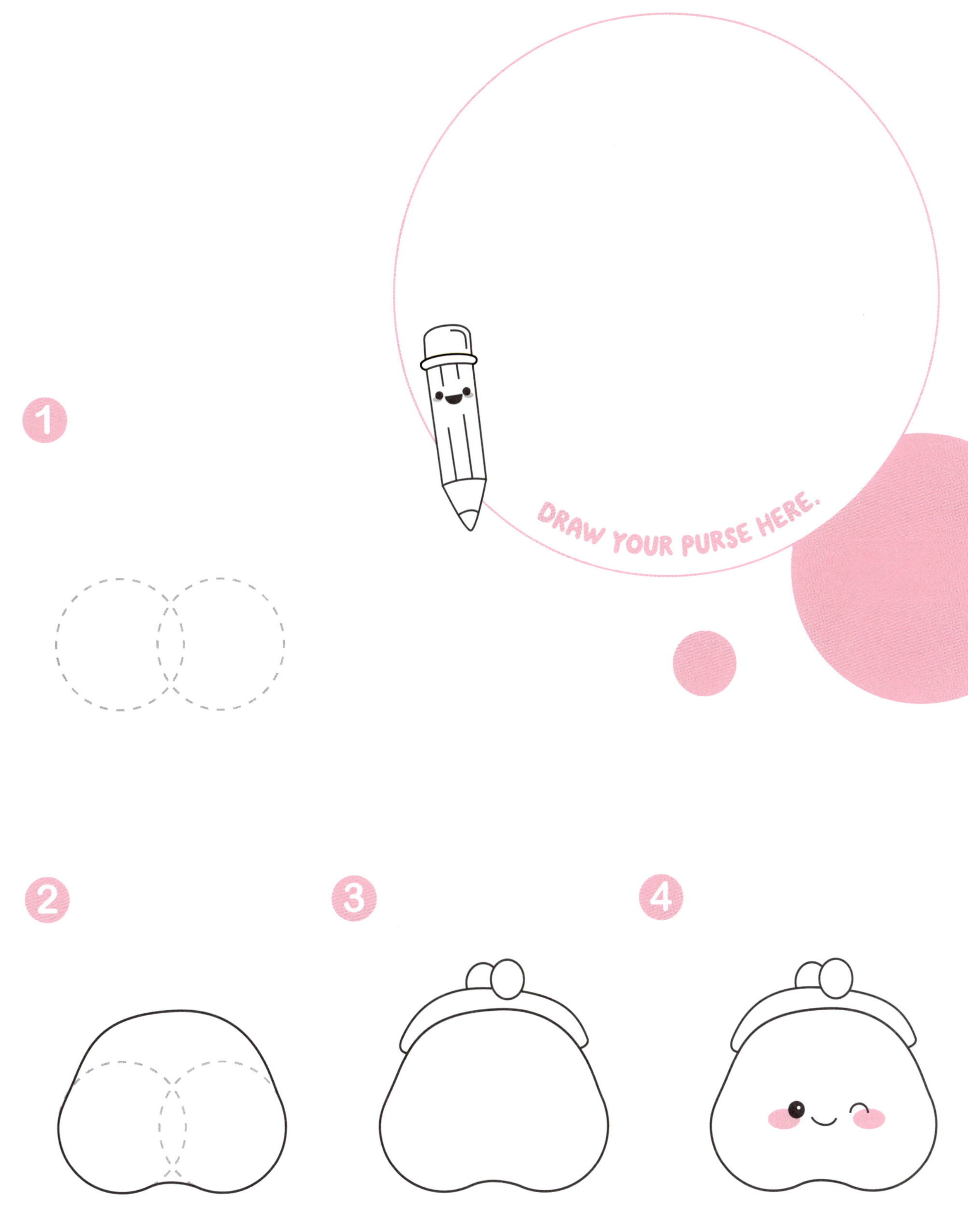
DRAW YOUR PURSE HERE.
1
2
3
4

Drills

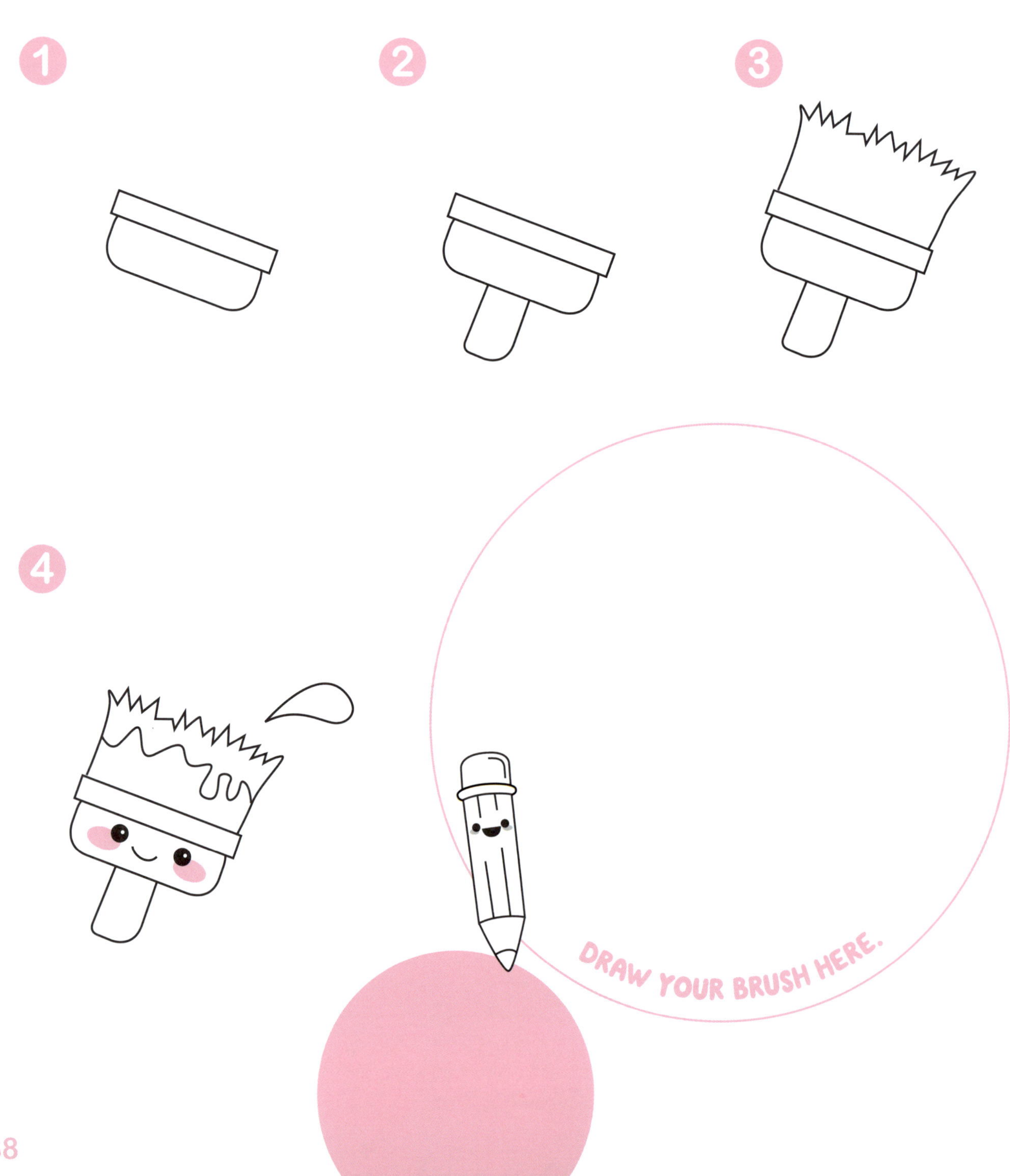

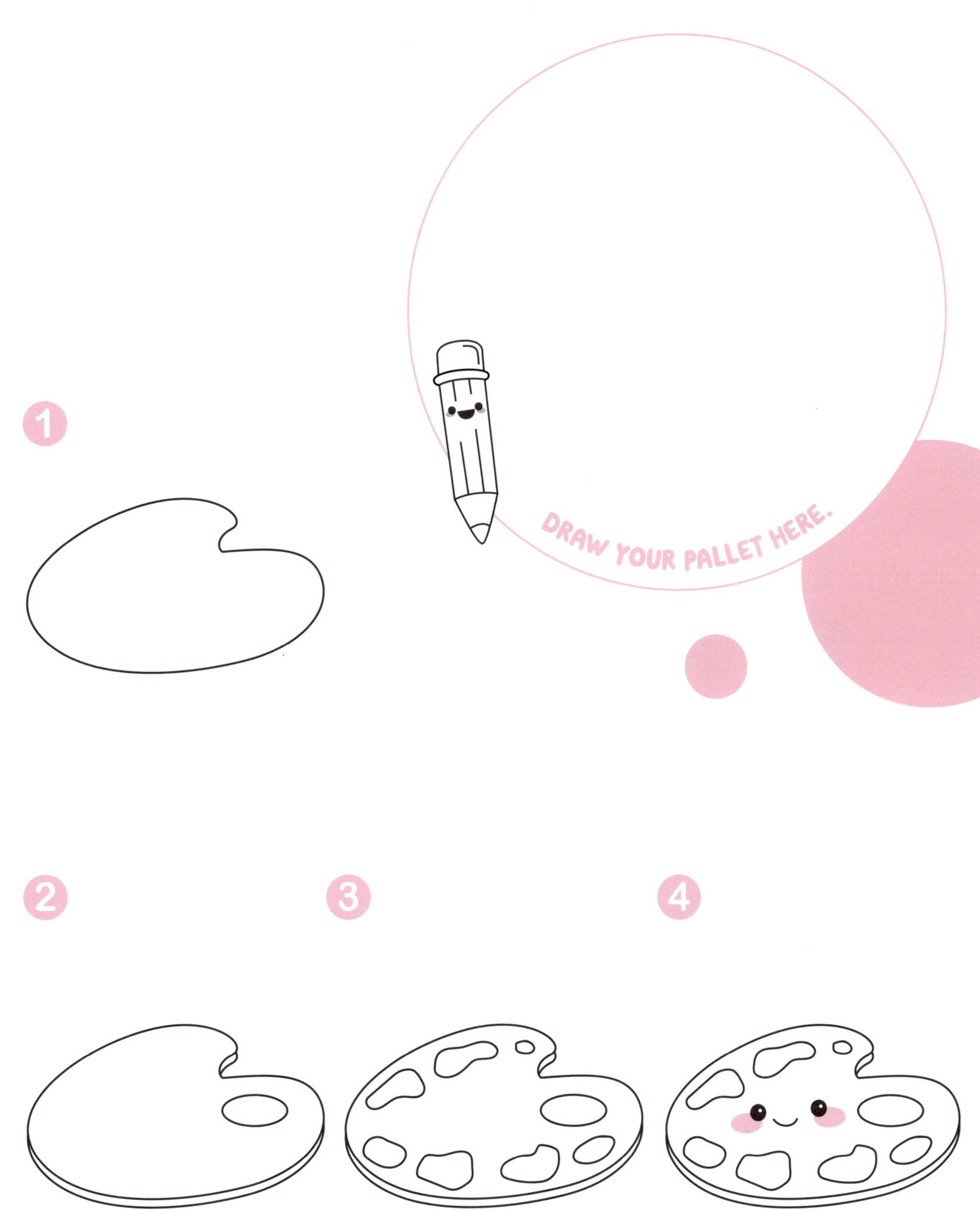
DRAW YOUR PALLET HERE.
1
2
3
4

Drills

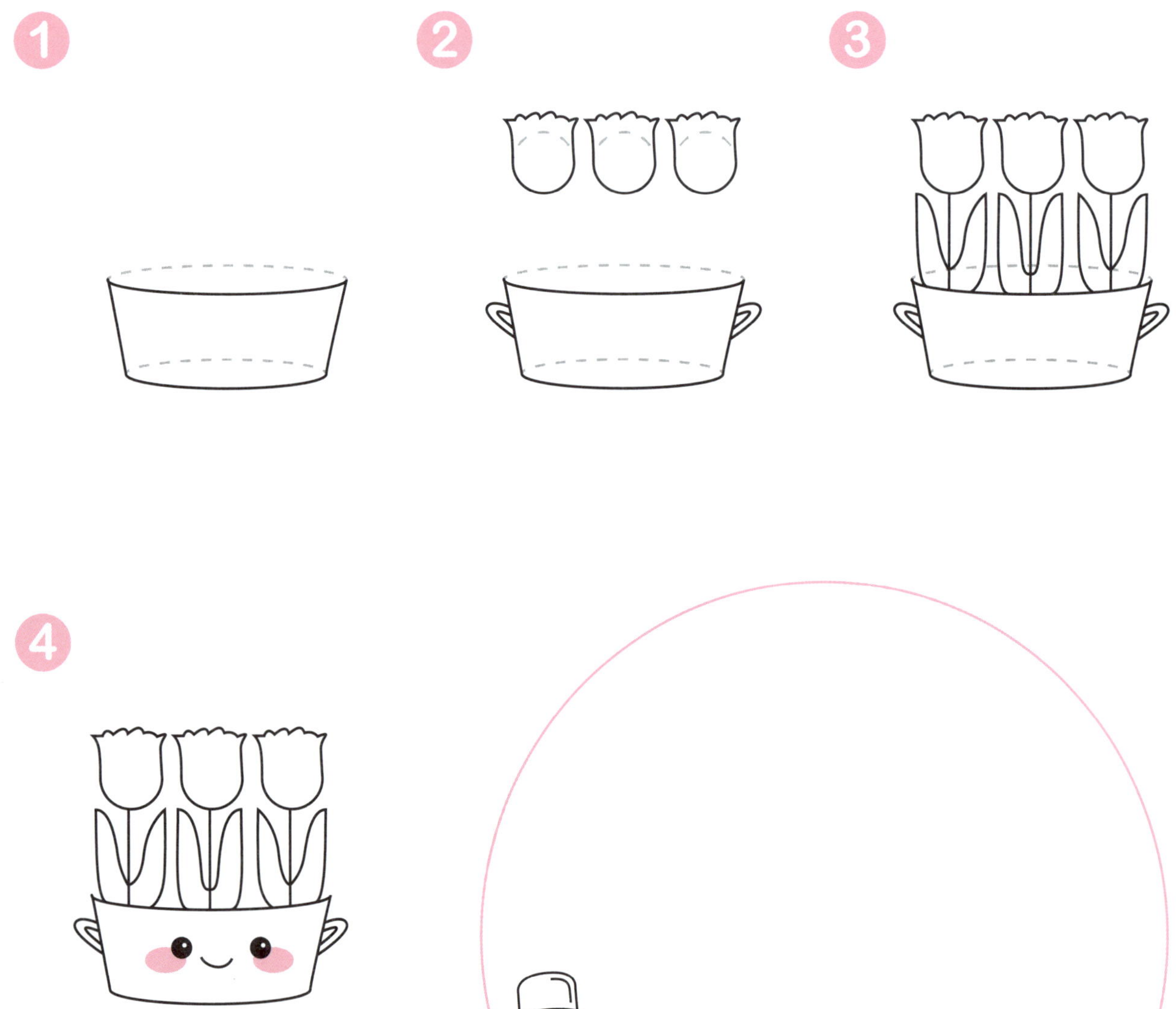

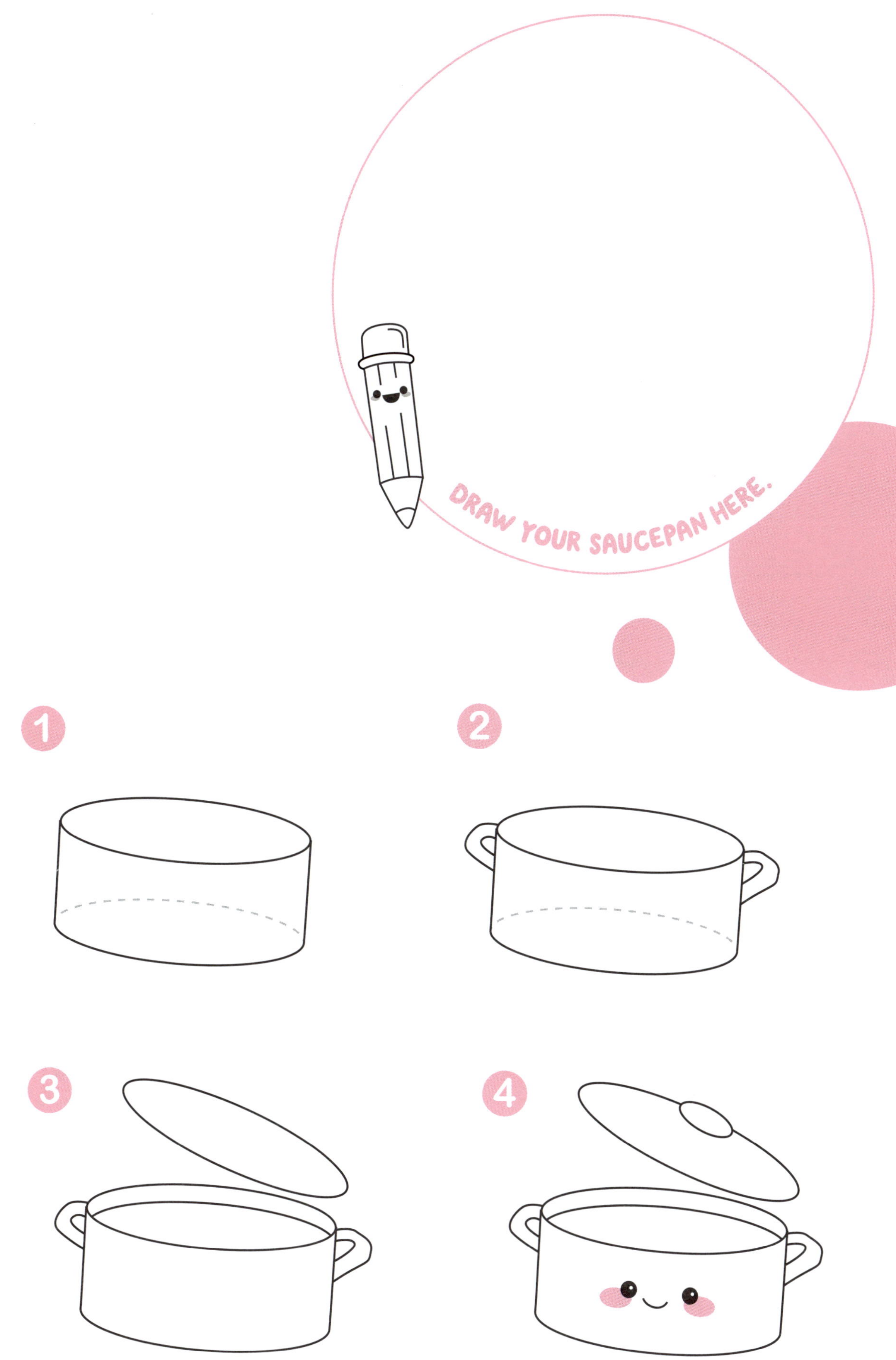
DRAW YOUR SAUCEPAN HERE.
1
2
3
4

Present

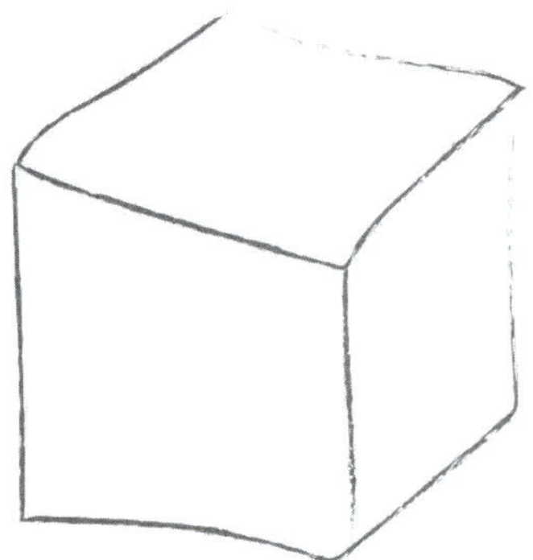

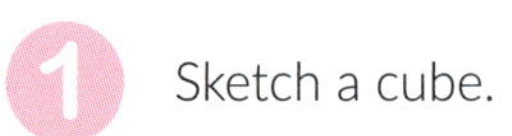

1 Sketch a cube.

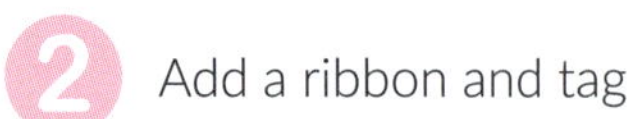

2 Add a ribbon and tag.

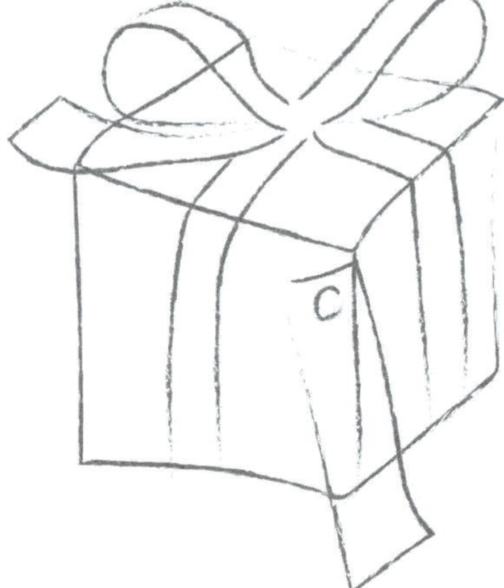

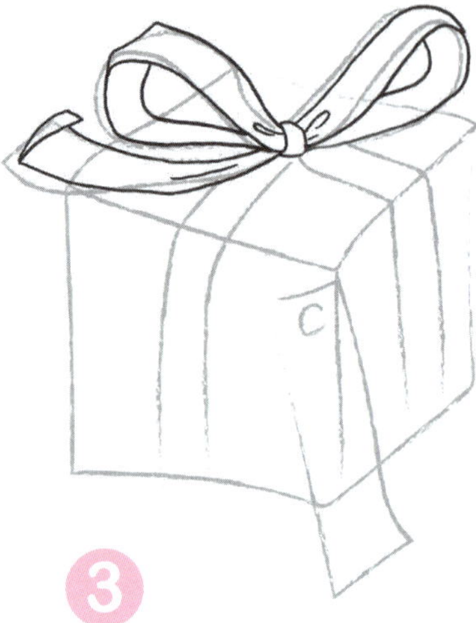

3 Use a fineliner to go around the bow.

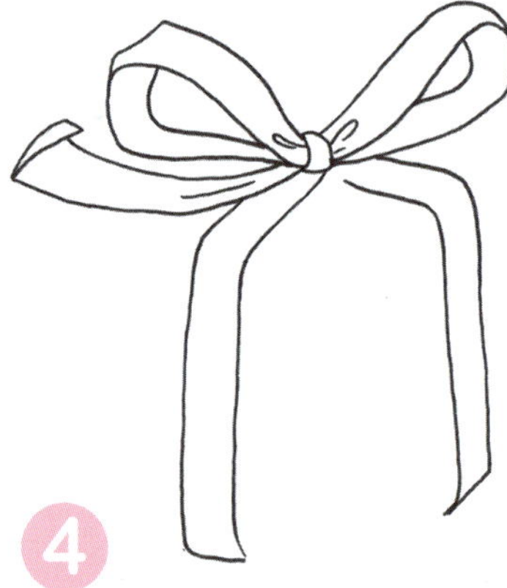

4 In the next step, draw the ribbon around the present.

5 Now draw the present, but leave space for the tag.

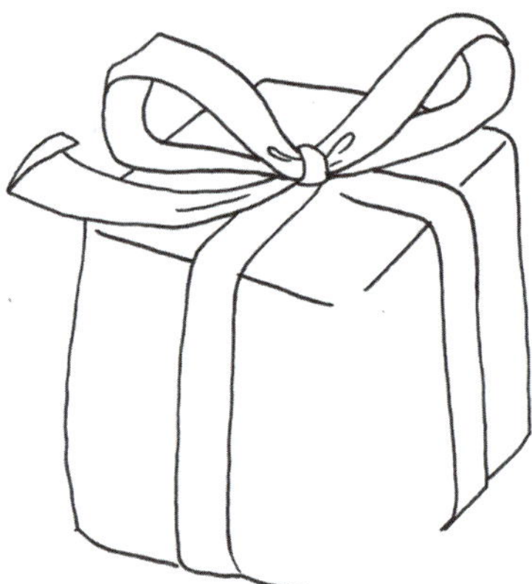

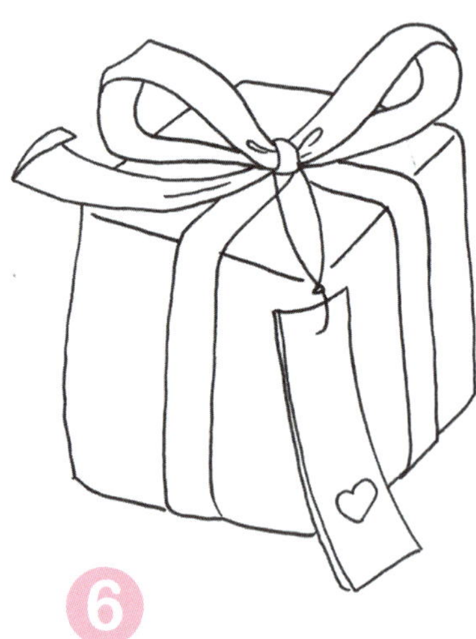

6 Draw the tag and the string to tie it to the present.

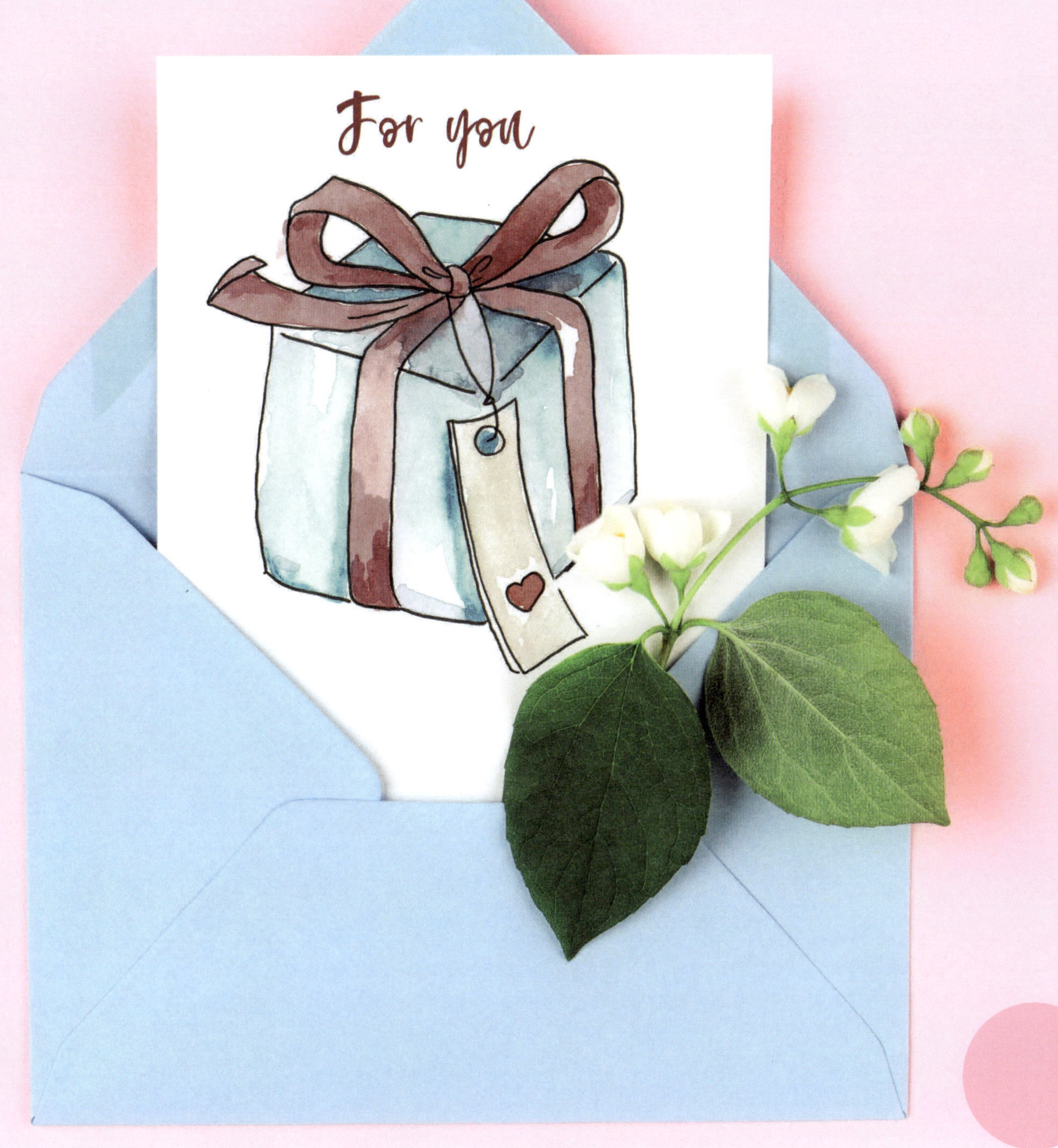

7 Paint your present in bright colours. If you find just two colours too boring, you can give the wrapping paper a pattern.

Ice Cream Cart

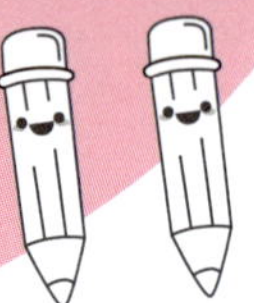

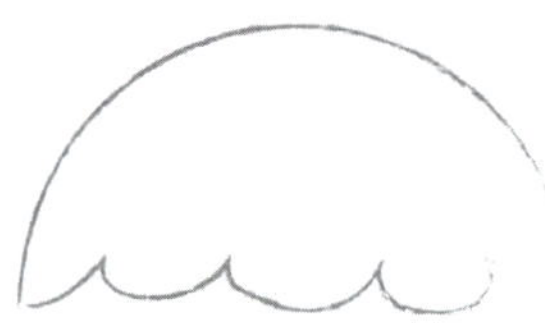

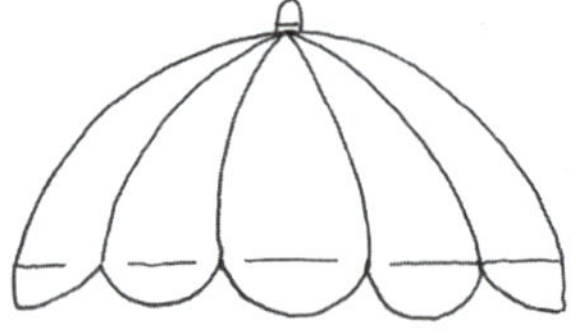

1 Sketch a semi-circle for the parasol and a square for the cart.

2 Sketch the parasol pole, the wheel and the handle.

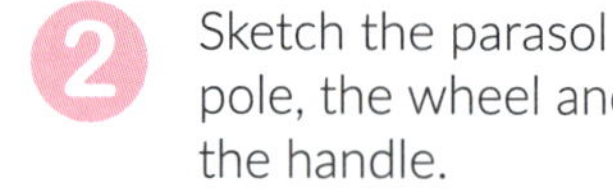

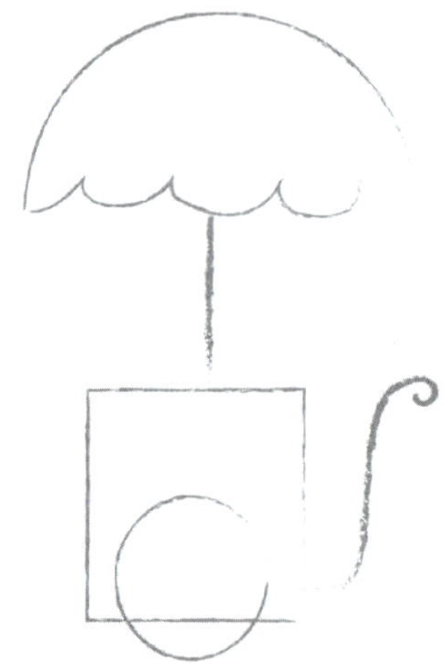

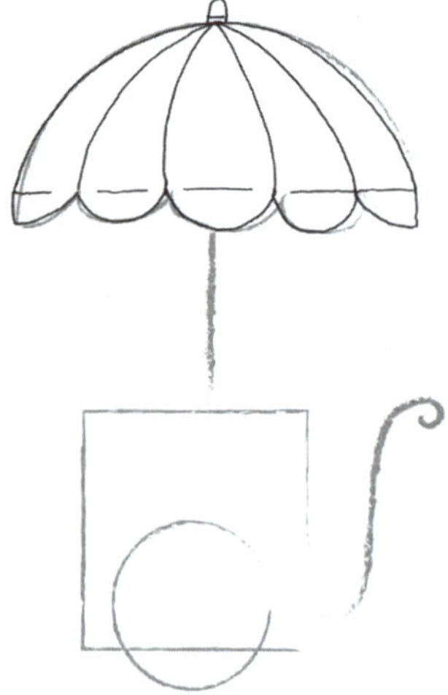

3 Use a fineliner to draw the outline of the parasol.

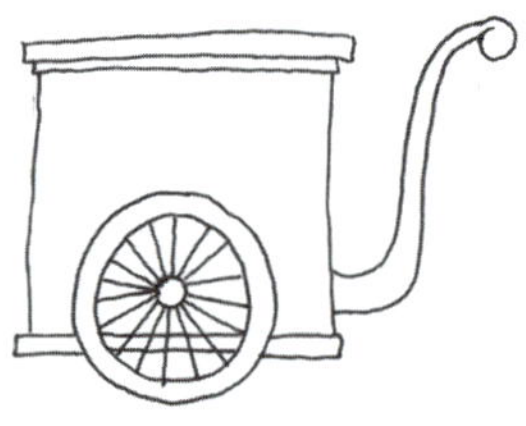

4 Now draw the cart with the wheel and the decorative handle.

5 Now add pretty bunting.

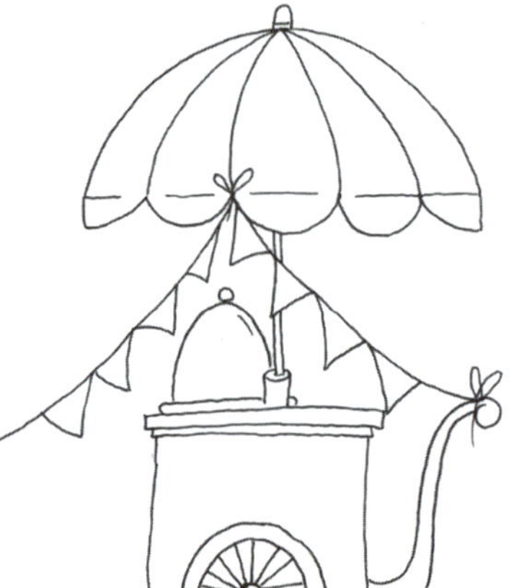

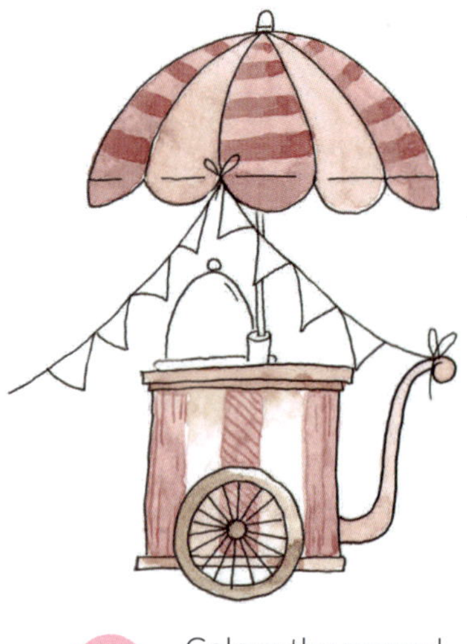

6 Colour the parasol and the cart in your favourite colours.

Add the remaining colourful elements to finish your cute ice cream cart.

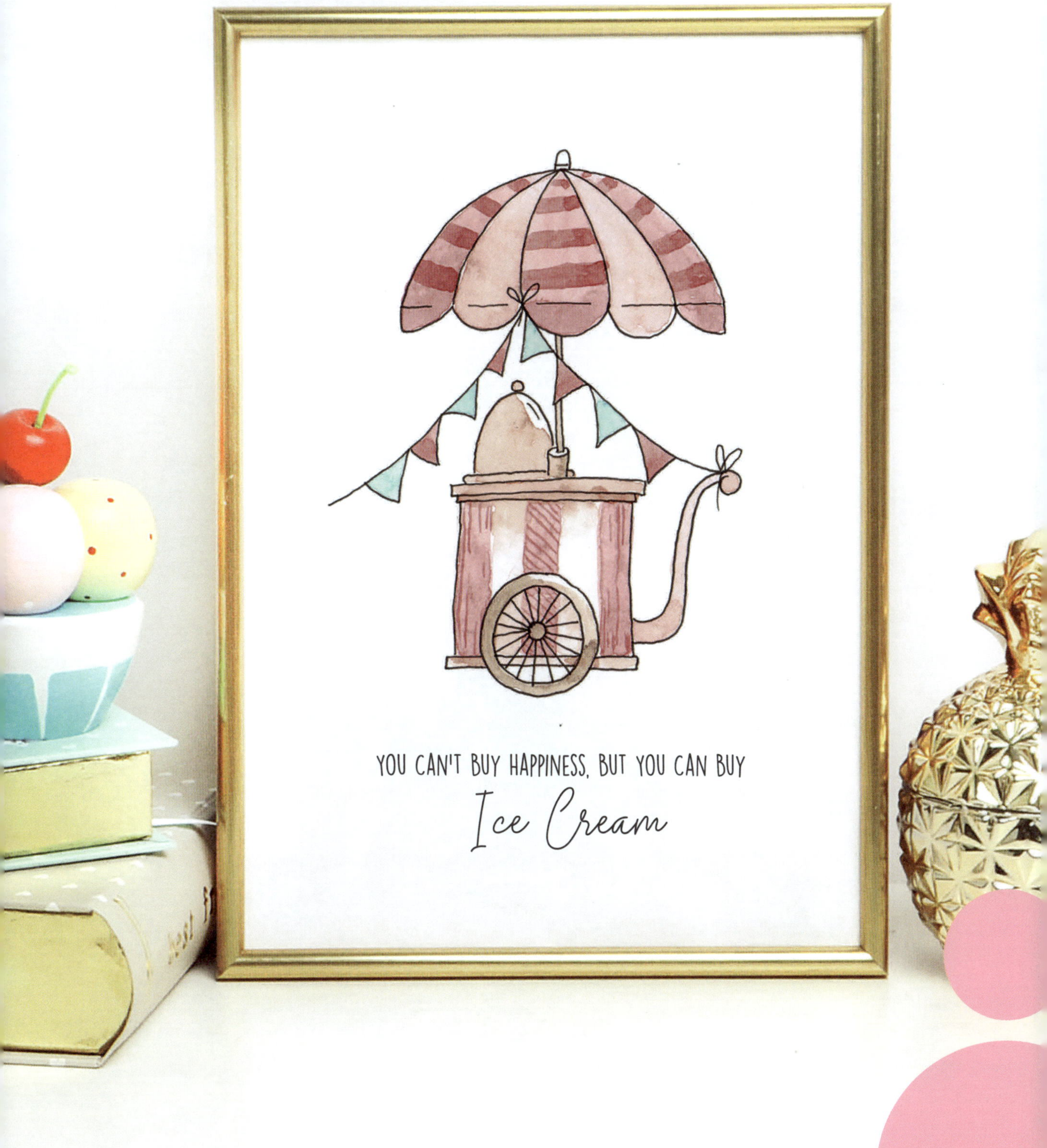

YOU CAN'T BUY HAPPINESS, BUT YOU CAN BUY

Ice Cream

Turtle in a Bottle

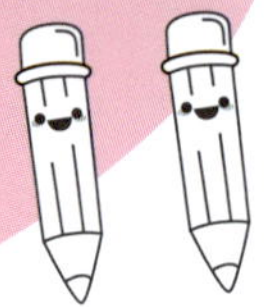

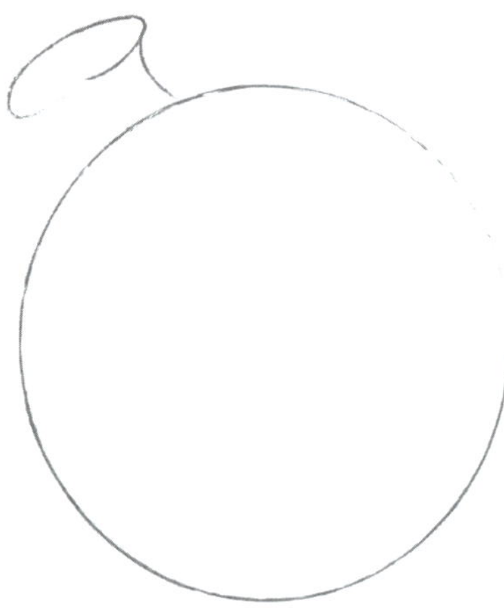

1 Sketch a large circle for the bottle and an ellipse for the bottle neck.

2 Sketch the turtle and the water inside the bottle.

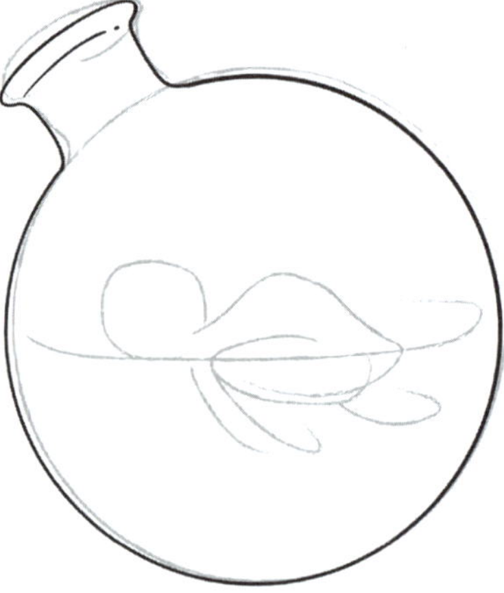

3 Use a fineliner to draw the outline of the bottle.

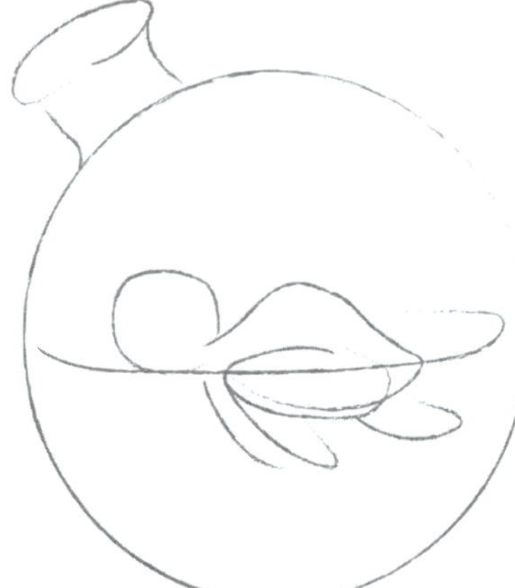

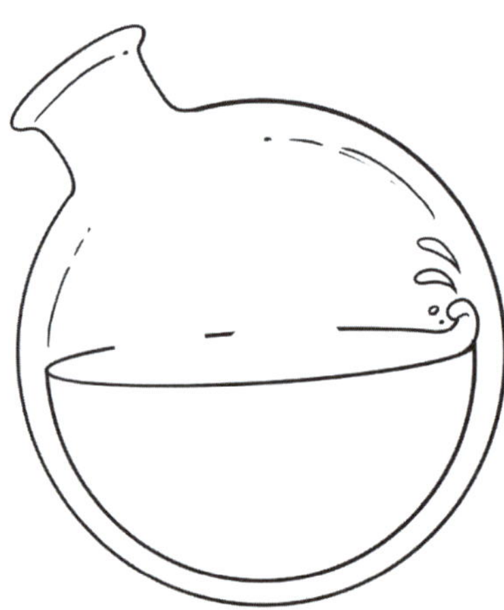

4 The surface of the water in the bottle is another ellipsis. The front part of the water is a full line, but the back line is broken where the turtle's head and body rise above the surface.

5 Draw a relaxed turtle in the water and carefully erase your sketch.

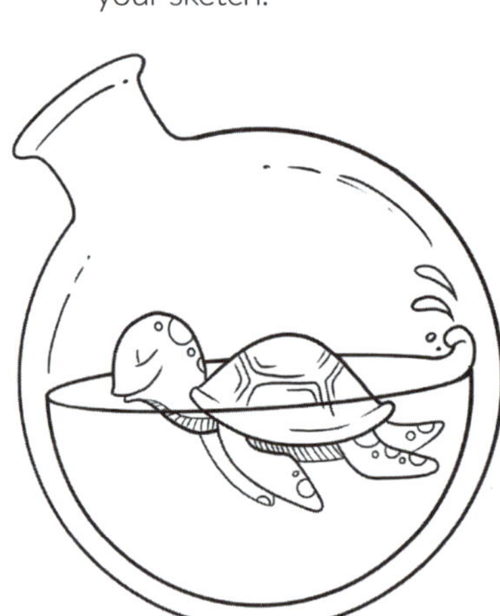

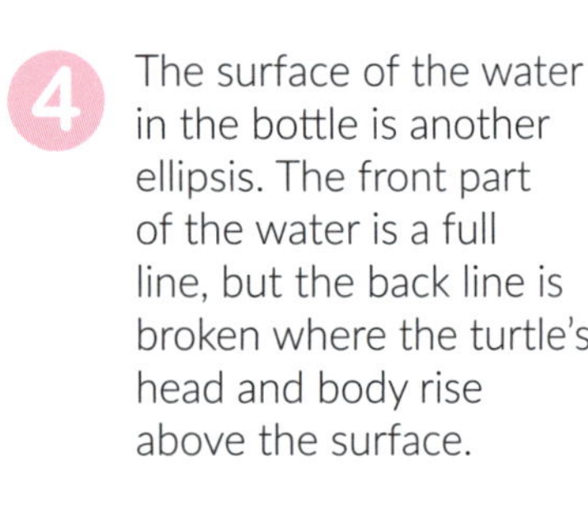

6 Draw a tag with a heart wrapped around the bottle neck.

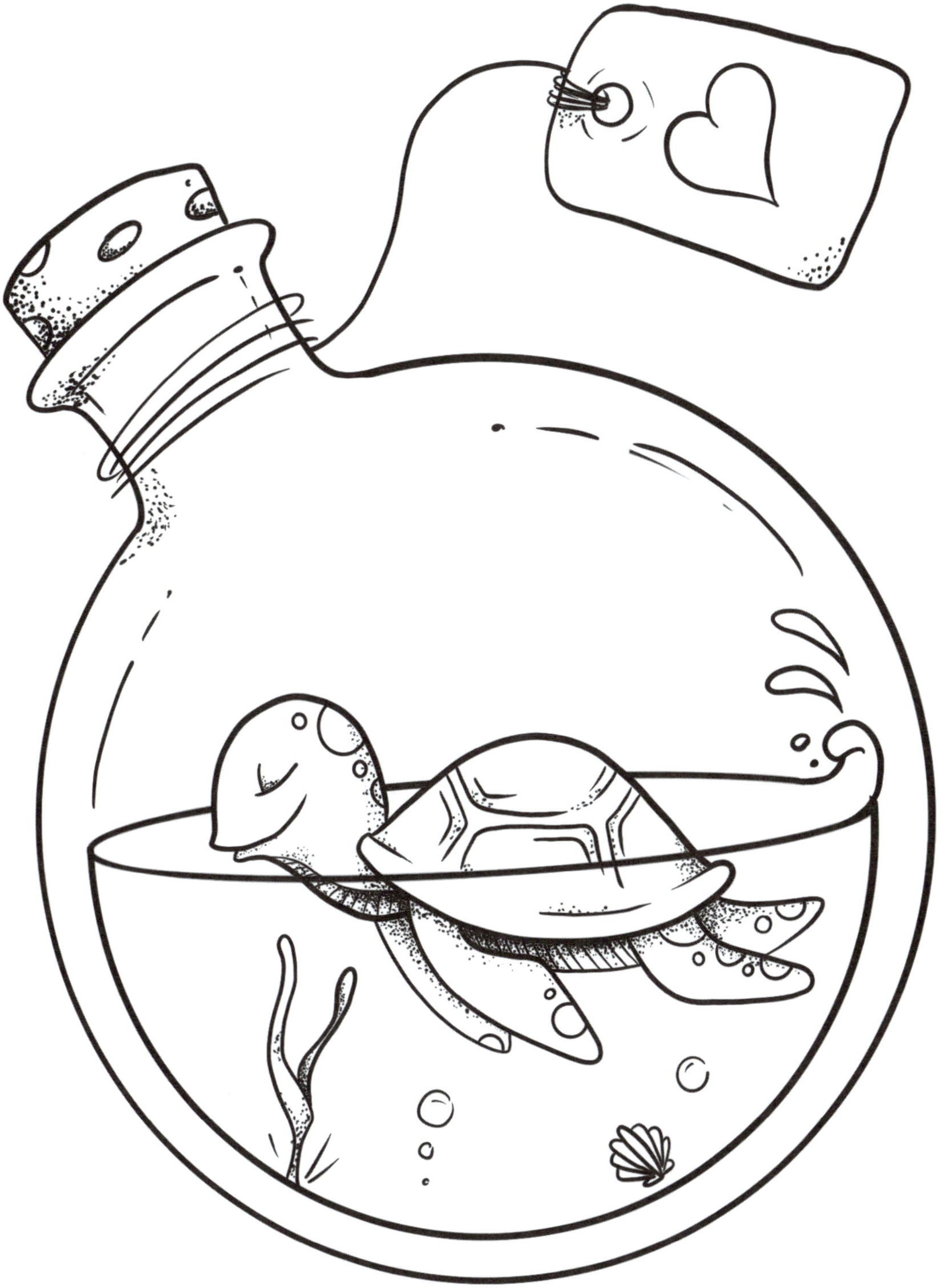

Add small dots to indicate shadows and close the bottle with a cork so that your cute turtle won't swim away.

Bubblegum Dispenser

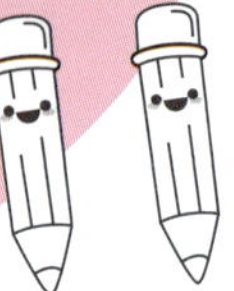
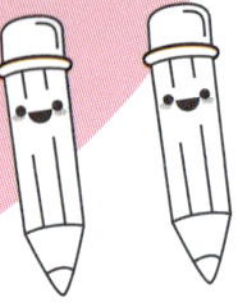

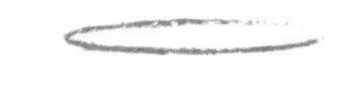

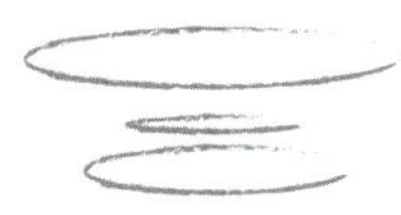

1 Sketch several parallel ellipses.

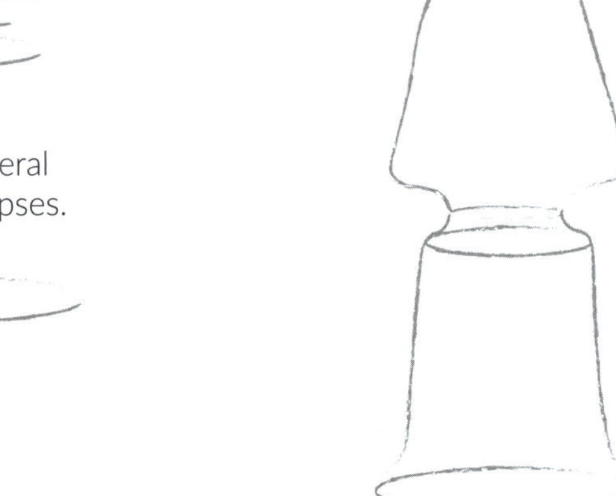

2 Connect the circles and sketch out your bubblegum dispenser.

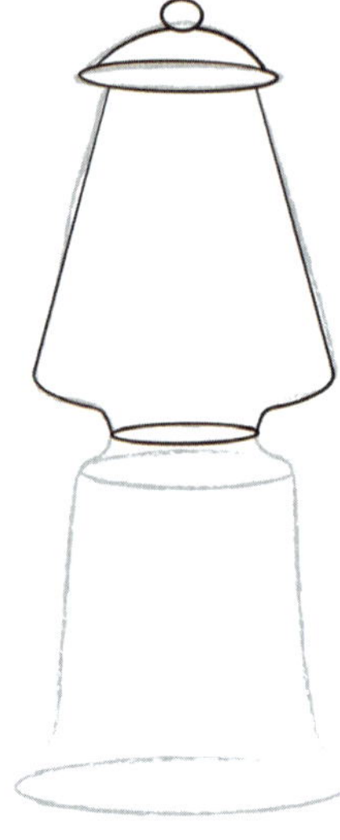

3 Use a fineliner to outline the top part of your bubblegum dispenser.

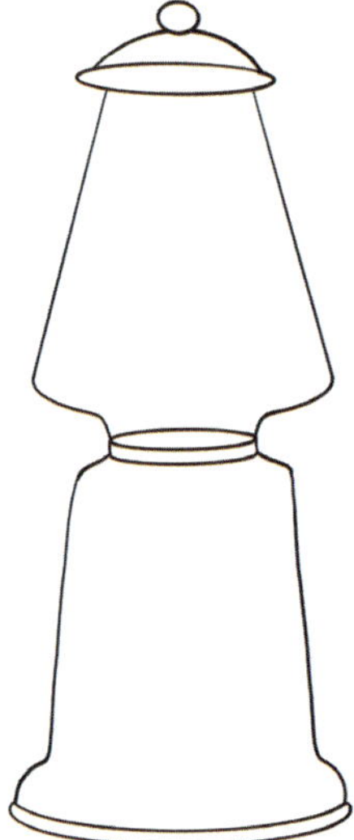

4 Finish drawing the outline.

5 Draw the opening and the handle.

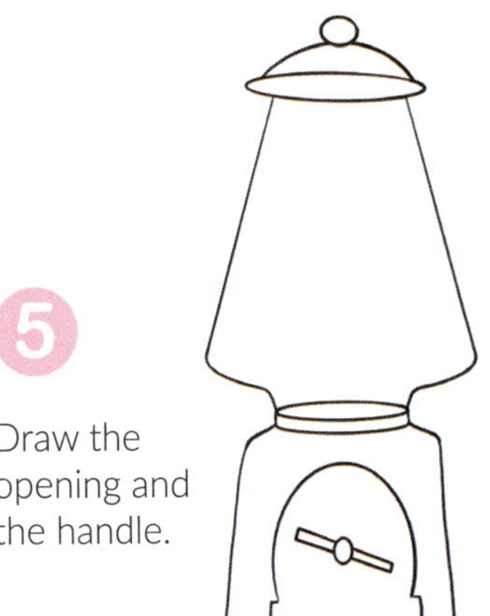

6 Fill the dispenser with flying hearts.

7

Colour your bubblegum dispenser in cheerful colours.

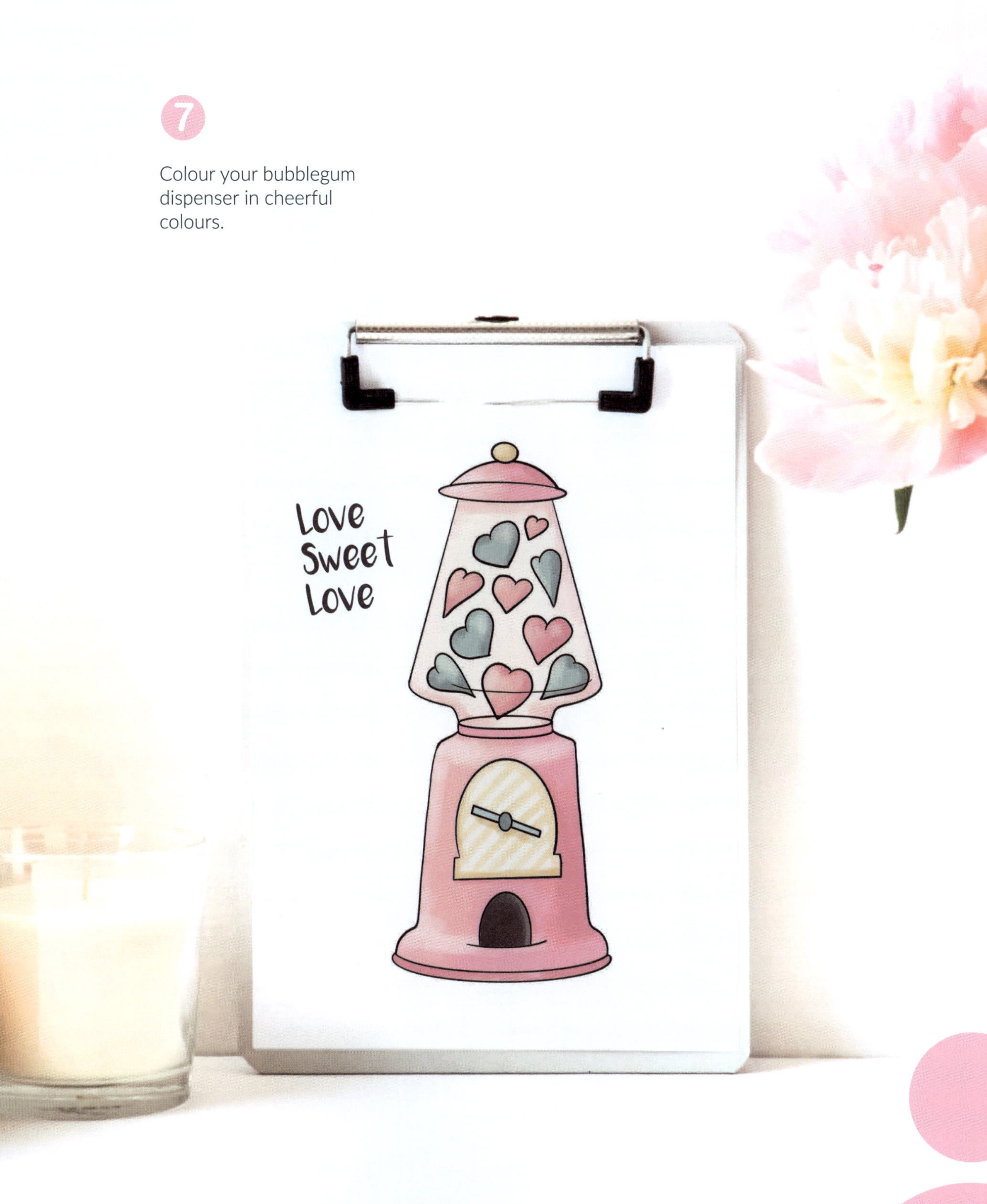

Flower wagon

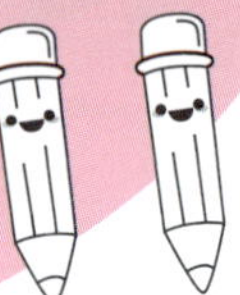

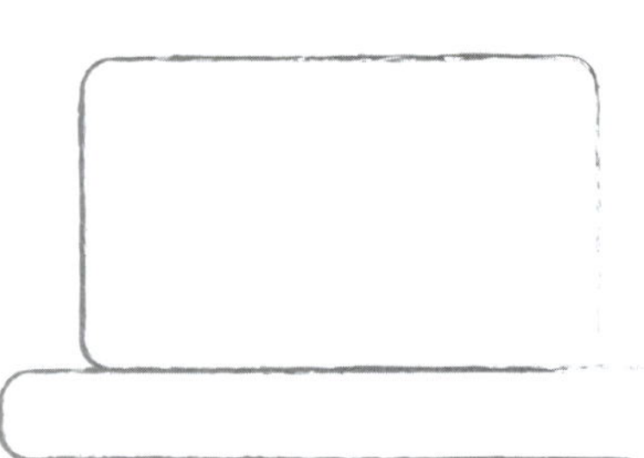

Sketch two rectangles for the wagon and the bumper.

2

Complete your sketch with flowers, roof, wheels and break lights.

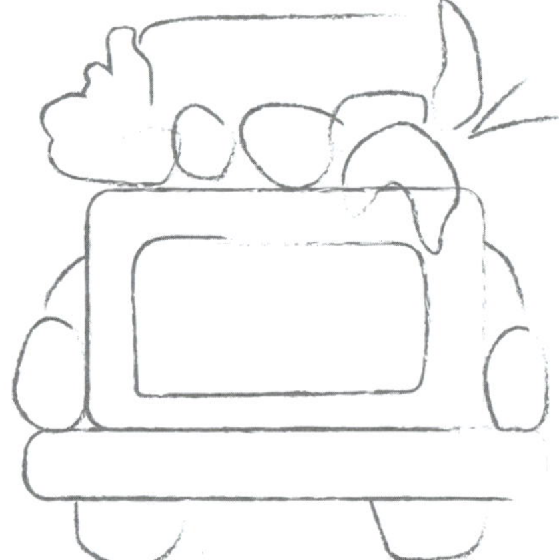

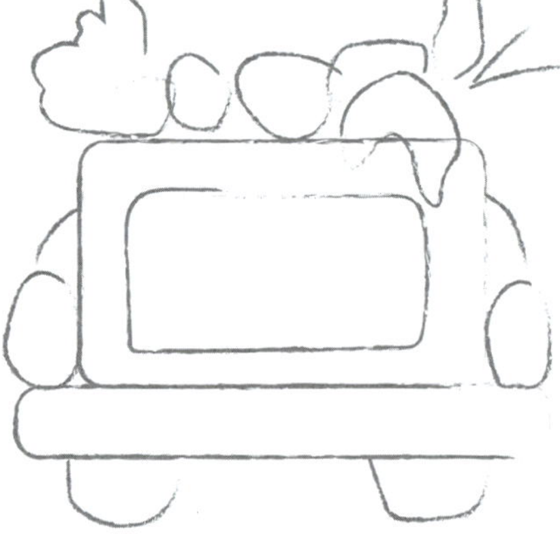

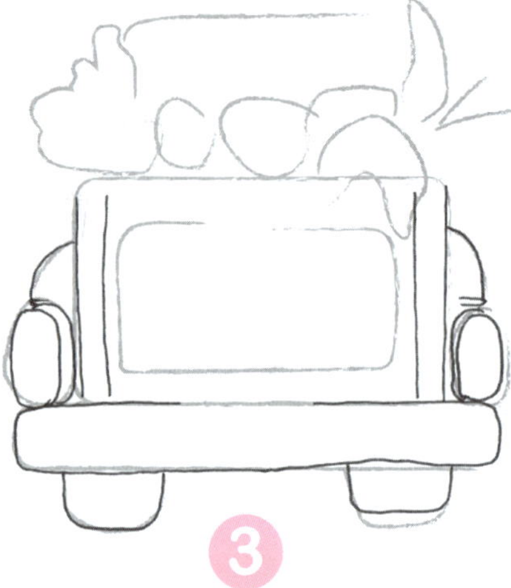

3

Use a fineliner to draw the outlines of the wagon.

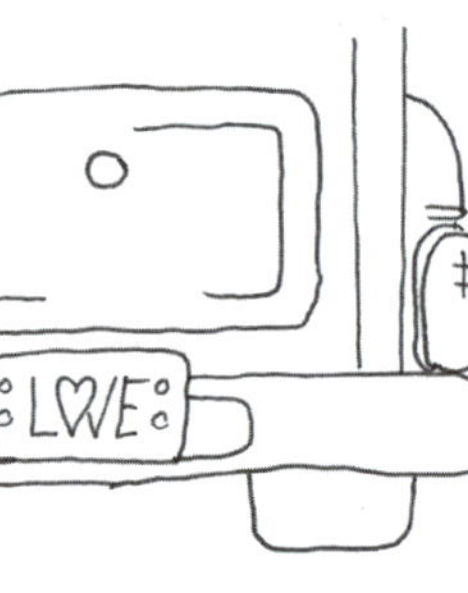

Add a few extra details.

Paint the first part of the wagon and leave it to dry well.

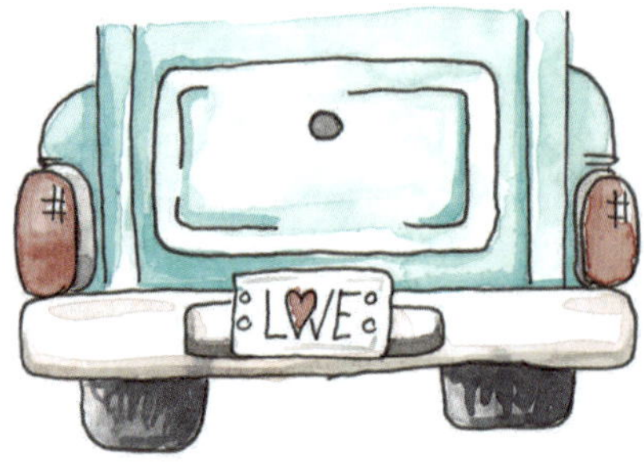

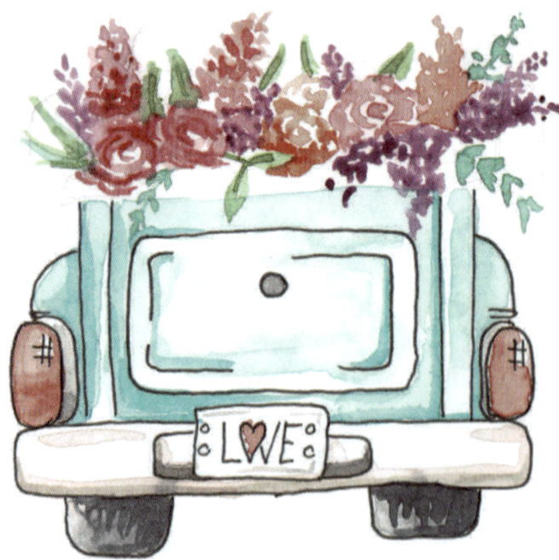

Paint flowers that poke out from the boot.

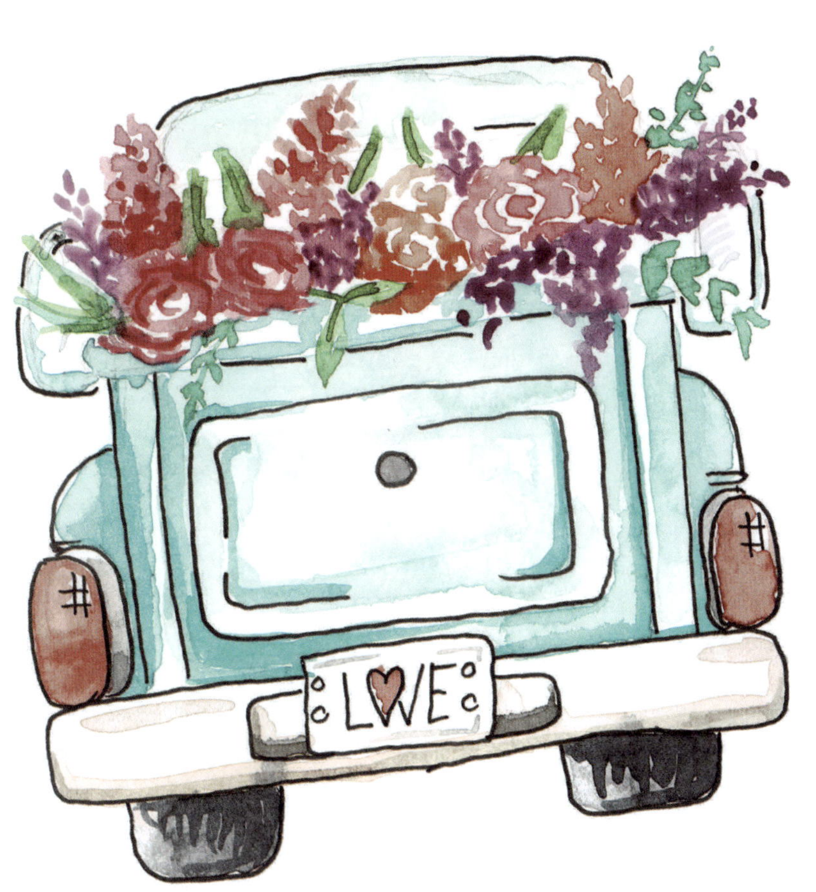

7 When the watercolour flowers have completely dried, you can paint the car roof and wing mirrors.

Little Bird House

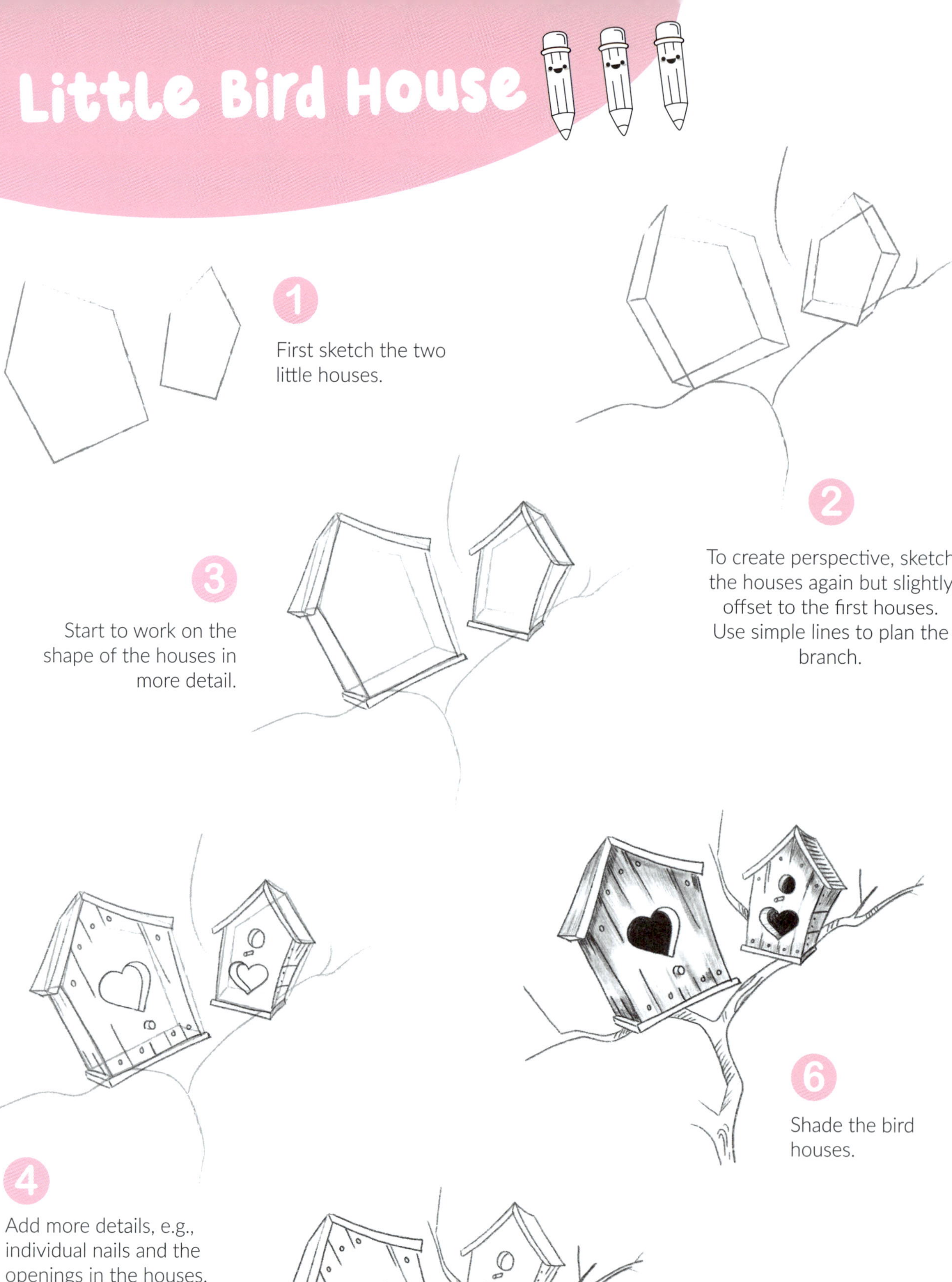

1

First sketch the two little houses.

2

To create perspective, sketch the houses again but slightly offset to the first houses. Use simple lines to plan the branch.

3

Start to work on the shape of the houses in more detail.

4

Add more details, e.g., individual nails and the openings in the houses.

6

Shade the bird houses.

5

Draw the branch, upon which the houses are placed.

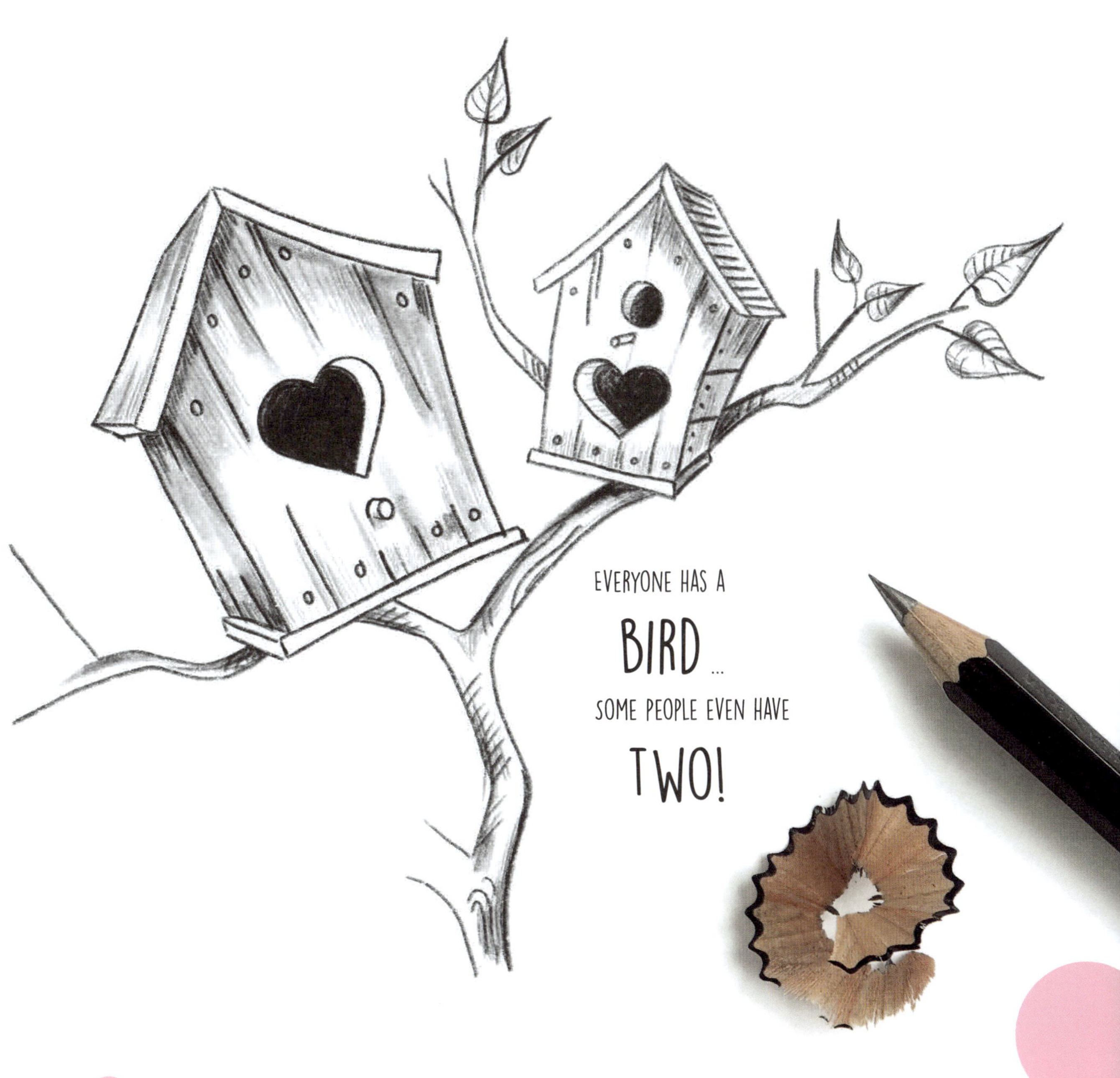

7

Finally, add more detail and shading to the branch to complete your sweet bird houses.

Flower Hot Air Balloon

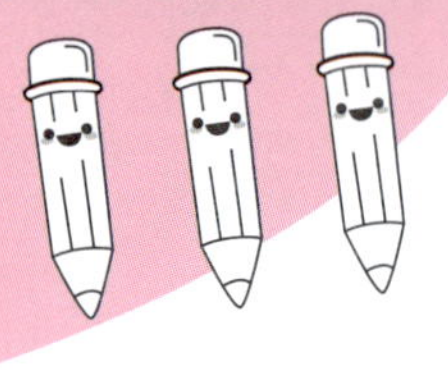

1 Start with one large circle and sketch a basket with an ellipse as the base.

2 Sketch three circles for the biggest flowers.

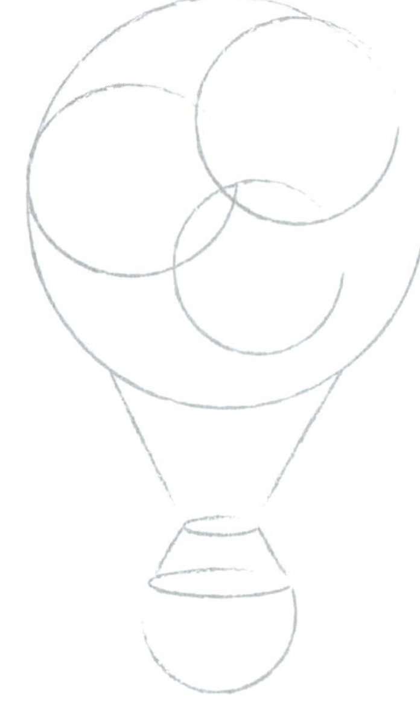

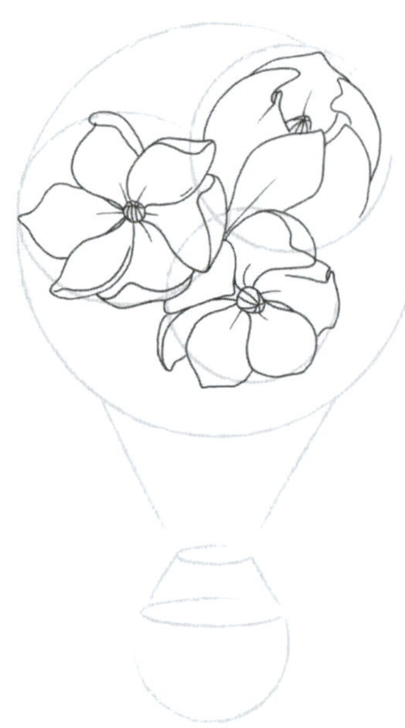

3 Start drawing the flowers with a fineliner.

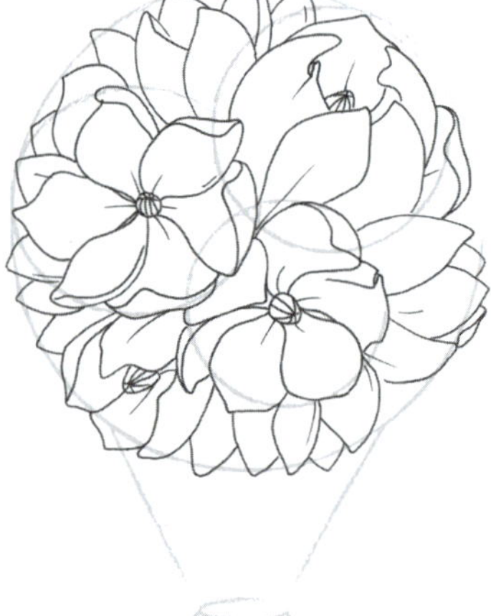

4 Fill the hot air balloon with more flowers around your large flowers.

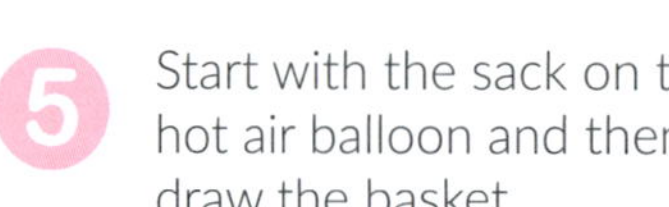

5 Start with the sack on the hot air balloon and then draw the basket.

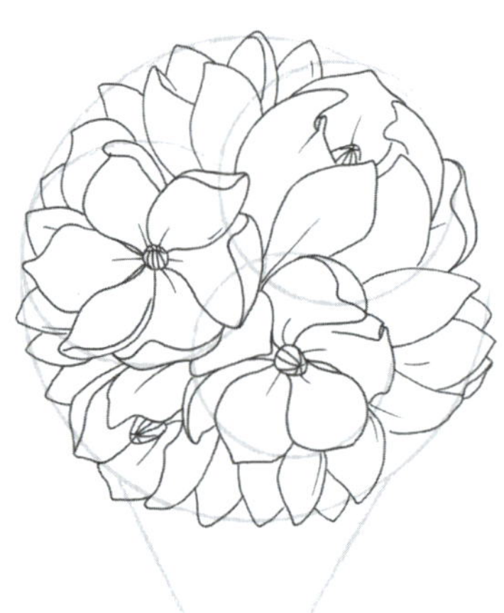

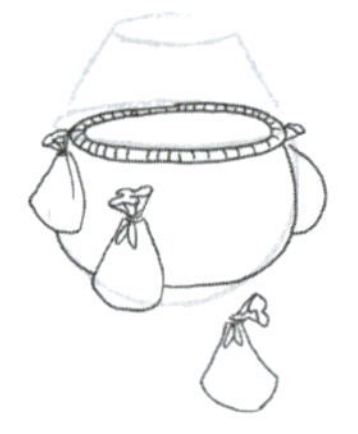

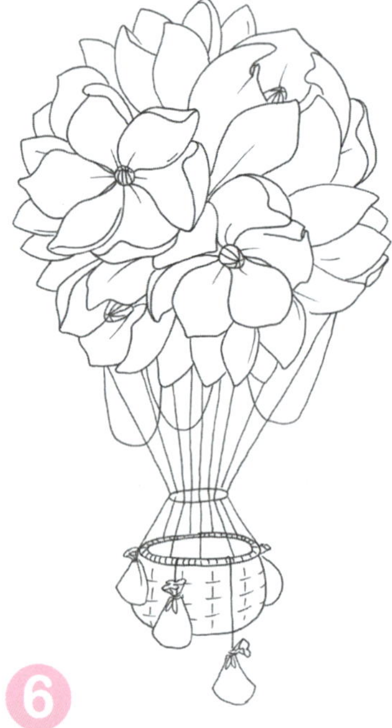

6 Refine your illustration by adding further details to the basket and the ropes.

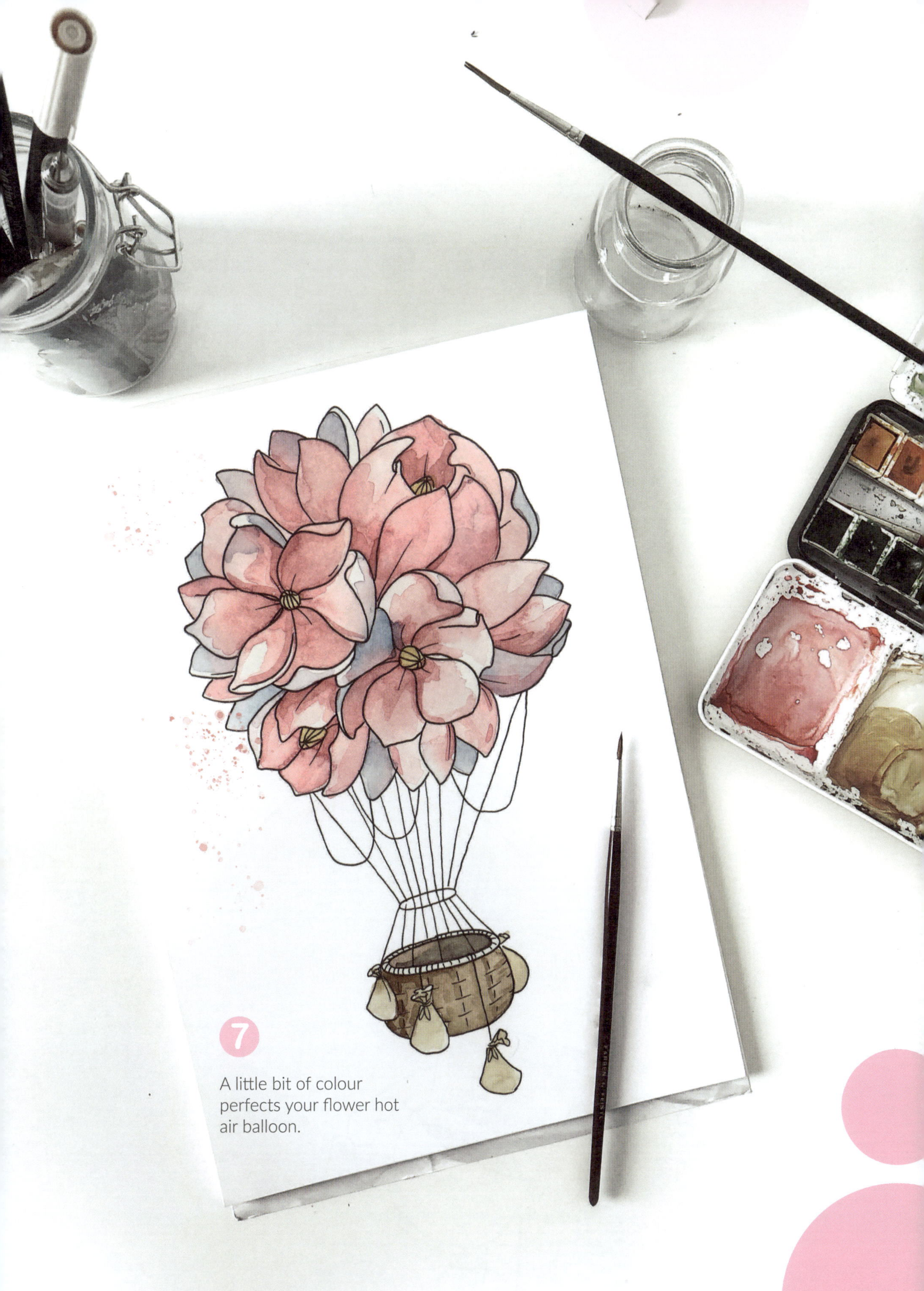

7

A little bit of colour perfects your flower hot air balloon.

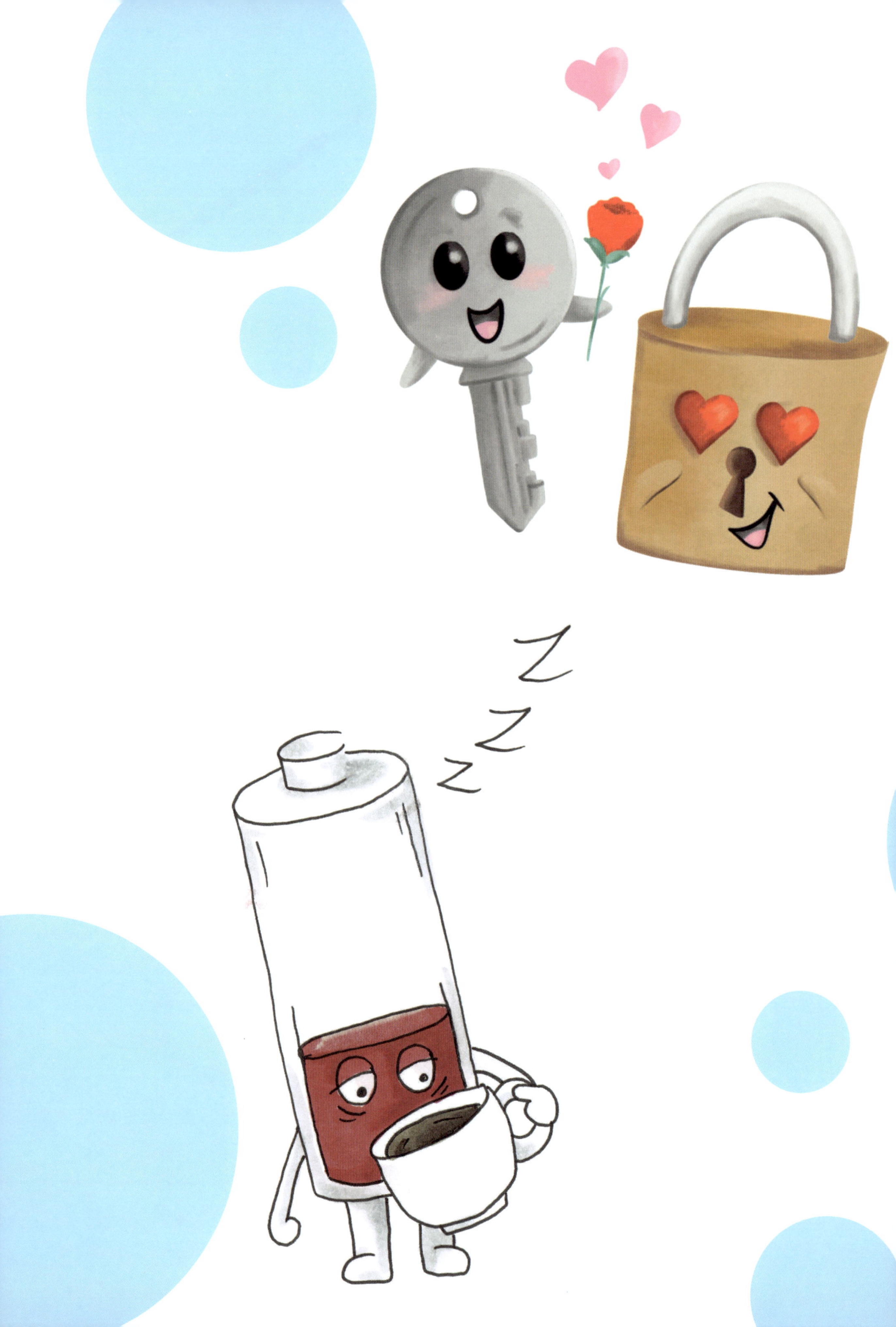

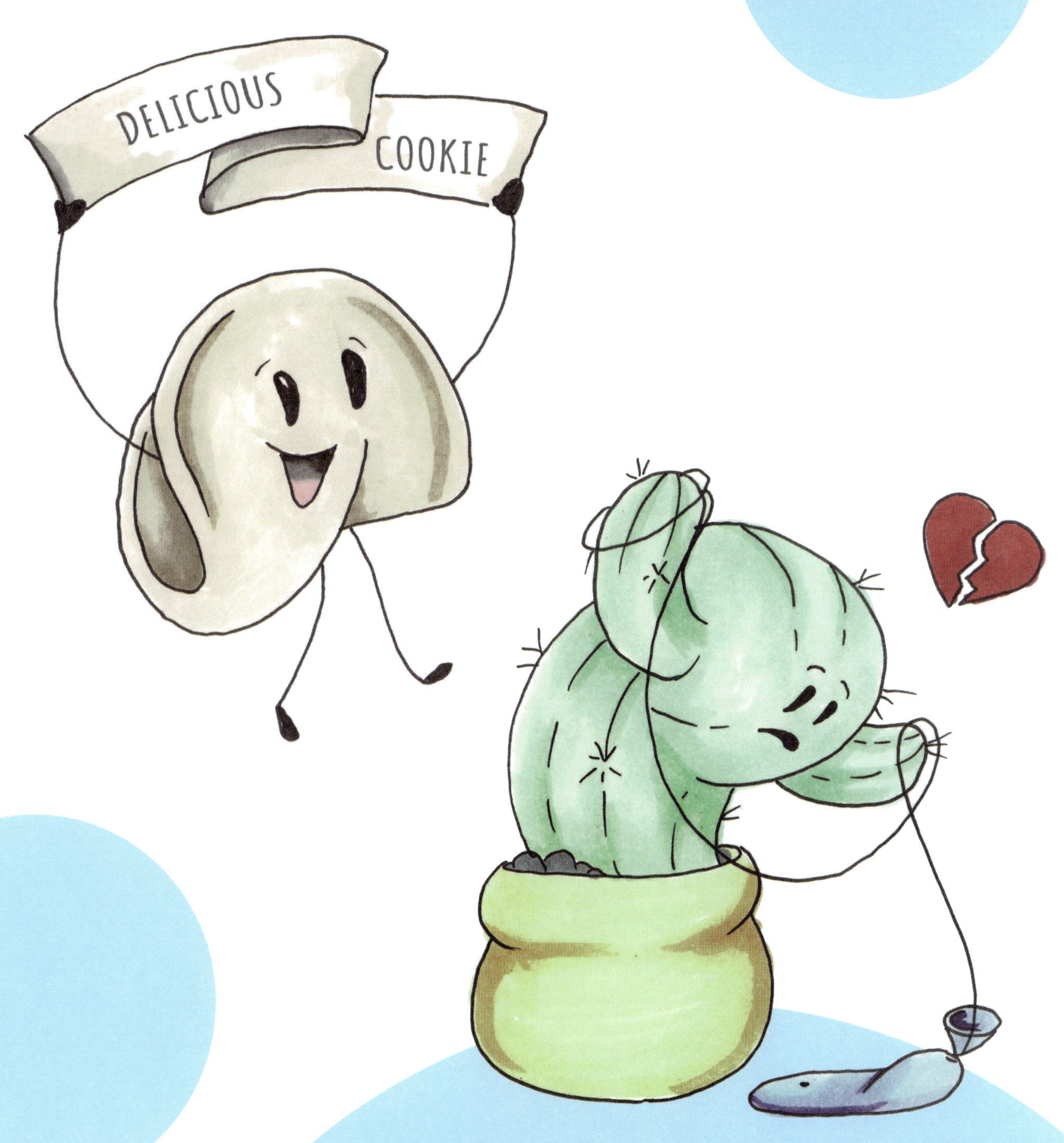

Cute Emotions

Drills

Our eyes reveal so much about us - as do our eyebrows and mouths. With just a few strokes and circles, faces can tell whole stories.

Give it a try! Draw each face and allocate it an emotion.

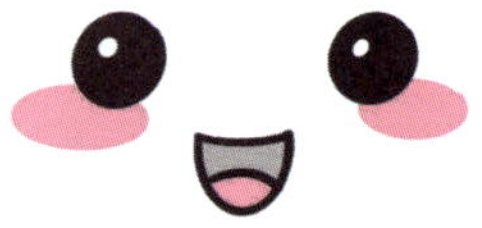

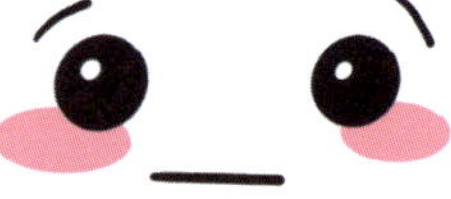

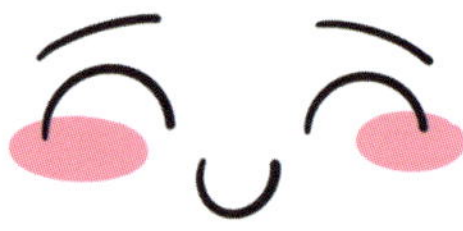

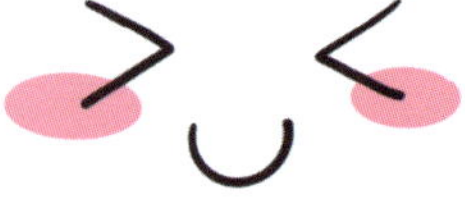

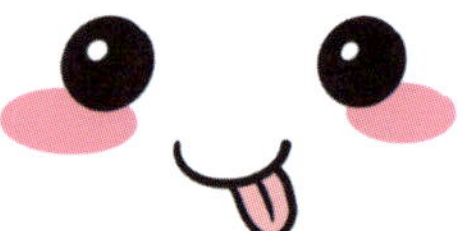

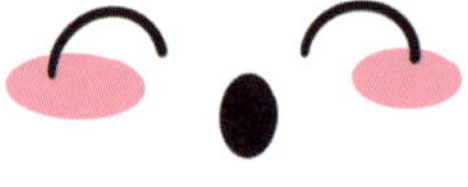

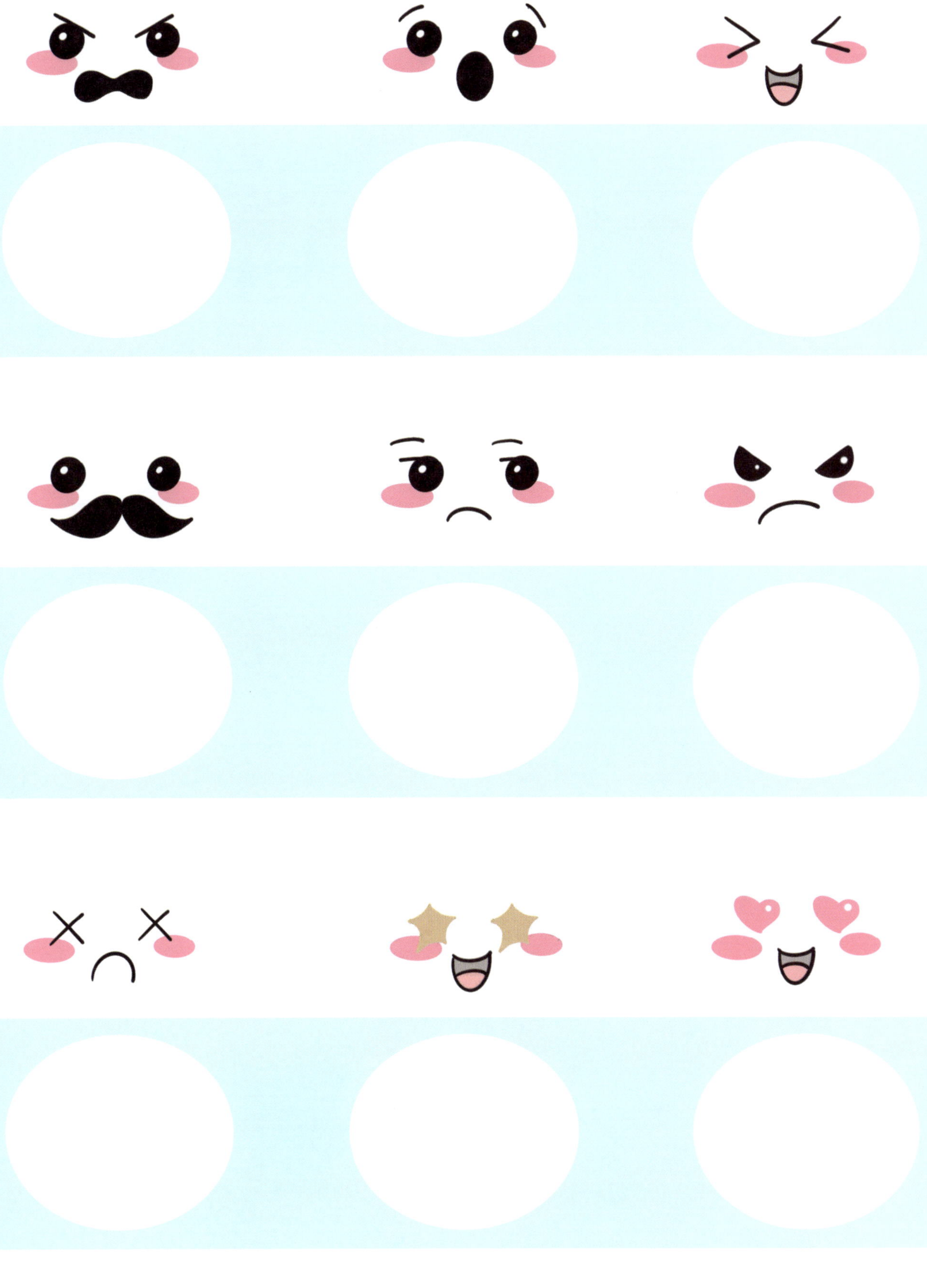

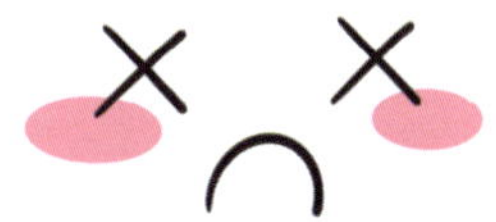
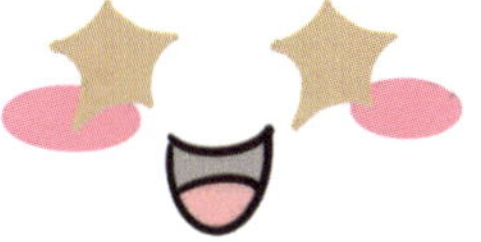
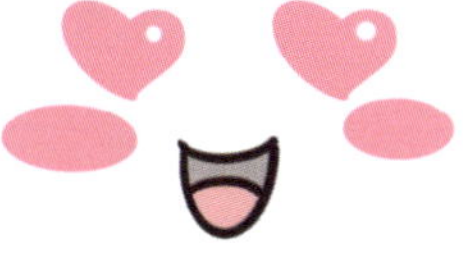

Drills

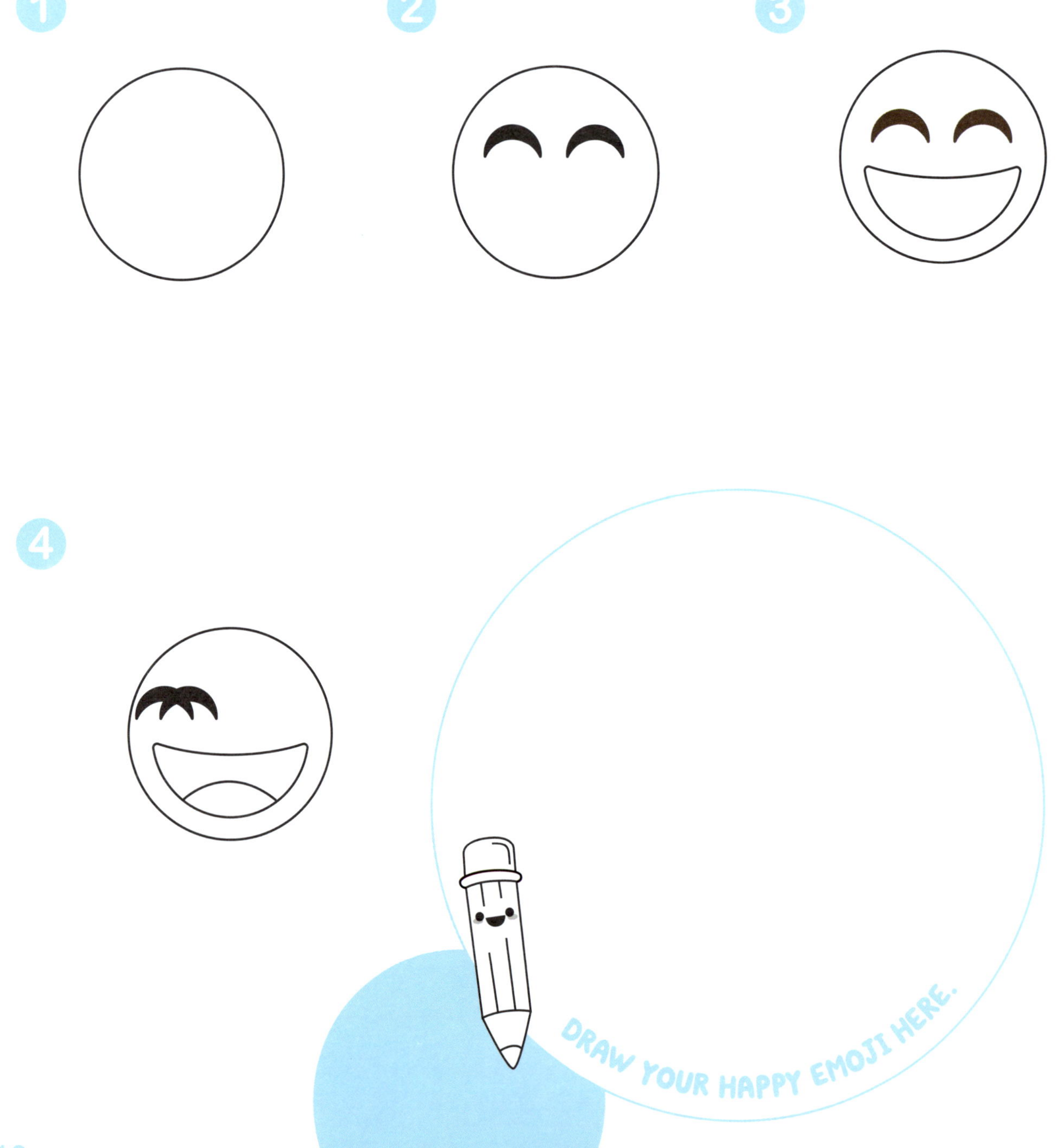

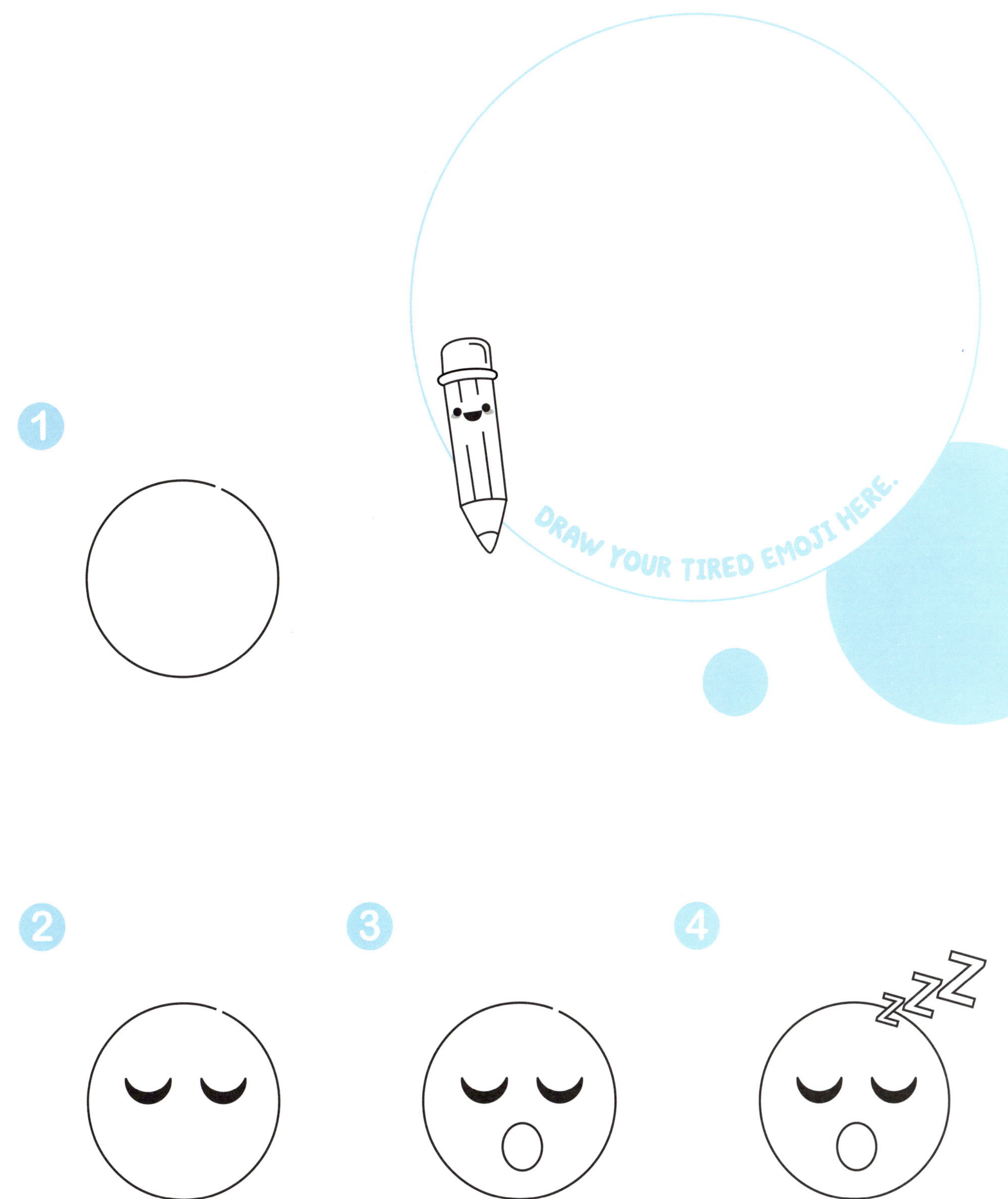
DRAW YOUR TIRED EMOJI HERE.
1
2
3
4

Drills

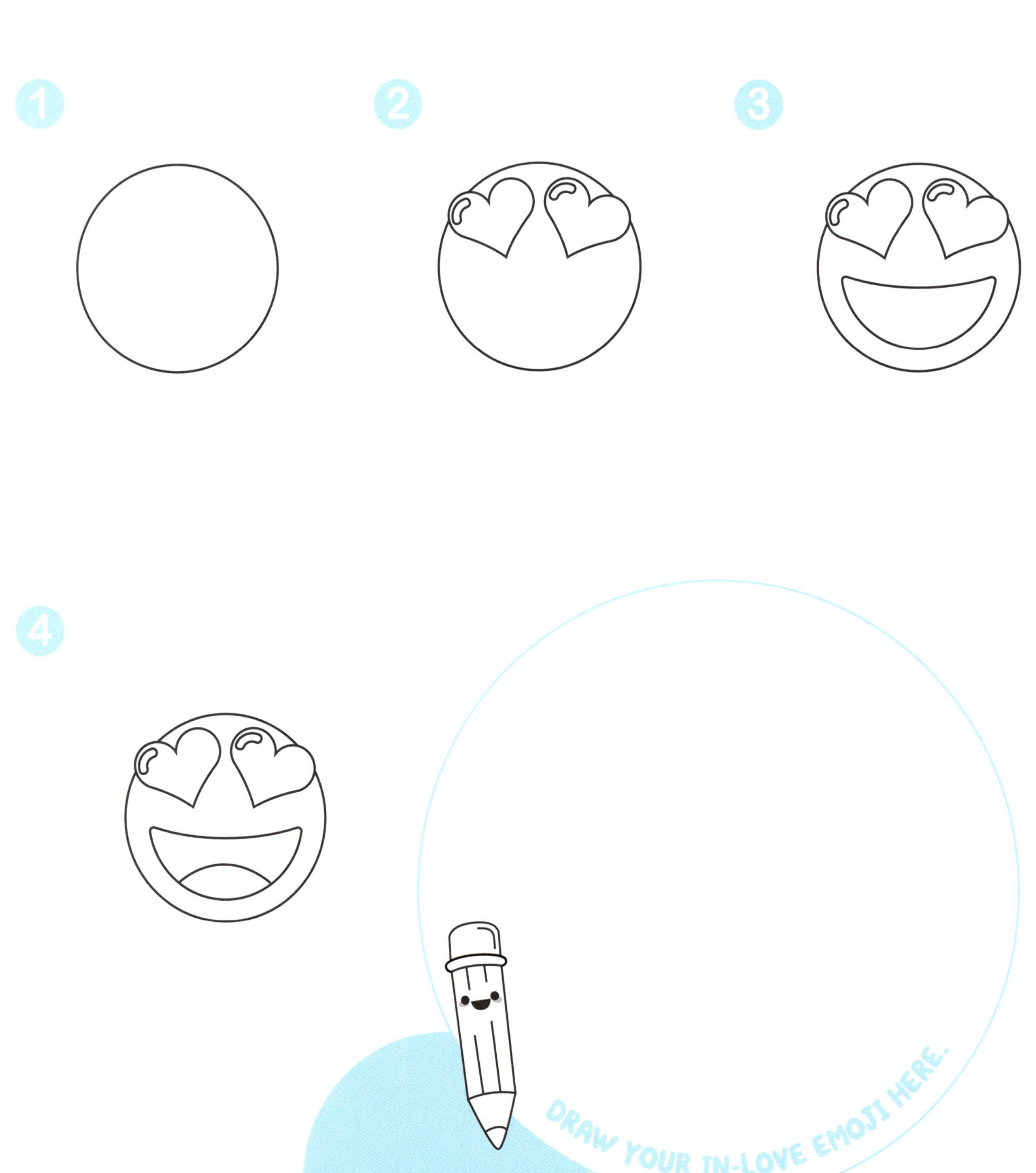

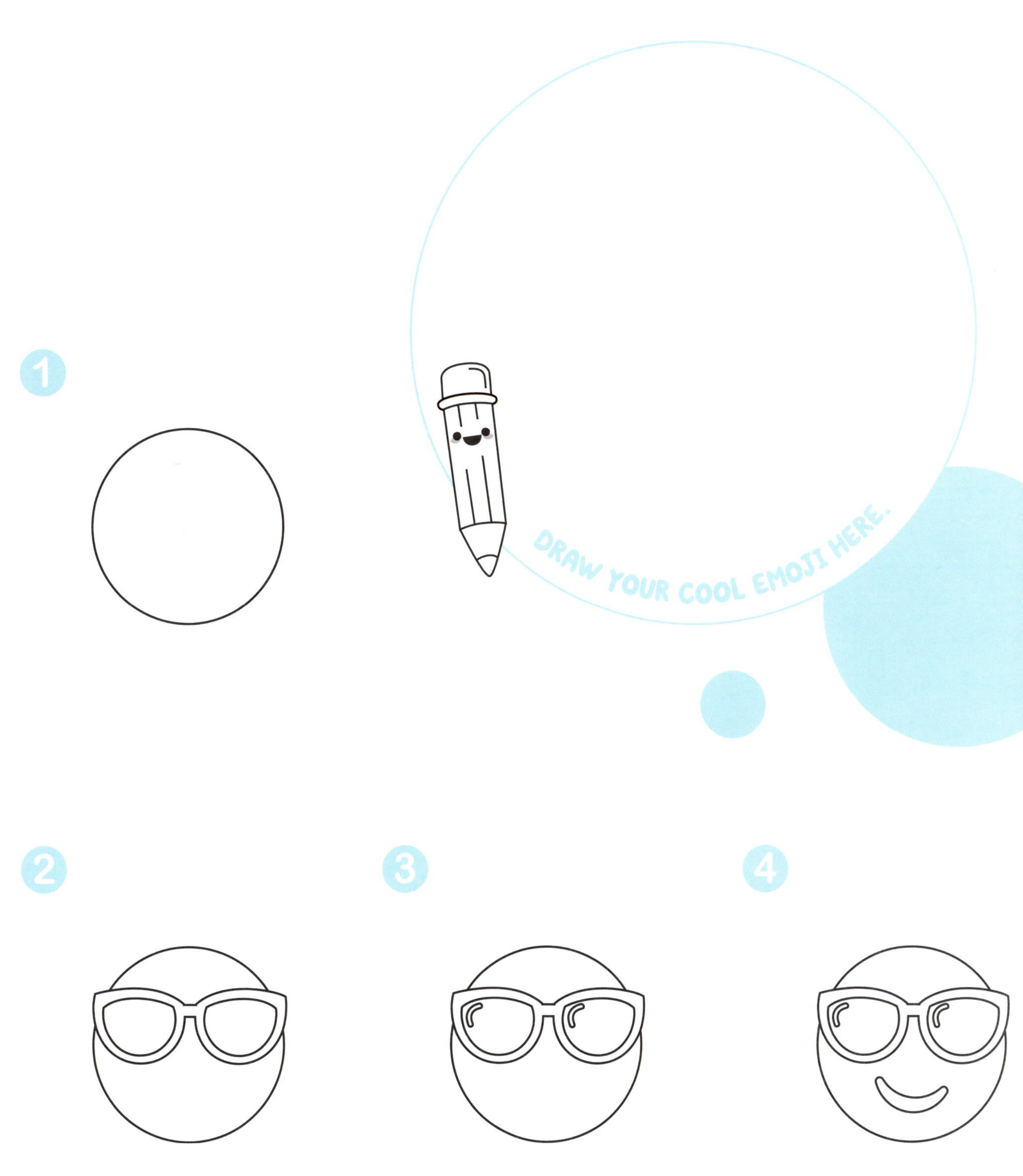
1
DRAW YOUR COOL EMOJI HERE.
2
3
4

Battery Empty

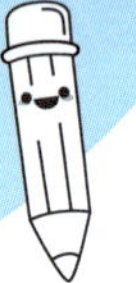

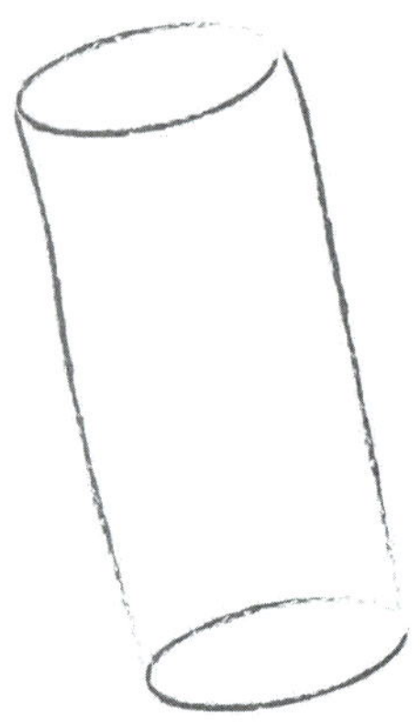

1 Sketch your battery with the help of two ellipses and join them together.

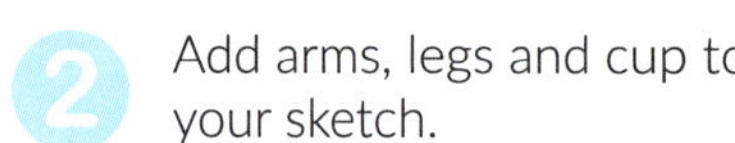

2 Add arms, legs and cup to your sketch.

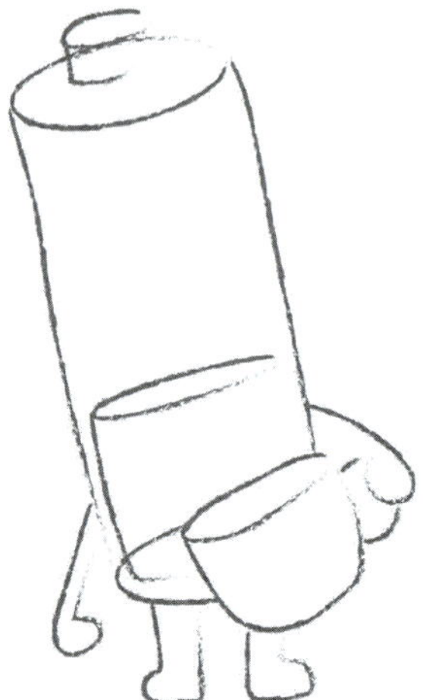

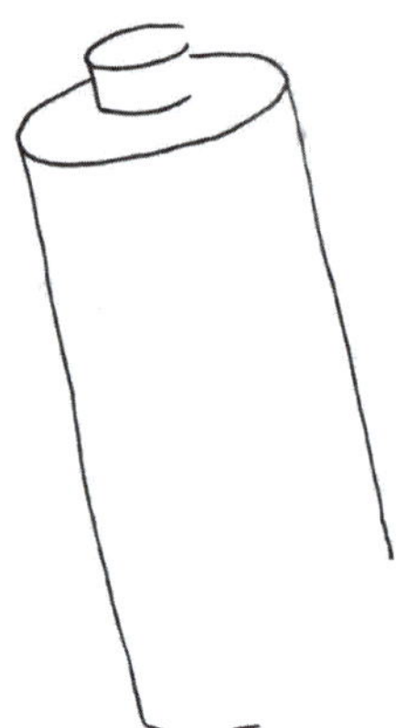

3 Use a fineliner to go around the outline of your battery.

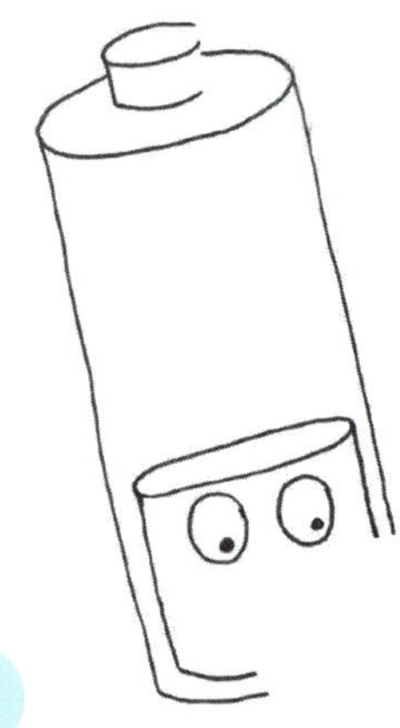

4 Now draw the charge status of your battery and its eyes.

5 Add the coffee, arms and legs to your battery.

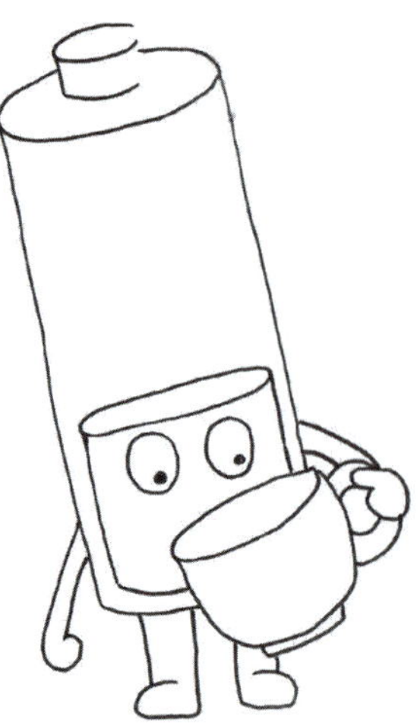

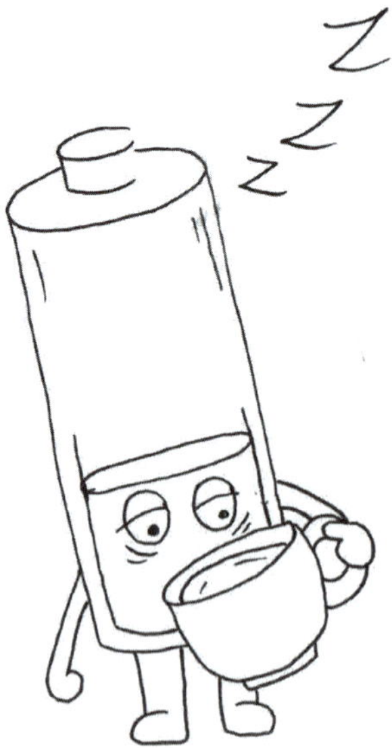

6 Add a few more details, such as eyelids and bags under its eyes.

7

Paint your battery to finish your cute tired battery.

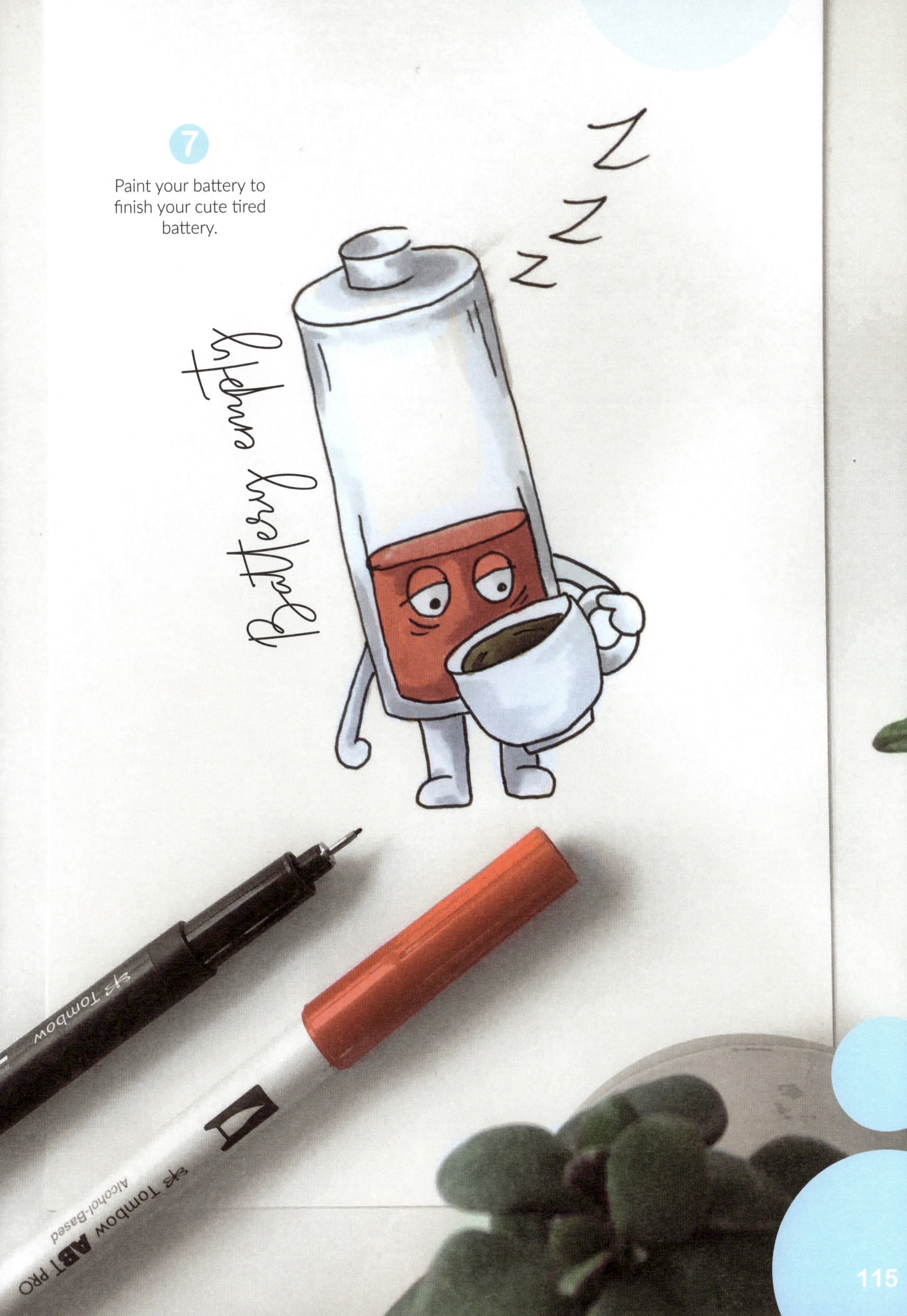

Cookie

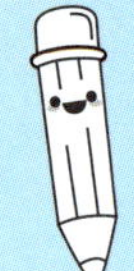

1 Sketch the shape of your cookie.

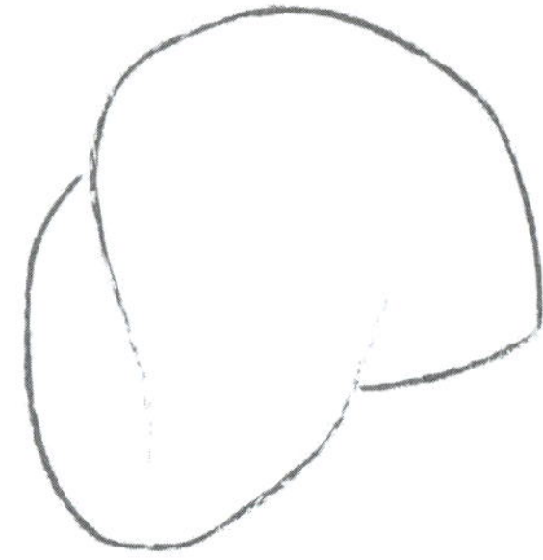

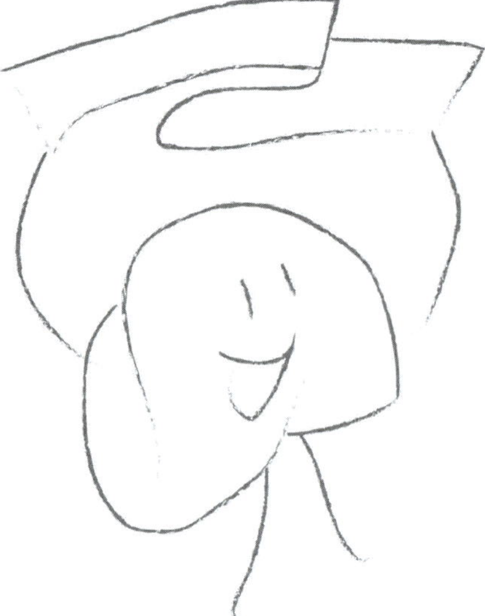

2 Sketch arms, legs, face and the slip of paper.

3 Start outlining the cookie with a fineliner.

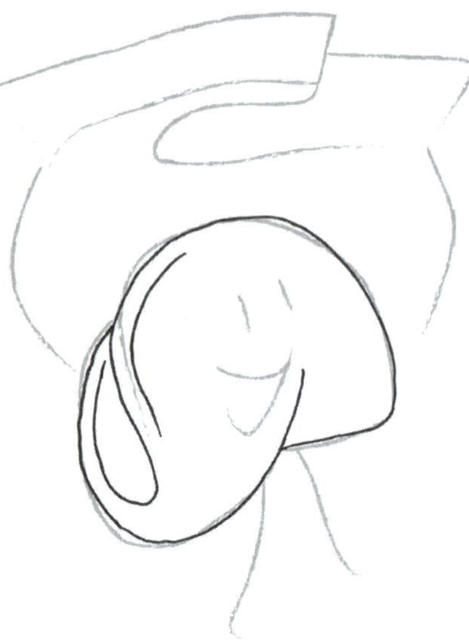

4 Draw a happy face on your cookie.

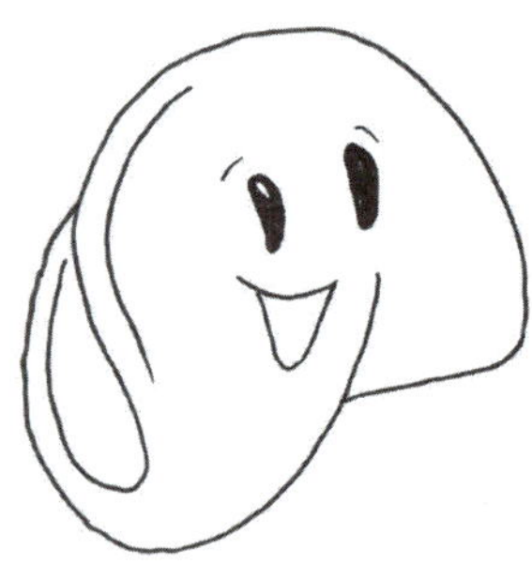

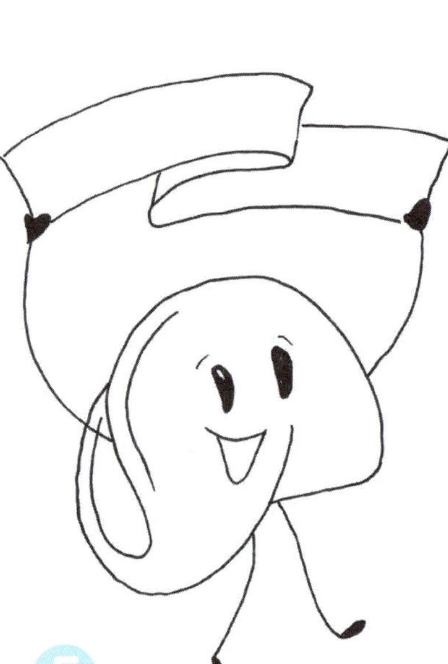

5 Draw the remaining elements for your cookie.

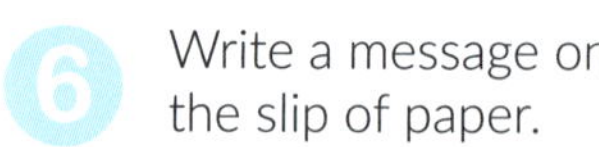

6 Write a message on the slip of paper.

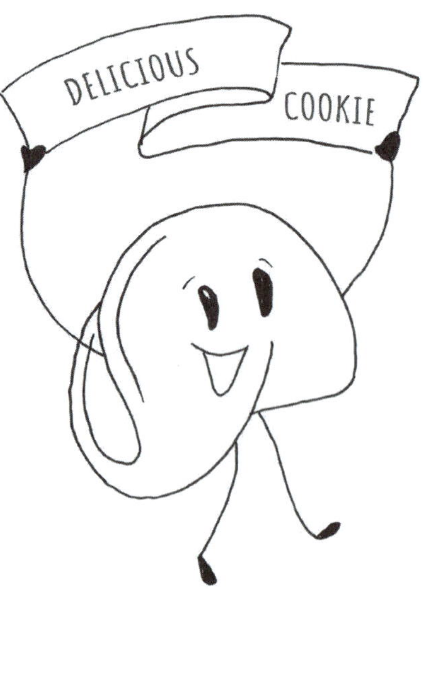

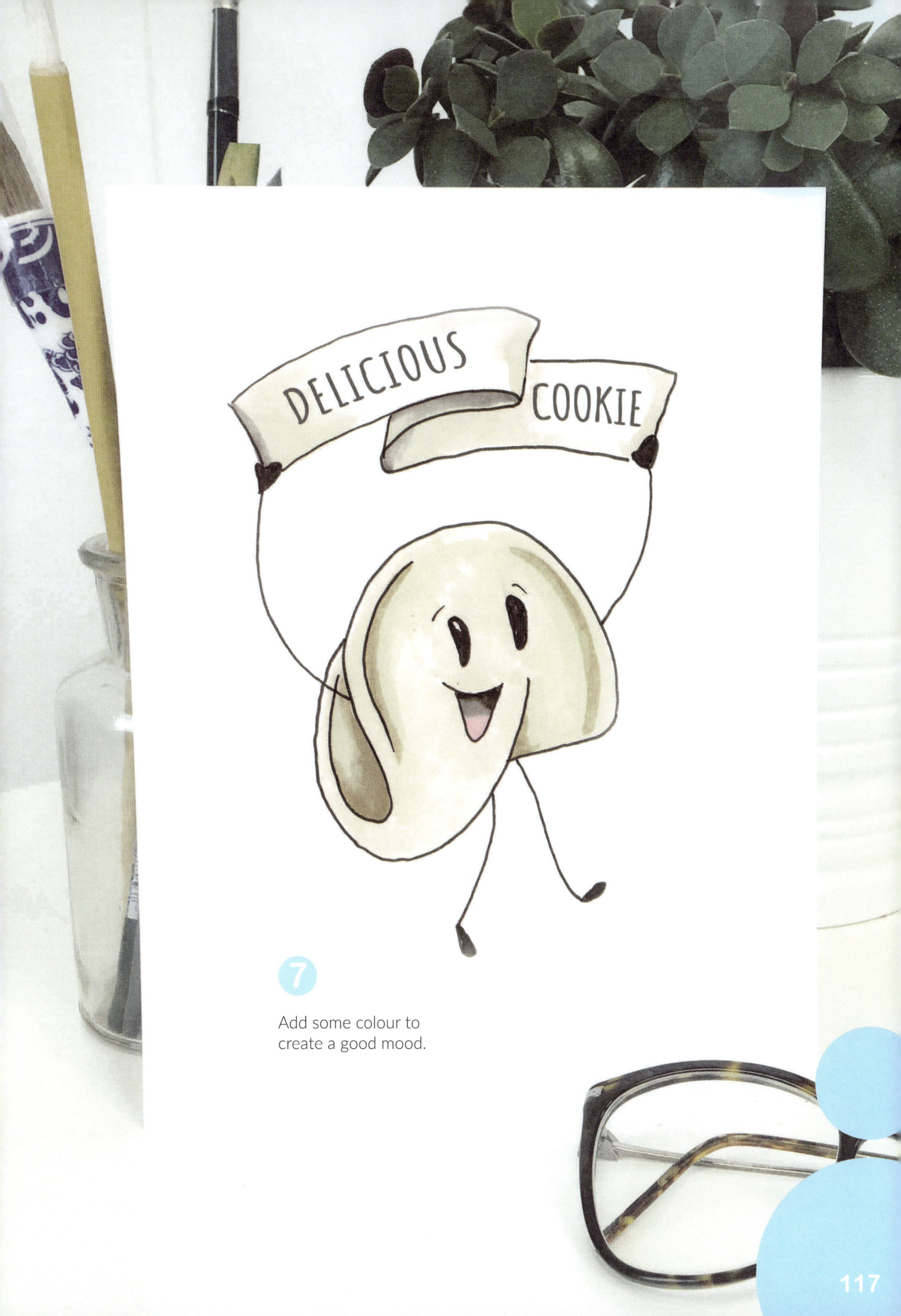

7

Add some colour to
create a good mood.

Love Key 

1 Sketch a circle for the key and a rectangle with an ellipse for the lock.

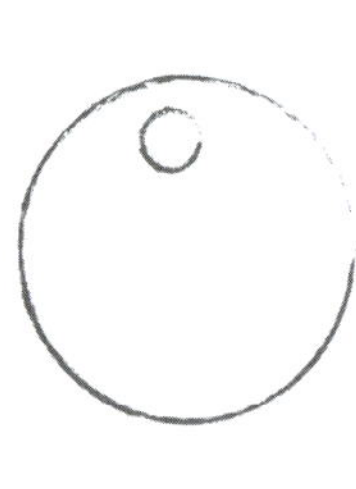

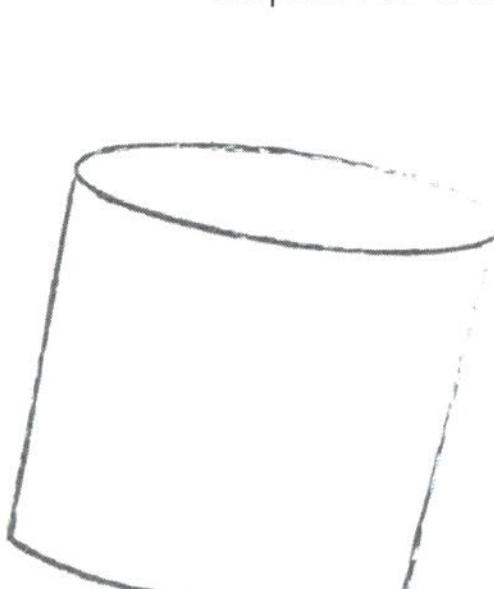

2 Complete your sketch.

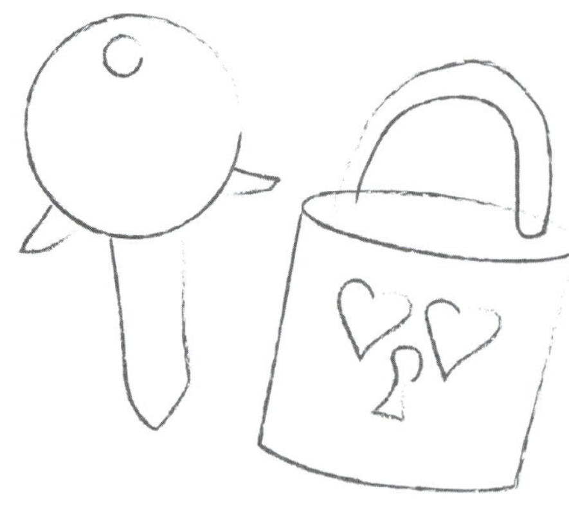

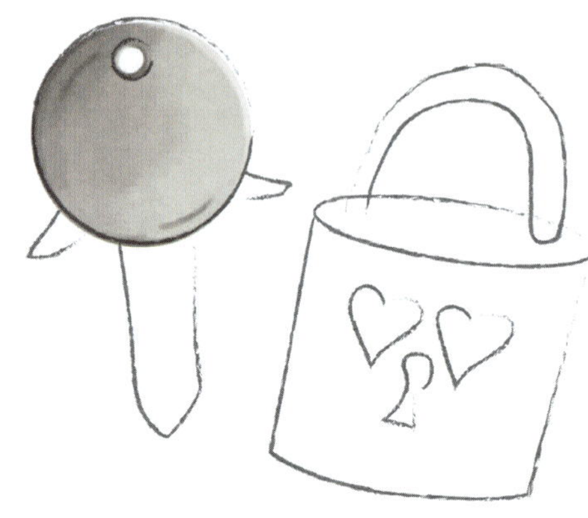

3 Start to paint the top of your key, paying attention to light and shadow.

4 Paint all grey parts of your key.

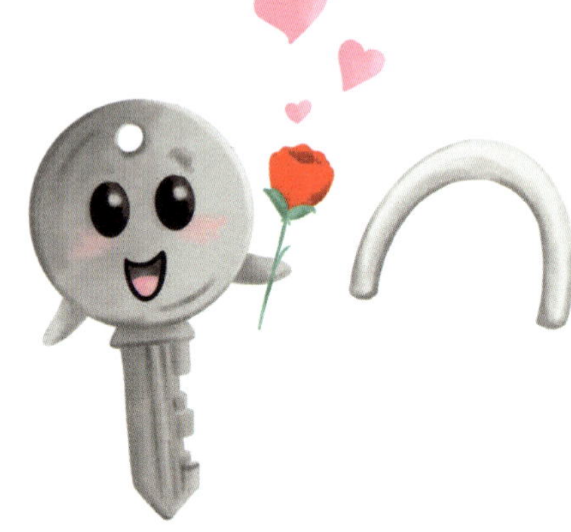

5 Give your key a face and put a flower in his hand. Then start with your lock.

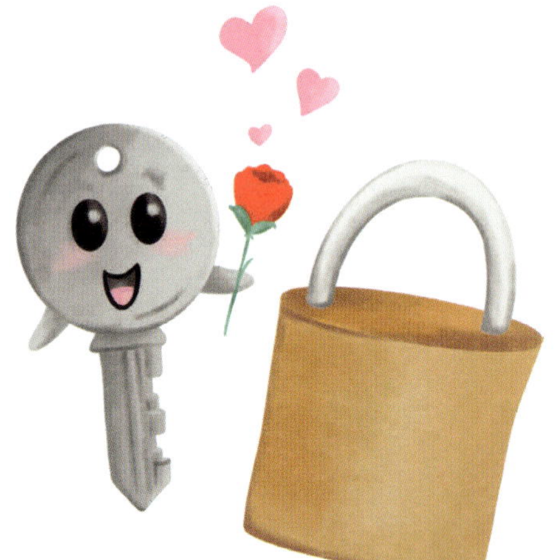

6 Paint the body of your lock in a lovely yellowy gold.

7

Finally add a keyhole and a face to the lock to finish your illustration.

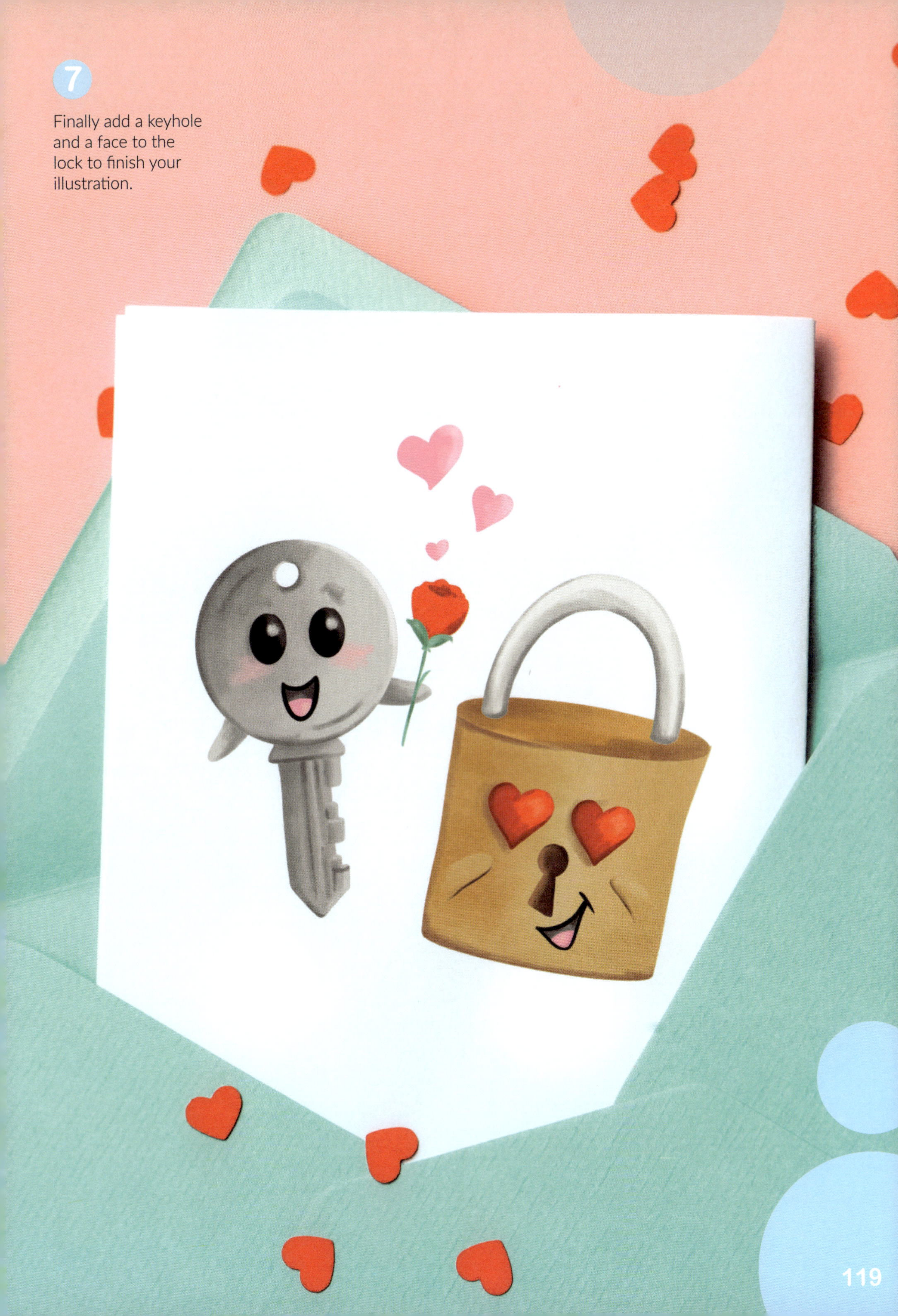

Love hurts

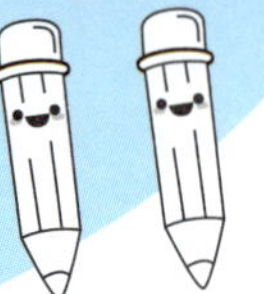

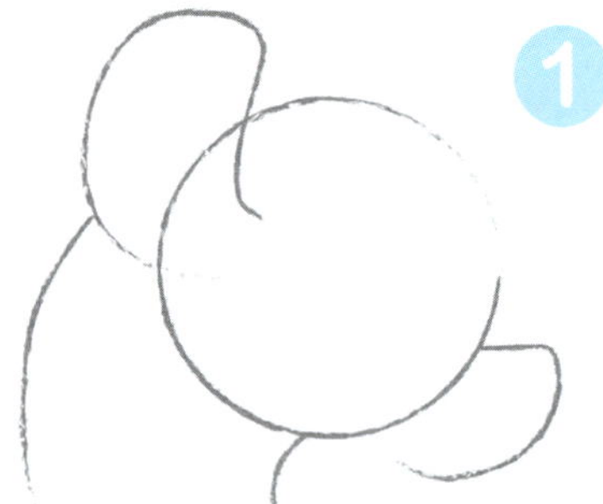

1 Sketch a circle for the head and add a body and arms to the sketch.

Now plan the pot and the burst balloon.

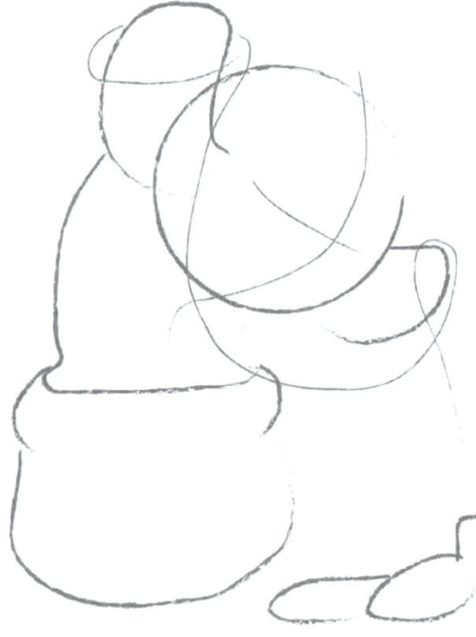

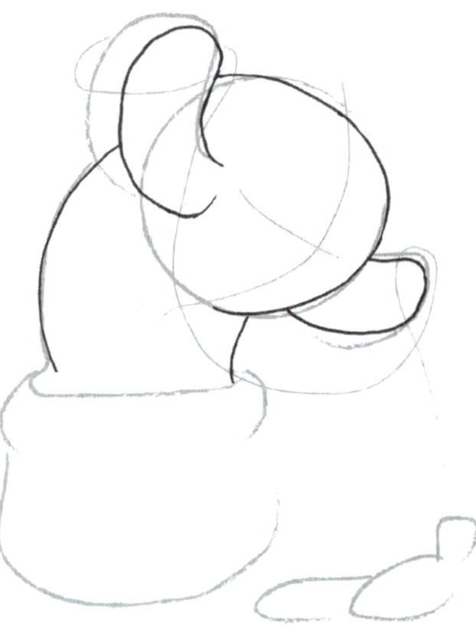

3 Use a fineliner to outline the top of the cactus.

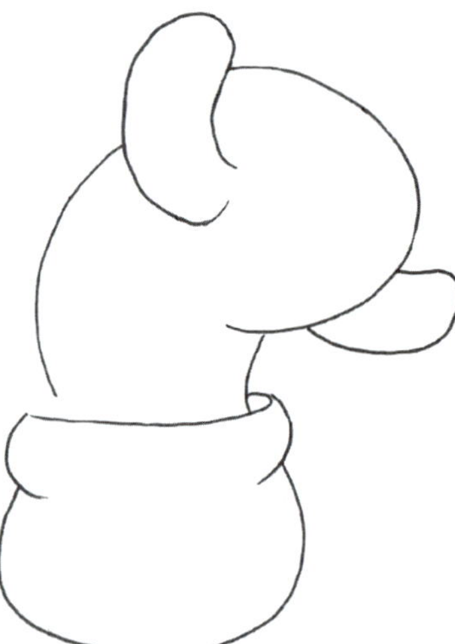

4 Continue outlining the pot in which the cactus is planted.

Add a few more cute details to your illustration.

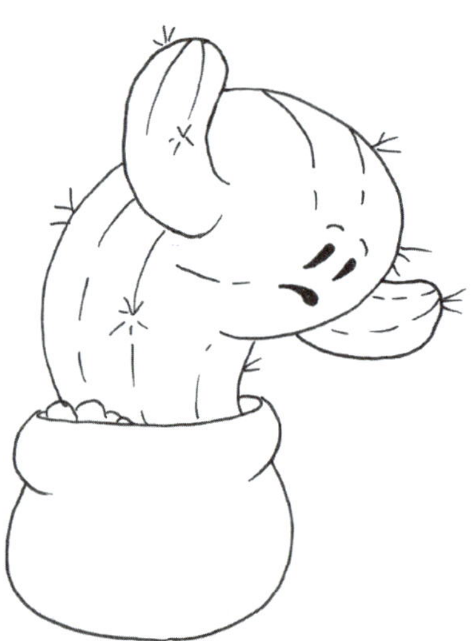

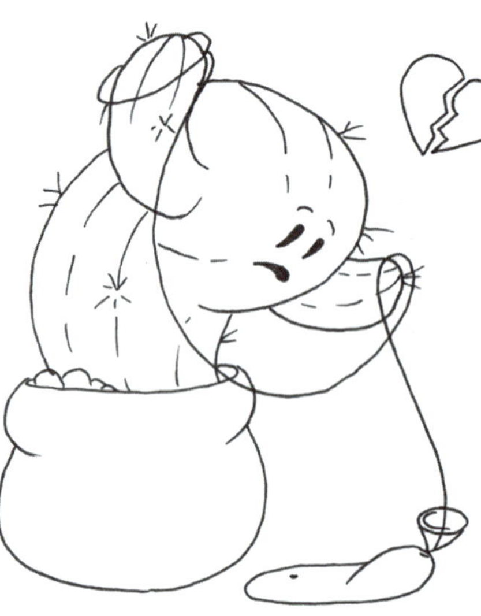

6 Draw the burst balloon with its string in the cactus' hand.

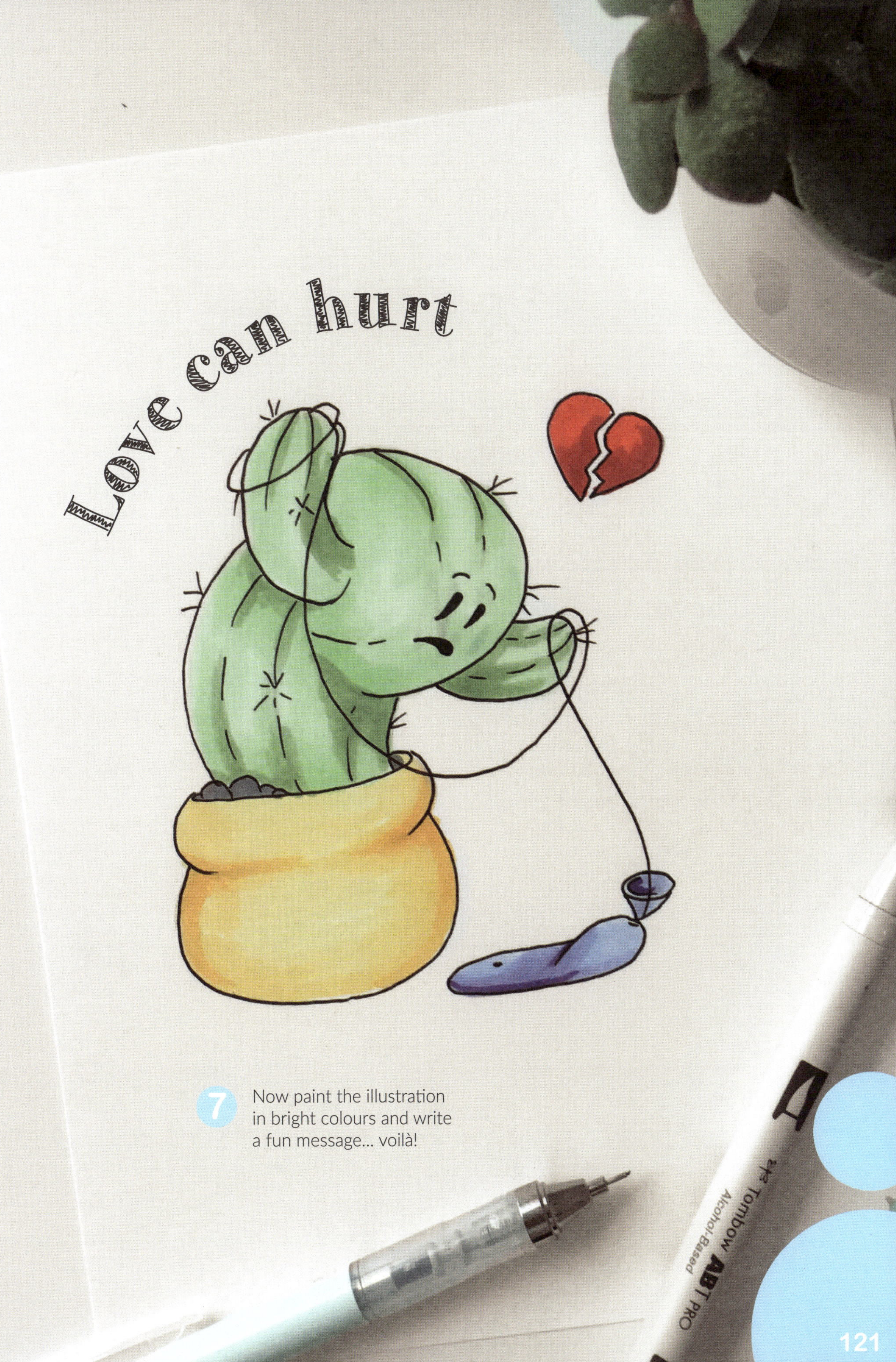

7 Now paint the illustration in bright colours and write a fun message... voilà!

Grumpy Cat

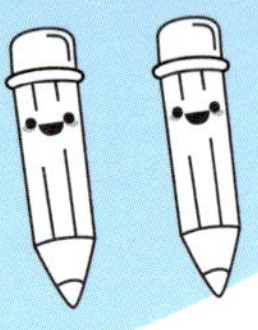

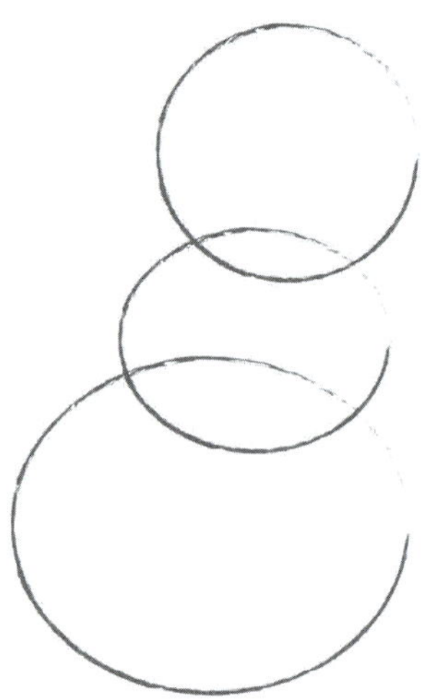

1 Start your sketch with three circles.

2 Join the circles, and sketch in the ears and tail. Draw guidelines to help you with perspective.

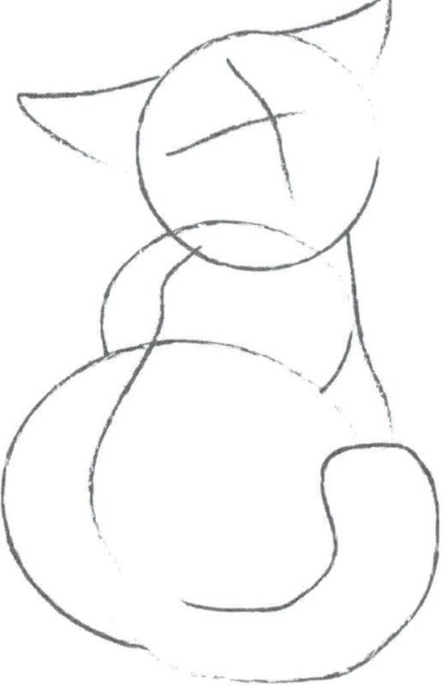

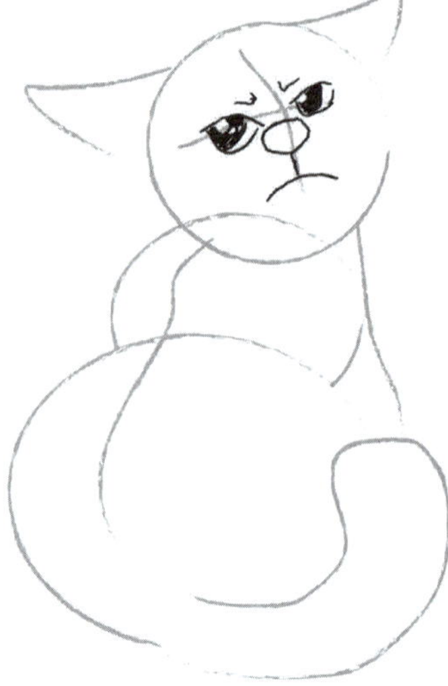

3 Use a fineliner to start drawing the face.

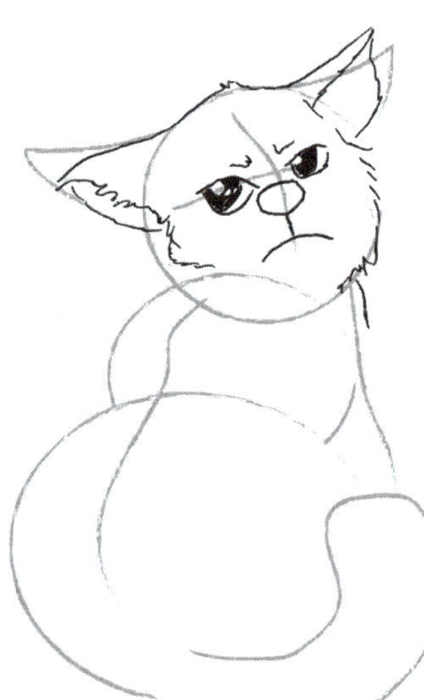

4 Then work on the head. Loose lines and strokes give the appearance of fluffy fur.

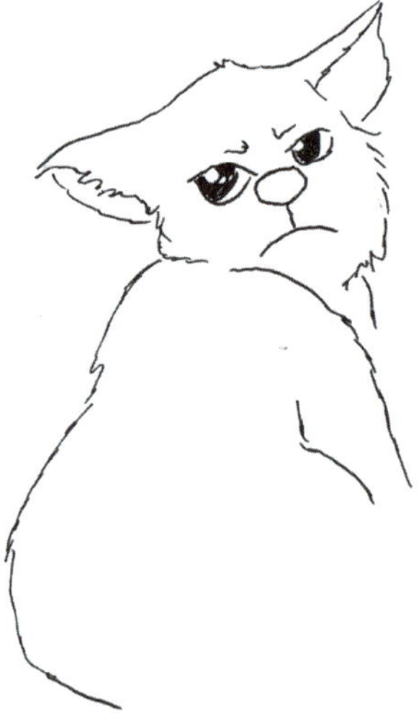

5 Draw the outline of the body, still ensuring the lines are loose.

6 Now just add the tail to complete your grumpy cat.

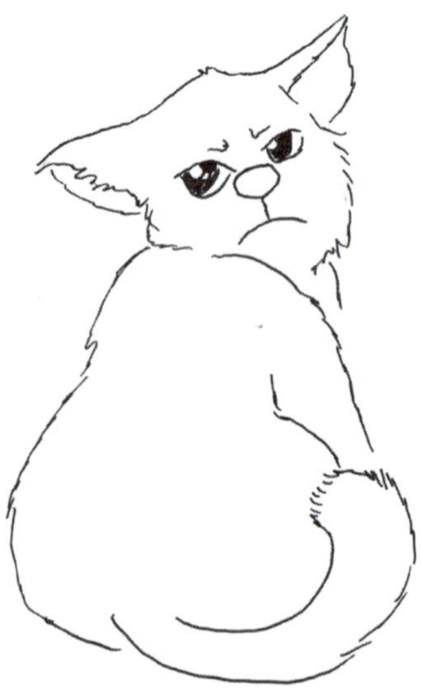

7

Paint your grumpy cat and add paint splats.

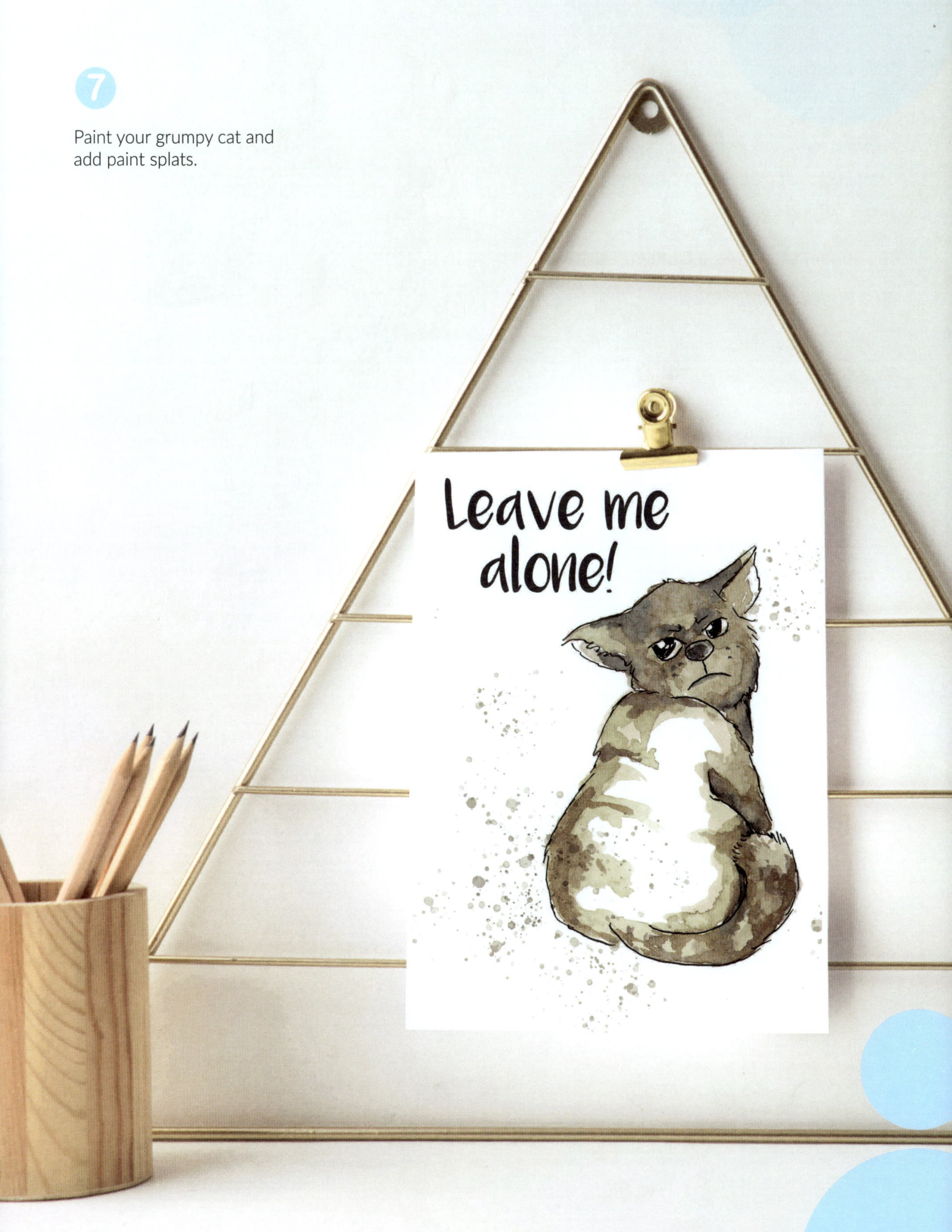

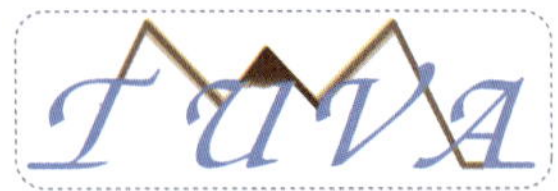

Tuva Publishing
www.tuvapublishing.com

Address Merkez Mah. Cavusbasi Cad. No71
Cekmekoy - Istanbul 34782 / Turkey
Tel +9 0216 642 62 62

The Super Cute Drawing Course

First Print October / 2022

Content Watercolour

Editor in Chief Ayhan DEMİRPEHLİVAN
Project Editor Kader DEMİRPEHLİVAN
Author Tanja GEİER
Graphic Designers Ömer ALP, Abdullah BAYRAKÇI, Tarık TOKGÖZ, Yuns GÜLDOĞAN

ISBN 978-605-7834-69-0

The original German edition was published as as Sooo Cute - Der supersüße Zeichenkurs Copyright © 2020 frechverlag GmbH, Stuttgart, Germany (www.topp-kreative.de)

This edition is published by arrangement with Anja Endemann, ae Rights Agency, Berlin, Germany

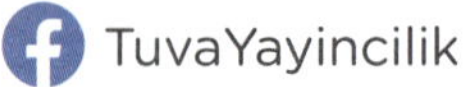

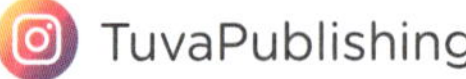

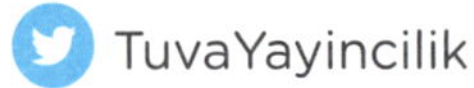

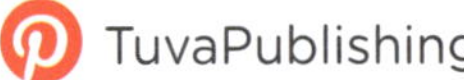

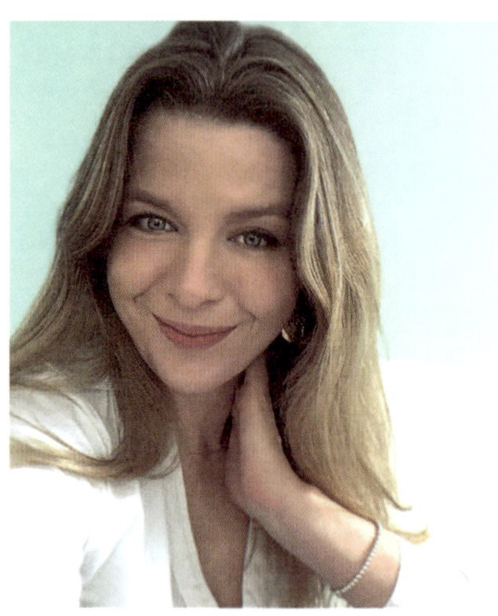

About the Author

My name is Tanja and I live in the beautiful area surrounding Munich. The stunning lakes and mountains have always been a reliable source of inspiration for new designs. In 2017, I took the leap into self-employment with my agency "Nice Day Communications" and my blog "Geliebtes Chaos". Since then, I have also rediscovered my passion for watercolours and I can barely imagine a day without painting. Under the name @missniceday on Instagram, you can follow my creative daily life and regularly watch me draw and paint.

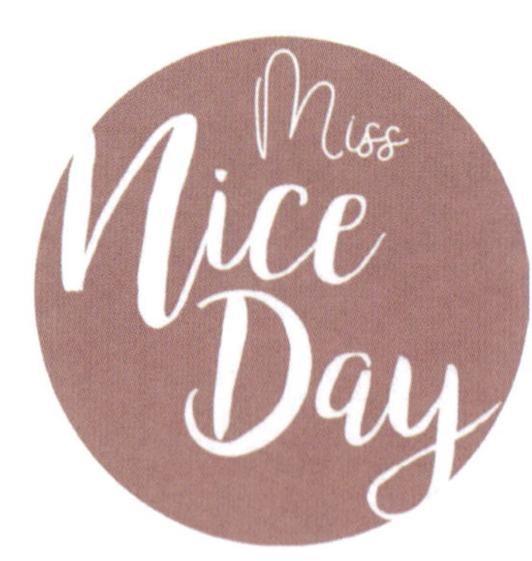